Praise for *Ordinary Girls*

"A skilled writer, Díaz is meticulous in her craft, and on page after page her writing truly sings. Her temporal leaps and switches in tense and point of view make the overall delivery both powerful and complex . . . This brutally honest coming-of-age story is a painful yet illuminating memoir, a testament to resilience in the face of scarcity, a broken family, substance abuse, sexual assault, mental illness, suicide, and violence."

—*The New York Times Book Review*

"Incredible . . . Beautiful . . . In gorgeous and propulsive prose, Díaz details a life full of painful and traumatic experiences—such as a chaotic and unstable home life and a mother who suffered from mental illness and addiction—but is also no less alive to joy and hope, overspilling with love in all its many complexities for family, friends, and the ordinary girls of the title—girls who were close, girls who were enemies, the girls she herself once was."

—Isaac Fitzgerald, *Today* (NBC)

"Jaquira Díaz's *Ordinary Girls* reaches deep into your heart and seizes your emotions from the very first sizzling paragraph. And as it carries you into some of Díaz's darkest shadows and out into variegated light, it refuses to let go. In fiercely honest prose, Díaz turns back every page of her life . . . The stunning beauty of Díaz's memoir grows out of its passion, its defiance, its longing, its love, and its clear-eyed honesty. Díaz's story hums with a vibrant beauty, shining a light out of the darkness that shadowed her life."

—*BookPage*, starred review

"A powerful memoir, heart-wrenching, inspiring, thoroughly engrossing . . . Through one family's story, we learn about challenges of poverty, migration, uprootedness, addiction, sexism, racism—but also about the triumphant, spirited storyteller who survives to tell the tale. Jaquira Díaz is our contemporary Scheherazade, telling stories to keep herself alive and whole, and us, her readers, mesmerized and wanting more. And we get it: there is more life packed on each page of *Ordinary Girls* than some lives hold in a lifetime." —Julia Alvarez, author of
How the García Girls Lost Their Accents and
In the Time of the Butterflies

"A fierce, unflinching account of ordinary girls leading extraordinary lives." —*Poets & Writers*

"[*Ordinary Girls*] belongs on your must-read lists. Díaz is a masterful writer . . . With refreshing honesty, she talks about despair, depression, love, and hope with such vibrancy that her vivid portrayal will stay with you long after the final page."
—*O, The Oprah Magazine*

"Outstanding. A powerful and lyrical coming-of-age story, *Ordinary Girls* is a candid illustration of shame, despair, and violence as well as joy and triumph. Against a Puerto Rican backdrop, this debut is compassionate, brave, and forgiving." —*Ms.* magazine

"At once heartbreaking and throbbing with life in a rich portrait that's anything but ordinary." —*Good Housekeeping*
(The 50 Best Books of 2019 to Add to Your Reading List)

"Díaz does not flinch with the hard-hitting details of growing up in communities that deserve our wholehearted attention. She complicates how we imagine girlhood and offers a beautiful memoir written with so much love, compassion, and intelligence. This book is a necessary read at a time where the system and the media is so often working against the survival of women of color. This book burns in the memory and makes one feel all the feelings. A triumph!"   —*Bustle* (Angie Cruz, author of *Dominicana*)

"Compelling . . . A must-read memoir on vulnerability, courage, and everything in between from a standout writer."
                                    —*Library Journal*, starred review

"A dynamic examination of the power of persistence."
                                    —*Time* (Most Anticipated Books of Fall 2019)

"Jaquira Díaz is an unstoppable force. Her writing is alive with power. I stand in awe of what she brings us. The future is here."
                —Luís Alberto Urrea, author of *The House of Broken Angels*

"Inventive . . . The literary bells and whistles give her story a broader interest than many memoirs . . . This book isn't just about the author's quest for self-determination; it's also about Puerto Rico's. An unusually creative memoir of a bicultural life."
                                    —*Kirkus Reviews*

"Díaz's resilience and writing abilities are far from ordinary; she's an emissary from an experience that many young women have. Listen."   —*Refinery29*

"There's a certain ferocity throughout the entirety of *Ordinary Girls*. For some of the book, it's humming like a hardworking engine—concealed under the hood, always present—but then there are moments when it combusts, bursting from the page in such a way that you, as a reader, have to pause and take a breath. *Ordinary Girls* is an electrifying, deftly paced debut." —*Salon*

"Every page of *Ordinary Girls* vibrates with music and lyricism. Díaz writes with raw and refreshing honesty, triumphantly mapping a way out of despair toward love and hope, to become her version of the girl she always wanted to be." —*Autostraddle*

"A whirlwind memoir. Like Maya Angelou's seminal 1969 memoir *I Know Why the Caged Bird Sings* before it, *Ordinary Girls* is brutally honest in a way that few books dare to be." —*Bitch*

"Every so often you discover a voice that just floors you—or rather, feels like it can bulldoze something in your very soul. This fall, that voice belongs to Jaquira Díaz." —*The Week*
(25 Books to Read in the Second Half of 2019)

"In her debut memoir, Jaquira Díaz mines her experiences growing up in Puerto Rico and Miami, grappling with traumas both personal and international, and over time converts them into something approaching hope and self-assurance. For years, Díaz has dazzled in shorter formats—stories, essays, etc.—and her entrée into longer lengths is very welcome." —*The Millions*
(Most Anticipated: The Great Second-Half 2019 Book Preview)

"In this vibrant and passionate debut, [Díaz] describes how she found a way to not only survive, but thrive." —*Book Riot*

"Jaquira Díaz writes about ordinary girls living extraordinary lives. And Díaz is no ordinary observer. She is a wondrous survivor, a woman who has claimed her own voice, a writer who writes for those who have no voice, for the black and brown girls 'who never saw themselves in books.' Jaquira Díaz writes about them with love. How extraordinary is that!" —Sandra Cisneros, author of *The House on Mango Street*

"Jaquira Díaz's *Ordinary Girls* is more than a memoir. It is an awe-inspiring, middle-finger-waving rejection of the cult and culture of shame that pervades Latinx communities . . . An unflinching yet compassionate dissection of the pain, love, and violence that cast Díaz's life in equal parts light and shadow . . . A love letter to the girls who have been stigmatized and silenced and hurt and left behind, to those of us whose families are both a source of incredible joy and immense pain, to all of us who contemplated dying more times than we could count and came back up for air at the last possible second . . . A homecoming for those of us who miss our pátria, a mirror for those of us looking for our ancestors . . . A history of Puerto Rico that trickles into the present, right up until the devastating aftermath of Hurricane María. And perhaps most importantly, *Ordinary Girls* is a reminder to keep surviving in whatever way we know how, so that we can one day write ourselves out of despair and into the people we could be—without shame." —*Women's Review of Books*

"Striking. Díaz's story is absolutely breathtaking."

—NBC Latino

"More so than many, *Ordinary Girls* will be treasured and studied not just for its testimony of survival, but also its stunning and refreshingly consistent strength of style. Every page shimmers with assuredness and the strength of somebody who has survived to tell this story but also knows that survival is a daily process. *Ordinary Girls* is a fierce, beautiful, uncompromising memoir about survival, motherhood, love, forgiveness, and identity. It's harrowing with a purpose."   —Popmatters.com

"A cry of hope . . . Díaz rises above her challenges, and ultimately, this book is the proof of her triumph."   —*The Rumpus*

"Jaquira Díaz's *Ordinary Girls* is a life story of astonishing honesty and beauty and power, a memoir of breath and rhythm and blood-red struggle, a book for everyone who has ever felt homesick inside their own skin, and for those who, like Díaz, sing the marvelous song of themselves at top volume."   —Karen Russell,
author of *Swamplandia*

"[A] candid and compelling memoir . . . Díaz's strength lies in how she can enliven the places she inhabits . . . While the story of a typical displaced girl's life could have been tragic, Díaz takes charge, changes her trajectory, and tells a tale of an individual who ultimately triumphs. Teens may relate to Díaz's adolescent struggles, including sexual curiosity, while being moved by her resilience."   —*Booklist*

"An intimate portrait . . . Moving swiftly from essay to essay, section to section, the stories that constitute Díaz's real life read with the pulse of short fiction—each word, sentence, and scene is vital and vibrant, meticulous in its structure and devastating in its poignance . . . *Ordinary Girls* is a triumph of a debut. A lyrical and generous book, Díaz lifts the voices of ordinary girls past, present, and future." —*Columbia Journal*

"Gripping . . . Díaz's empowering book wonderfully portrays the female struggle and the patterns of family dysfunction." —*Publishers Weekly*

"Díaz blazes a bold path from the depths of the heart and guts of girls up through their fiercely beautiful throats into unstoppable song. *Ordinary Girls* risks dipping into family fractures, identity traumas, and the strained lines between cultures with language so fierce in places I bit my tongue, so tender in places I felt humming in my skin. Sometimes the repressed, oppressed girl, against all odds, goes back to get her own body and voice. This book will save lives." —*Lidia Yuknavitch, author of The Book of Joan*

"Through her honest and vibrant writing, Díaz navigates through life to discover her identity in a world full of challenges." —*SheReads.com*

"Díaz delivers a poignant account of her life, and the colloquial prose style longs to be read aloud. If you're a fan of Roxane Gay or Sandra Cisneros, then make sure *Ordinary Girls* is the next memoir you pick up." —*Paperback Paris* blog

"Every once in a while, a truly electric debut memoir comes along, and this fall, *Ordinary Girls* is it. It's the story of an ordinary girl; it's the story of all the extraordinary girls. Díaz is a skilled writer; the depth of layering is strong, from the details to the larger structures of identity, white supremacy, colonialism, and brown, queer, and femme resilience and resistance." —*BuzzFeed*

ORDINARY GIRLS

ORDINARY GIRLS

/I/\I//\I//\I//\I//\I//\I//\I//\I//\I//\I//\I//\I//\I//\I//\I//\I//\I//\I//\I/

A MEMOIR

Jaquira Díaz

ALGONQUIN BOOKS OF CHAPEL HILL 2020

Published by
ALGONQUIN BOOKS OF CHAPEL HILL
Post Office Box 2225
Chapel Hill, North Carolina 27515-2225

a division of
WORKMAN PUBLISHING
225 Varick Street
New York, New York 10014

The interview on page 321 was first published in the
Paris Review Daily on December 12, 2019.

Library of Congress Cataloging-in-Publication Data
Names: Díaz, Jaquira, author.
Title: Ordinary girls : a memoir / Jaquira Díaz.
Description: First edition. | Chapel Hill, North Carolina :
Algonquin Books of Chapel Hill, 2019.
Identifiers: LCCN 2019009593 | ISBN 9781616209131 (hardcover)
Subjects: LCSH: Díaz, Jaquira—Childhood and youth. | Díaz, Jaquira—Family.
| Lesbian authors—Puerto Rico—Biography. | Racially mixed women—Puerto
Rico—Biography. | Families—Puerto Rico. |
Mentally ill women. | Substance abuse.
Classification: LCC PS3604.I176 Z46 2019 | DDC 818/.603—dc 3
LC record available at https://lccn.loc.gov/2019009593

ISBN 978-1-64375-082-8 (PB)

10 9 8 7 6 5 4 3 2 1
First Paperback Edition

Versions of the following stories have previously been published as follows:

"El Caserío," as "Malavé," in the *The Los Angeles Review*

"La Otra" in *Longreads*

Excerpts of "Monster Story," as "Baby Lollipops," in *The Sun* magazine, and as "Monster Story," in *Ninth Letter*

"Ordinary Girls" in the *Kenyon Review* and *The Best American Essays 2016*

Excerpts of "Fourteen, or How to be a Juvenile Delinquent," as "Fourteen," in *Passages North*, and as "How to be a Juvenile Delinquent," in *Slice Magazine*

Excerpts of "Girls, Monsters," as "Girls, Monsters," in Tin House's *Flash Fidelity*, and "Season of Risks," in *The Southern Review*

Excerpt of "Beach City," in *Brevity*

"Secrets" in *The Southeast Review*

"Mother, Mercy," as "My Mother and Mercy," in *The Sun* magazine

Excerpts of "Returning," as "Bus Ride, 1999," in *Juked*, as "How Memory Is Written and Rewritten," in the *The Los Angeles Review of Books*, as "Inside the Brutal Baby Lollipops Murder Case that Shook South Florida," in *Rolling Stone* online, and as "You Do Not Belong Here," in *Kenyon Review Online*

Para Abuela, para Mami, para Puerto Rico,
and for all my girls.

We're going to right the world and live. I mean live our lives the way lives were meant to be lived. With the throat and wrists. With rage and desire, and joy and grief, and love till it hurts, maybe. But goddamn, girl. Live.

—SANDRA CISNEROS, "Bien Pretty"

CONTENTS

Girl Hood   1

GIRL HOOD

We were the girls who strolled onto the blacktop on long summer days, dribbling past the boys on the court. We were the girls on the merry-go-round, laughing and laughing and letting the world spin while holding on for our lives. The girls on the swings, throwing our heads back, the wind in our hair. We were the loudmouths, the troublemakers, the practical jokers. We were the party girls, hitting the clubs in booty shorts and high-top Jordans, smoking blunts on the beach. We were the wild girls who loved music and dancing. Girls who were black and brown and poor and queer. Girls who loved each other.

I have been those girls. On a Greyhound bus, homeless and on the run, a girl sleeping on lifeguard stands, behind a stilt-house restaurant, on a bus stop bench. A hoodlum girl, throwing down with boys and girls and their older sisters and even the cops, suspended every year for fighting on the first day of school, kicked out of music class for throwing a chair at the math teacher's son, kicked off two different school buses, kicked out of pre-algebra for stealing the teacher's grade book. A girl who got slammed onto a police car by two cops, in front of the whole school, after a brawl with six other girls.

And I have been other girls: girl standing before a judge; girl on a dock the morning after a hurricane, looking out at the bay like it's the end of the world; girl on a rooftop; girl on a ledge; girl plummeting through the air. And years later, a woman, writing letters to a prisoner on death row.

And the girls I ran with? Half of them I was secretly in love with. Street girls, who were escaping their own lives, trading the chaos of home for the chaos on the streets. One of them had left home after being molested by a family member, lived with her brother most of the time. Another had two babies before she was a junior in high school, and decided they were better off with the father—a man in his thirties. Only one had what I thought was a perfectly good set of parents at home: a dad who owned a restaurant and paid for summer vacations abroad, a mom who planned birthday parties and cooked dinner. They were girls who fought with me, smoked out with me, got arrested with me. Girls who snuck into clubs with me, terrorized the neighborhood with me, got jailhouse tattoos with me. Girls who picked me up when I was stranded and brought me food when I was starving, who sat with me outside the emergency room after my boy was stabbed in a street fight, who held me, and cried with me, at my abuela's funeral. Hood girls, who were strong and vulnerable, who taught me about love and friendship and hope.

Sometimes in dreams, I return to those girls, those places. And we are still there, all of us, roller-skating on the boardwalk, laying out our beach towels on the sand, dancing to Missy Elliott's "Work It" under the full moon.

We are women now—those of us who are alive, the ones who made it. For a while there, we didn't know if any of us would.

PART ONE

////\\//\\//\\//\\//\\//\

Madre Patria

Origin Story

Puerto Rico, 1985

Papi and I waited in the town square of Ciales, across from Nuestra Señora del Rosario, the Catholic church. He was quiet, stern-faced, his picked-out Afro shining in the sun, his white polo shirt drenched in sweat. Papi was tall and lean-muscled, with a broad back. He'd grown up boxing and playing basketball, had a thick mustache he groomed every morning in front of the bathroom mirror. Squinting in the sun, one hand tightened around his ring finger, I pulled off Papi's ring, slipped it onto my thumb. I was six years old and restless: I'd never seen a dead body.

My father's hero, Puerto Rican poet and activist Juan Antonio Corretjer, had just died. People had come from all over the island and gathered outside the parish to hear his poetry while his remains were transported from San Juan. Mami and Anthony, my older brother, were lost somewhere in the crowd.

During the drive from Humacao to Ciales, I'd listened from the backseat while Papi told the story: how Corretjer had been raised in a family of independentistas, how he'd spent his entire life fighting for el pueblo, for the working class, for Puerto Rico's freedom. How he'd been a friend of Pedro Albizu Campos, "El Maestro," who my father adored, the Puerto Rican Nationalist Party leader who'd spent more than twenty-six years in prison for attempting to overthrow the US government. How he had spent a year in "La Princesa," the prison where Albizu Campos was tortured with radiation. After his release, Corretjer became one of Puerto Rico's most prominent activist writers.

In the car, Mami had lit a cigarette and rolled down her window, her cropped, blond waves blowing in the wind. She took a long pull from her cigarette, then let the smoke out, her red fingernails shining. My mother smoked like the whole world was watching, like she was Marilyn Monroe in some old movie, or Michelle Pfeiffer in *Scarface*. Every time we left the house, my mother was made up from head to red-pedicured toes, her hair colored, her eyes dramatically set in eye shadow and a thick coat of mascara, with lipstick to match her nail polish.

While my mother smoked, not paying attention to my father's story, Anthony slept beside me in the back, his mouth half open. My brother had no interest in stories, but I lived for Papi's tales of magic and Boricua Robin Hoods, imagined myself as a character in them, riding a black horse into battle, slicing conquistadores in half with my razor-sharp machete.

It was my father who'd taught me to tie my shoelaces like rabbit ears, to catch fireflies at dusk, to eat ensalada de pulpo bought from chinchorros on the side of the road in Naguabo and Luquillo, to play chess. He'd told me stories of coconut palms that bowed to the sun, of jíbaros like his uncles and grandfather, who got up before daylight to cut cane in the cañaverales. Stories of machetes, sweat, and sugar, before paved roads and indoor plumbing and

English. Stories of women: Lucecita Benítez, one of Puerto Rico's most famous singers, who sang about race and liberation; Lolita Lebrón, who fought among men, taking up arms after La Masacre de Ponce; Yuíza, a Taíno cacica who would be resurrected, rising from ash and clay and blood to avenge the death of her people. His tales were spun of history and wind and poetry.

The funeral procession approached, a caravan of cars led by a white hearse—every car flying a Puerto Rican flag—moving slowly uphill toward the plaza, closer to the church, where arrangements of roses and lirios and carnations already waited. The crowd grew, hundreds of people approaching the square, some of them waving Puerto Rican flags. Papi watched them, never looked away, even when I yanked his hand this way and that way or when I tugged on the hem of his shirt, even as I picked up pebbles and flung them across the plaza at the pigeons. Not even to wipe the tears from his eyes. I wanted to ask about his tears, to remind him of what I'd heard Mami say while Anthony, during one of his tantrums, thrust himself against the walls of our apartment, then the floor: Los hombres no lloran.

Papi and I moved through the crowd, the two of us zigzagging in between couples and families and students in their school uniforms, all of them waiting for their turn in front of the open casket. When we'd finally made our way to the front, I saw the man in the casket for the first time: in his seventies, balding, patches of white hair on the sides, pale, white mustache. I tried to memorize the lines around Corretjer's mouth, the shape of his forehead, the arch of his eyebrows. I wanted to trace my fingers along the creases of his unmoving face, commit them to memory.

I don't know how long Papi and I stood there in front of that open casket, as if in a trance, as if waiting for the rise and fall of Corretjer's chest, my father voiceless, sweat trickling down his face. But I was sure of one thing: that I wanted everything my father wanted, and if he loved this man, then I would love him, too.

Months after Alaina was born, Anthony in the second grade, Mami working at a factory in Las Piedras, I spent my days at home with Papi. Abuela took care of Alaina while Mami worked, so I had Papi all to myself. He'd sit up in bed, reading to me from Juan Antonio Corretjer's *Yerba bruja* or Hugo Margenat's *Obras completas* or Julia de Burgos's *El mar y tú,* a mug of café con leche in his hand. My father, who'd been a student at the University of Puerto Rico, had spent his college days writing protest poems and studying literature and the work of independentistas and activists.

I loved books because Papi loved books, and his were the first I tried to read. I was a kid trying to learn my father's secrets, whatever mysteries he'd found in those pages that kept him from me for so many hours each day. Imagine my disappointment when I discovered that Manuel Puig's *El beso de la mujer araña* didn't involve a masked superhero using her spider powers to save innocent people from muggers or mad scientists. Or that Mario Vargas Llosa's *La ciudad y los perros* was not about a society made up entirely of dogs.

In my father's books, I got lost in stories: children who sprouted eagles' wings, a baby born with the curled tail of a pig, a man who spent a hundred years on an island prison mourning the loss of his lover but never aged a day, a woman who carried a pistol into a government building and opened fire.

One morning, I woke to find Papi in the bedroom I shared with Anthony, sitting at my desk, his back to me. He pulled dollar bills, wrinkled and folded, from a black garbage bag, unfolding them, lining them up in stacks. Our bedroom was cramped with our twin beds, Alaina's crib, stacks of Papi's books in a corner, our toys littering the floor. From my bed, under a nautical bedspread sewn by my mother, I watched him counting and bundling and fastening them with rubber bands, until the desk was covered with money.

There was another morning, and another, and another, and I learned not to ask questions, not to let slip what I knew about the money, about Papi's hiding places: the top shelf in our closet, which Anthony and I couldn't reach, the small suitcase under my parents' bed, my father's toolbox.

Every afternoon when my mother came home from the factory, my father left and went to the little plaza in El Caserío. And every afternoon I begged him to take me along, but he refused. I could play outside, but la plaza, he said, was no place for a girl.

"How come Anthony *always* gets to go?" I would ask Mami, yelling, slamming my fists on the kitchen counter. Anthony was never banned from any place, always got what he wanted because he was a boy.

But Mami, she didn't take no shit. She'd pull me by the arm, the half-moons of her sharp fingernails biting into my skin, and shut me right up. She'd leave me sobbing, longing for something to lift this burden of girlhood.

ONE AFTERNOON, OUTSIDE our apartment building, I kicked off my chancletas and ran around on the front lawn, barefoot, looking for moriviví. It grew all over the neighborhood, a small plant with leaves that closed like tiny fists when you touched them, faking their own death, reopening when left undisturbed. I leaned down to touch it, running my fingers over it, until my friend Eggy, who lived two blocks over, showed up on his bike.

"Wanna go for a ride?" he called from the street. Eggy was my best friend, always wandering the streets because his mom didn't pay him or his brother Pito any mind. He was brown, a dash of freckles across his nose and cheeks, his Afro always unkempt, his T-shirts always either too small or too big, with holes on the front. Eggy was too smart for his own good, always knew everybody's business: whose husband crashed their car into a barbershop, who kissed who behind the elementary school, which boys got caught looking up the girls' skirts on the playground.

I glanced back at our building, our balcony, our apartment's open windows. Mami had told me to stay where she could keep an eye on me, but Papi was in the plaza, and I was dying to see what he did there, why girls weren't allowed. So I climbed up on Eggy's handlebars.

"Don't drop me!" I said.

Eggy pedaled hard, making a left toward the building across the street, then past his building. We rode around to the back, the wind slapping my head, my curls blowing in my face. I held on to the handlebars, my bare feet in the air.

When we finally got to la plaza, a small square surrounded by two-story buildings, shaded by ceiba trees and flamboyanes, I hopped off the bike.

Next to one of the buildings, children's clothes were drying on a clothesline. A homeless man slept on a discarded sofa, baking under the sun. Four hustlers, three men and one woman, played dominoes around a makeshift card table made from a large paint bucket and four milk crates used as chairs. Papi was standing among his stone-faced friends. Tecatos walked up to Papi, said something I couldn't hear, handed him money, then disappeared behind the buildings.

"You know what they're doing, right?" Eggy asked.

"What are they doing?"

"Your dad is selling them perico."

I knew what perico was, just like I knew what tecatos were— Eggy had told me. His mother, he'd said, had sold all her jewelry and their TV to get perico. She would've sold the food in their fridge, if they'd had any.

Eggy got off his bike, leaned it against the building.

I looked for my brother among the men, feeling betrayed, wondering how much he knew, if this was a secret he and Papi shared, something else they kept from me. But Anthony was not around.

My face hot, upper lip sweaty, I turned and started walking back home.

"Where you going?" Eggy called after me.

I kept walking, ignoring his question. Bare feet on the grass, then the sidewalk, on tiptoes, trying not to step on broken glass while crossing the street. As I reached the front of my building, I found one chancleta there, right where I'd left it. The other one gone. I leaned down and ran my fingers over all the morivivi. They each shriveled, leaf by leaf, dying their fake deaths. And me, pretending I'd been there all along, in case Mami looked out the window, stepped out on the balcony, asked where I'd been.

DURING THE WARM nights in El Caserío, I lay in the hammock on our first-floor balcony, listening to the coquis' songs as they echoed through the whole neighborhood. Every night, at all hours, Papi's friends came asking for him. I fetched my father when I saw them approaching, watched as he took their balled-up dollar bills and handed them their baggies over the railing. Some of them came by every day. Some of them, a few times a day.

I was rocking myself in the hammock when one of them strolled right up to our balcony, a man with a curved, jagged scar on his face extending from the corner of his lips all the way up to his eye.

"Is your father home?" he asked.

"No," I said, even though my father *was* home. I lied without hesitating, without knowing why. Maybe I thought I was protecting my father. Maybe I sensed that something about this man was dangerous.

"Do you want to see what I'm holding?" the man asked, stepping closer. He looked past me, through the door into our living room. "I have something for you."

I got up out of the hammock and walked over, thinking that maybe he'd hand me a few crumpled dollar bills to give my father. I wanted so much to believe him. But when I looked at his pants, down below his waist, he pulled out his dick.

It wasn't like the ones I'd seen before—my brother's, a baby cousin's, or Eggy's, which I saw once when he pulled it out and started pissing on a dead toad. Eggy's had been no big deal. I'd been more interested in the toad, its carcass torn open and full of live maggots. Those other ones had been small, shriveled-up things. But this was something else. This was a grown man's dick, swollen and thick and veiny. Horrifying.

At first I thought it was a mistake, that he'd meant to pull something out of his pocket and it somehow slipped out. But then, the smile on his face, the serrated edges of his sickle feather scar. I stumbled back.

"Papi!" I screamed at the top of my lungs. The man tore past the side of our building toward the cañaverales behind El Caserío.

Papi came out to the balcony, barefoot, wiping sleep from his eyes. But how could I explain what had just happened? From my mother, I'd learned that a girl's body was special, that I should stay away from men, who were not to be trusted, that I should not let boys see my private parts, or let them show me theirs. How could I explain what the man had done without admitting that I'd stupidly let him? Years later I'd remember this moment, how I'd thought it was my own fault. How, ashamed, I thought of it like a secret that needed to be kept.

Standing there, heart pounding in my chest, I said nothing as my father rushed over, as he wrapped his arms around me, as he asked, "What's wrong?"

I held my stomach, willing the tears to come, as Papi asked again and again, "What's wrong? Where does it hurt?"

But I kept it to myself, just cried and cried, wilting like morivivi in his arms.

I ADORED MY father. He was the center of my universe, and I wanted, more than anything else, to be the center of his. That whole year, I had Papi mostly to myself during the day. But when I didn't, at least I had his books.

In my father's books, I would learn about the genocide of the Taínos, about our island's Taíno name, Borikén, which then became Borínquen, and later, Puerto Rico. About Africans who were brought through the Transatlantic slave trade, including part of our black family, although most of my father's side came from Haiti right after the Haitian Revolution, and settled in Naguabo. In my father's books, and in my father's own stories, I would find our history:

Ponce, 1937

AFTER PEDRO ALBIZU Campos' first imprisonment in La Princesa, members of the Puerto Rican Nationalist Party and civilians organized a march in protest. Puerto Ricans wanted independence from the United States, and from Blanton Winship, the US-appointed governor, who had not been elected by the people. They secured all the necessary permits, invited a marching band, gathered with their families after church. Men, women, and children headed toward the parade, where they would celebrate Palm Sunday with music and palm fronds.

Hundreds of people marched as the band played "La Borinqueña." They were met by hundreds of police officers in riot gear who shot their Tommy Guns directly at the crowd of unarmed civilians. Under Winship's orders, the cops surrounded the demonstrators, leaving them no route for escape.

The shooting lasted about thirteen minutes, some people say. Others insist it was fifteen.

The police murdered nineteen people, and wounded about 235, including a seven-year-old girl, a man shielding his young son, and an eighteen-year-old boy looking out his window.

Witnesses said that as the cops walked by the dead or dying, they beat them with their clubs. Most of the victims who lay dead on the street, the evidence showed, were shot in their backs while running away from the gunfire.

Although an investigation by the US Commission on Civil Rights found that Governor Winship had ordered the massacre, none of the murderers were ever convicted, or even prosecuted. [1]

This was our history, I would eventually learn. We'd come from uprisings against colonial rule, slavery, massacres, erasure. We'd carried histories of resistance, of protest.

AND I WOULD also learn that my father, even though he spent his days selling perico, was imagining some other life. All that time lost in his books, all those nights writing poetry and painting, every single dollar he stashed away—Papi dreaming of another place, where his kids could play outside, where he didn't have to sell dope anymore. One day, he would tell me all his secrets, all the stories not meant for children: the other woman he'd loved, the baby who died before I was born, the army days. And I would write it all down, determined to remember.

Prohibido olvidar.

El Caserío

This is where I begin. I come from poverty, from El Caserío Padre Rivera, the government housing projects, and there are stories here I never want to forget.

In El Caserío, Anthony and I spent most summer days playing outside. It was a world of men, of violence, a place too often not safe for women or girls. There were shoot-outs in the streets, fourteen-year-old boys carrying guns as they rode their bikes to the candy store just outside the walls. We watched a guy get stabbed right in front of our building, watched the cops, who we called "los camarones," come in and raid places for drugs and guns. Outsiders were not welcome. Outsiders meant trouble.

We were poor, like everybody who lived there, but we didn't know any better. At times, El Caserío was like the Wild West, but what you didn't know unless you lived there was that most people were just trying to raise their families in peace, like anywhere else. The neighbors kept an eye on all the kids, fed them, took them to school, took them trick-or-treating on Halloween. All over the neighborhood, people told stories. El Caserío was where I learned about danger and violence and death, but it was also where I learned about community.

El Caserío was made up of clusters of two-story cinderblock buildings, each with four apartments on the first floor, and four on the second. Every apartment had two balconies, one facing the front yard, one facing the back. Some buildings, like ours, faced the street, but some had a view of the plaza, or the basketball courts, or the elementary school at the end of the main street.

We sometimes played cops and robbers, but Anthony and his friends didn't want girls around—I had to beg them to let me play. I was always the robber, always the one to get shot down by the cops. Because they were boys, they got to carry the guns and do all the shooting. Girls were not supposed to carry weapons—knives or guns or machetes—so how was I supposed to rob a bank? Still, they showed no mercy, shooting me six, seven times. I had to lie on the sidewalk, pretend I was dead.

Most days I ran wild around El Caserío, dying to hang out with the boys, or my brother when he was around, to be the boy I thought my father wanted. But my brother was nothing like me. I was tanned from days spent in the summer sun, and everything about me was messy. I spent hours climbing the tangled branches of the flamboyanes, riding my bike in the street. I ran around with Eggy, barefoot, splashing in puddles, catching lizards, digging our hands into the mud, pulling up earthworms. Sometimes we'd shoot hoops. If there were no boys around, I'd play double Dutch with the triplets who lived in the next building over, singing along to our Spanish version of the Jackson Five's "Rockin' Robin."

My brother was the favorite, who never got in trouble for pushing me down, for knocking me upside the head, for tripping me as

I walked by. Eventually, I learned to defend myself, to outrun him, to hit him back. Anthony was chubby, with my mother's piercing blue-green eyes, blond hair, fair skin. He didn't climb trees, or run through the flooded streets during rainstorms, or hang upside down from the monkey bars—that was all me. My brother mostly stayed inside, watching TV or drawing. He could draw anything in under a minute. With a pencil and paper, he'd take one look at you and turn you into a cartoon. He'd draw cities and underwater worlds and the Millennium Falcon. He'd draw our family: Mami with a round pregnant belly, Papi with boxing gloves and high-tops, Abuela stirring a giant pot of sancocho, and me, with a parrot's beak for a nose, two red devil horns, and a pointed tail. I was just like Papi, with his wide nose, with dark eyes, tight curls, skin that browned easily after a little bit of sun. I was the wild one, always running, always dirty, sweaty, a tomboy. Anthony was blue-green, light, golden. I was brown, brown, brown, like tierra. But even though we had a white mother, Abuela reminded us that we were a black family, and that every single one of her grandchildren was black, no matter how light-skinned we might look to the world. Even Anthony, with his golden hair and light eyes.

One afternoon, Anthony and I met the other boys outside our building—Pito and Eggy and a bunch of other kids. Pito, the oldest of all the Caserío street kids, was the shot caller. He was in sixth grade, but smaller than most of the other kids, with a short Afro and a face full of freckles. Eggy was taller, less freckled, and not so bossy.

"You better be ready for war," Pito said. He tossed a pebble back and forth from one hand to the other.

Pito decided that we'd all be Taínos, that it was our duty to defend our island from the Spaniards who came to murder and enslave us. If Pito said climb a tree, we climbed. If he told us to break into the neighbor's apartment, we broke in. So when he said we were going to wage a war against el viejo Wiso, we ran around El Caserío looking for rocks and pebbles to use as bullets and grenades, enough to take down an entire army.

El viejo Wiso spent all day sitting on his second-floor balcony, looking out at the barrio. He sat there quietly when we rode our bikes in front of his building, and when Pito started a small fire on the lawn so we could cook a can of Spam like soldiers did in the old days of war.

Across from Wiso's building was the tallest tree in El Caserío, a ceiba with a trunk thicker than my torso. Everybody said el viejo Wiso was toasted, and we kids were supposed to leave him alone, stay out of his way. But Pito claimed Wiso had killed hundreds of Taínos in Vietnam, which is what made him crazy, and now we were going to make him pay.

Pito filled the pockets of his jeans with rocks, small pebbles, and pieces of broken glass. Some of the boys didn't have pockets, so they stuffed my overalls' pockets with their ammunition, even though I was forbidden from throwing rocks. (According to Pito and Anthony, everybody knew girls couldn't throw.) When Pito gave the order, we marched our way across the narrow, cracked sidewalks, cutting through patches of grass and weeds and morivivi, all the way to el viejo Wiso's building on the other side of El Caserío. He was exactly where we expected, just sitting there on his balcony, fanning himself with his worn, gray, newsboy cap.

When Pito threw the first rock, it landed in the middle of the front yard. Wiso didn't move.

"Attack!" Pito ordered, one fist raised over his head.

And then, all at once, the boys started flinging rocks, hurling them at the planters and the rusty bike el viejo Wiso kept on his balcony, some of them landing in the yard or hitting the neighbor's windows. Anthony and Eggy and Pito picked my pockets for their rocks, throwing one after another and another.

"Get up!" Pito shouted. "Come down and fight!"

But Wiso still didn't move.

I pulled a rock from one of my pockets, got ready to fling it, but Anthony snatched it without a word, as if I was just handing it to him. I watched him throw it as I scrunched my face under the sun. He bit his bottom lip, something he did when he was trying to concentrate, and sent it flying over the lawn, his bushy blond locks lifting in the wind.

When everyone ran out of ammo, Pito scanned the lawn for more rocks, turned all my pockets inside out. He searched the ground beneath the ceiba tree, until he found exactly what he was looking for: an empty beer bottle. He grabbed it, measured the distance between the balcony and his throwing arm, and without another word, he flung it, hard.

It landed right in the middle of the balcony, shattering into a million pieces, glass exploding like shrapnel.

Slowly, Wiso rose from his chair. He dropped his hat right there and stepped back into his apartment. We watched, wide-eyed and nervous, waiting for him to come back out, maybe with a pot of hot water to throw at us, like some of the viejas when they were fighting with their husbands, or the mailman, or the neighbors.

But suddenly, without warning, Pito took off, pushing boys out of the way, running in the same direction we'd come from. Eggy grabbed my arm, pulled me, hard. And that's when I saw it: el viejo Wiso crossing the lawn, headed right for us, a machete in his hand.

Then we all took off. Most of the boys split, peeling off toward their own apartments. Eggy, Anthony, and I followed Pito, who was heading toward Abuela's place. It was home base, Abuela's house, where we all went for lunch or snacks, where we all took refuge when we were in trouble, when we were hiding from our parents or each other, or when los camarones came in to raid places or take someone away.

I cut through the same spots of patchy grass and morivoví, all the boys yelling, "This way!" and "Faster!" and "Get out of the way!"

I followed Pito. Maybe because he was older and I thought he'd have a plan. Maybe I thought he wouldn't let Wiso chop my head off. After all, he was brave. He was the boss.

A FEW WEEKS later, after everybody had heard how Wiso came after us with the machete, they found him in pieces. Limbs, torso, head severed. His body had been left in a saco, inside a dumpster a few blocks from our building. They said he'd been dead at least a week. Eggy was the one who told me, his eyes glossy and wide with excitement, as if he was retelling the end of *Star Wars* or *Jaws*.

Some people said Wiso owed somebody money, one of the hustlers around El Caserío. Some said he was just a crazy old man who must've chased the wrong tecato with his machete. Some suspected the wife.

People went around El Caserío telling their stories of el viejo Wiso, wanting to be connected to him in death, even if they had no connection in life: "He sprayed me with a hose as I walked out of my building" or "I knew him before he went to Vietnam." Even us kids: "He almost chopped our heads off!"

Later, we would go back to climbing the flamboyanes, back to playing in the streets. We would forget about Wiso, the machete, its polished blade gleaming in the sunlight. We would forget the stories of Vietnam. Our parents would set us free, let us run wild, like they could not imagine a future where the street kids in El Caserío would no longer point toy guns at each other, but real ones, where the boys were no longer boys.

It would be decades before I really thought about how much violence found its way into our childhood games, how it had been us kids who drove Wiso to attack, taunted him, targeted him, until he picked up that machete and walked out of his house determined to hack us all to pieces. Or how he'd lived in that apartment with his wife, spent his days watching the ceiba, watching the leaves fall, the neighbor's bony backyard chickens strutting by with their pollitos. Or who he was before they shipped him off to fight in someone else's war, how maybe he'd been the kind of man who stepped back in his apartment for a piece of stale bread to crumble and toss over the balcony for the birds. Or how else the story could've played out: In some other version, the girl is left behind by all the boys. She runs as fast as she can toward her abuela's house, but trips over her chancletas on the sidewalk. She falls or maybe she doesn't. She gets back up or maybe she never gets the chance. The boys run and run and run, the sun on their faces, the sour smell of caña burning somewhere in the distance, until finally, that front door opens. That front door *open*.

In some other version, there is no front door. There is no girl. There is just Wiso, alive.

La Otra

The first time she saw my father, my mother knew he was hers. She was in high school. He was in college. She lied about her age. She had always looked older, my mother, and by the time she was fourteen, Grandma Mercy was already leaving her to care for two of her sisters, twelve-year-old Xiomara and one-year-old Tanisha, while she was at work.

My father says he didn't know my mother's real age, that she'd told him she was eighteen, that he found out only when Mercy caught them in bed. My mother says he didn't really find out until they were applying for their marriage license a week later, when he finally got a look at her birth date.

My father had been a college activist, protesting the naval occupation of Culebra, studying literature, writing poems about American colonialism in Puerto Rico. My mother—so young, so desperate to leave her abusive mother, so in love with my father— would've done anything to keep him.

Sometimes when I write this story, I think of my mother as the villain, tricking my father, knowing the exact time my grandma

Mercy would come home from work, leaving the bedroom door unlocked, forcing him to become a husband, a father, when what he really wanted was to read books and write poems and save the world. How maybe I wouldn't be here if Grandma Mercy hadn't threatened to have him thrown in jail.

Sometimes it's my father who is the villain. The brilliant college student who pretended not to know my mother's age as he slithered his way into her bed. How he decided to ignore the school uniform folded neatly and left on a chair in the corner of her bedroom.

They are different people now, divorced more than twenty-five years. But no matter how much they've changed, there is always this: My mother loved my father obsessively, violently, even years after their divorce. My father was a womanizer, withdrawn, absent. And it was after three children, after leaving Puerto Rico for Miami, after eleven years of marriage, after my father left her for the last time, that my mother started hearing voices, that she started snorting coke and smoking crack. But each time I write and rewrite this story, it's not just my mother's intense, all-consuming love for my father that destroys her. It's also her own mother, Grandma Mercy. And her children—my older brother, my little sister, and me. Especially me.

BY THE TIME my mother was twenty-two, she had three children. She'd already been a mother for a third of her life. It was 1985. These were the days of Menudo and "We Are the World," the year Macho Camacho gave a press conference in a leopard-skin loincloth as Madonna's "Like a Virgin" blared from radios across the United States. In one month, the space shuttle Challenger would explode while all of America watched on television, entire classrooms full of kids, everyone eager to witness the first teacher ever launched into space.

In those days, Mami teased her blond hair like Madonna, traced her green eyes with blue eyeliner, applied several coats of black mascara, apple-red lipstick, and matching nail polish. She wore skin-tight jeans and always, no matter where she was going, high heels. She dusted her chest with talcum powder after a bath, lotioned her arms and legs, perfumed her body, her hair. My mother loved lotions, perfume, makeup, clothes, shoes. But really, the truth was my mother loved and enjoyed her body. She walked around our apartment butt-ass naked. I was more used to seeing her naked body than my own. *You should love your body*, my mother would say. A woman's body was beautiful, no matter how big, how small, how old, how pregnant. This my mother firmly believed, and she would tell me over and over. As we got older, she would teach me and Alaina about masturbation, giving us detailed instructions about how to achieve orgasm. This, she said, was perfectly normal. Nothing to be ashamed of.

While my father only listened to salsa on vinyl, Héctor Lavoe and Willie Colón and Ismael Rivera, my mother was all about Madonna. My mother was Puerto Rican but also American, she liked to remind us, born in New York, and she loved everything American. She belted the lyrics to "Holiday" while shaving her legs in the shower, while making us egg salad sandwiches served with potato chips for lunch. She talked about moving us to Miami Beach, where Grandma Mercy and most of our titis lived, about making sure we learned English.

On New Year's Eve, she made me wear a red-and-white striped dress and white patent leather shoes. It was hideous. I looked like a peppermint candy. She styled my hair in fat candy curls and said she wanted me to look like Shirley Temple. I had no idea who Shirley Temple was, but I hoped she didn't expect me to be friends with her. I wasn't trying to be friends with girls in dresses and uncomfortable shoes.

I knew that these were things meant for girls, and that I was supposed to like them. But I had no interest in my mother's curtains, or her tubes of red lipstick, or her dresses, or the dolls Grandma Mercy and Titi Xiomara sent from Miami. I didn't want to be Barbie for Halloween, like my mother suggested. I wanted to be a ninja, with throwing stars and nunchucks and a sword. I wanted to kick the shit out of ten thousand men like Bruce Lee. I wanted to climb trees and catch frogs and play with *Star Wars* action figures, to fight with lightsabers and build model spaceships. I didn't have a crush on Atreyu from *The NeverEnding Story*, like my brother said, teasing me. I wanted to *be* Atreyu, to ride Falkor the luckdragon. When I watched *Conan the Destroyer*, I wanted to be fierce and powerful Grace Jones. Zula, the woman warrior. I wanted her to be the one who saved the princess, to be the one the princess fell for in the end.

(Years later, would I think of Zula during that first kiss, that first throbbing between my legs? It would be with an older girl, the daughter of my parents' friends. We'd steal my mother's cigarettes, take them out back behind our building, and light them up. She would blow her smoke past my face, stick her tongue in my mouth, slide her hand inside my shorts. How she'd know just what to do without me having to tell her—this was everything, this butch girl, so unafraid, getting everything she wanted. And how willing I was to give it to her.)

OUR NEW NEIGHBOR arrived in the middle of the night, carried her boxes from somebody's pickup into her living room, then waved goodbye as it drove away. She arrived in silence, filling the empty space of the apartment next door, where nobody had ever lived as long as I could remember, hung her flowerpots from hooks on the balcony. She arrived with almost nothing, just those plants and some furniture and her daughter Jesenia, a year older than me.

The morning after, Eggy and I were outside catching lizards, holding onto them until they got away, leaving their broken-off tails still wriggling between our fingers. She stepped out on her balcony, watering her plants with a plastic cup.

"Guess you have a new neighbor," Eggy said.

La vecina, as we learned to call her, was nothing like Mami. She wore no makeup, a faded floral housedress and out-of-style leather chancletas like my abuela's, her curly brown hair in a low ponytail. She had deep wrinkles around the corners of her eyes, although she didn't look as old as Abuela. When she looked up at Eggy and me, she smiled.

"Hola," she said. "Where's your mom?"

"Working," I said.

She pressed her hand to her cheek. "And she lets you play outside by yourself?"

"Sure," I said.

We talked for a while, la vecina asking us questions about the neighborhood, about the basketball courts, about what time the grano man came by on Sunday mornings. Eggy and I answered question after question, feeling like hostages until my father emerged.

"Buenas," Papi said.

La vecina introduced herself, and Papi walked over, shook her hand over her balcony's railing. They got to talking, ignoring me and Eggy, Papi smiling, the way he never smiled. My father always had a serious look on his face, a look that made him seem angry, even when he was happy. And he was always trying to look good, ironing his polo shirts, grooming his mustache every morning, massaging Lustrasilk Right On Curl into his hair before picking it out, even if he was just lying around the house on the weekend. The only time my father dressed down—in shorts, tank tops, and his white Nike Air Force high-tops—was when he played ball or when we went to the beach.

La vecina laughed at something he said, and my father patted his Afro lightly. When I saw the opening, I tapped Eggy on the shoulder and we took off running toward the basketball courts.

MY MOTHER WORKED long shifts at an electronic parts factory in Las Piedras. Sometimes, when Mami was at work and Anthony at school, Papi took me to Abuela's house for lunch. Abuela lived in the next building over, and Mami usually dropped off Alaina at her house before her shift. Abuela's kitchen always smelled like fried meat and café, her bedroom a blend of Maja soap, bay rum, and Bal à Versailles perfume. The second bedroom belonged to my tío David, who was a priest at the Catholic church in the city and only came home occasionally.

In Abuela's apartment, where he'd lived before he and Mami got married, before we were born, Papi was at home. He had a special bookcase there, and some books I was not allowed to touch— expensive signed first editions on the top shelf, stories not meant for children on the second. That bookcase was his refuge, where he sometimes went when Mami was yelling or flinging plates across the room. He'd sit in Abuela's kitchen, turning pages, always with his café. I would do the same, take a book off the lower shelf, sit at the table trying to make out which words I knew, as if this would transfer a sort of magic to me—secrets only Papi knew.

Abuela always said that I was like Papi's tail, that when he came into a room, I was usually not far behind. *You are just like your father*, she'd say, knowing how much I loved hearing that. She'd tell me stories about Papi as a kid. Cano, my father's nickname, given to him by my tío David when he was a baby, meant "light." When he was born, my father had been a light-skinned baby with very light hair, and my uncle, three years old at the time, found that hilarious.

Cano, Abuela told me, would climb guayaba trees to steal fruit, sneak out of the house to run through the cañaverales with the street kids. He was always getting in trouble: Cano throwing down with the school bully to defend my tío, the quiet, Jesus-loving kid who refused to fight. Cano getting whooped with a belt by the assistant principal for smacking another kid upside the head. Cano, who'd spent only a short time in the army. Cano the prankster, the papichulo with a girlfriend in every other town, always finding trouble. Cano, who—before any of us were born—had taken off to New York for a couple of years after trouble finally found *him*.

EVERY TIME I ran into la vecina, she wanted to talk. She lived alone with her daughter, Jesenia, she told me. Jesenia wasn't in school yet, but she would be starting in a couple of days. Jesenia was shy. Jesenia loved to watch TV. *Do you want to watch a movie with Jesenia? Do you want to jump rope with Jesenia?* I hadn't seen this Jesenia yet, but I was already done with her.

One morning, Mami at work, Papi asleep on the couch, la vecina caught me leaving our apartment. She was sweeping the front steps when I came out, and called after me when I tried to sneak past her. "Jaqui, wait!" She leaned the broom against her door and sat on the stoop, tapping the space next to her.

I exhaled dramatically, then plopped down on the step.

"Where were you headed?" she asked.

"Out."

"Is your brother at school?"

"Yes."

"Is your mom at work?"

"Yes."

"When does she come home?"

"I don't know."

"Does she come home at night?"

I rolled my eyes. "Yes, she comes home at night."

"Is your father home?"

"He's sleeping."

"Does he take care of you when your mother's not home?"

I studied her face, trying to figure out why all the questions about my parents. "Sometimes Abuela takes care of us."

"Who makes dinner for you?"

"Abuela," I said. "And sometimes Papi."

"What do you like to eat?"

"Ice cream."

She laughed. "What about your father?"

I shrugged. "He likes arroz con pollo, I guess."

At first it felt like being interrogated, but after a while, I was so happy to have a grownup listening to me talk about myself, I let it all out. I told her about the kioskos on the beach where Papi took me to eat ensalada de pulpo. I told her all about how Anthony almost died when he was born, how they kept him in the hospital for two months because he was so little, how he'd had machines to help him breathe. I told her how Anthony and I were always fighting, how I wasn't supposed to go to the plaza, but I still snuck over there sometimes. She listened to every word I said, *really* listened, even laughed when I made a joke. Then, I don't know what made me do it, but I told her about the tecato who came up to our balcony and pulled out his dick.

"Do you know who he was?" she asked.

"No, but I've seen him before."

"Did you tell your father?"

"No."

"You know," she said, "if you ever need to, you can talk to me." She looked right into my eyes and waited.

"Okay," I said. And I believed her.

ANTHONY, ALAINA, AND I shared a cramped bedroom—linoleum covering the concrete floors, aluminum persianas, spiderweb cracks on cinderblock walls. Anthony's twin bed against one wall, mine against the opposite, Alaina's crib in the middle. The thick smell of something burning in the air, wafting from the cañaverales, from the nearby mills where they made sugar and guarapo de caña.

I woke up sweaty, Anthony still snoring, Alaina sitting up, crying softly, her chubby fingers in her mouth, brown curls stuck to her moist forehead. Pedro Conga's "Soy Peregrino" blared from the record player in our living room.

I could hear Mami and Papi arguing in the kitchen. My mother slamming plates and silverware in the sink, asking over and over about la otra, a dirty fucking whore she could smell all over him, this woman who had taken the money *she* worked for, the money *she* brought home to take care of her children while my father was chillin' with his homeboys in la plaza.

My father denied everything. There was no smell on him. He had not spent the night with another woman. He'd gone out with friends and was too drunk to drive home. She was imagining things. She was making shit up. How could she think that he would ever do something like that? It was ridiculous. It was *crazy*.

"Don't you call me crazy!" my mother yelled, then she started screaming, like she really *was* crazy, the sound of it threatening to crack the cinderblock walls around us. A few years later, I would listen to my mother screaming, just like this, during another one of their fights. All of us already living in Miami Beach, Anthony, Alaina, and I hiding in the bedroom, our parents hurling coffee mugs and ashtrays at each other, yanking the phone off the wall, turning over the dining room table. My father already so fed up with Mami, with all of us, he would accuse her of making shit up, call her foolish, ridiculous, *crazy*. And my mother, not even thirty and already in the snares of schizophrenia and addiction and three kids at war with each other, with themselves, Anthony pounding on me, depression already like a noose around my neck.

. . .

ANOTHER DAY, LA VECINA'S apartment door wide open, she caught me as I was coming home from the basketball courts, sweaty and breathless, my face hot from the sun.

"Hey, Jaqui!" she called after me, "come in and play with Jesenia!"

I didn't know how to say no to her, and I didn't think she'd like it if I told her that Eggy and I always avoided Jesenia when we saw her riding her bike out front. Jesenia and her Jesenia dresses, one in every color of the rainbow, and her folded-down ankle socks. Jesenia with ribbons in her hair. Jesenia and her stupid pigtails. She was everything I wasn't. I had a mass of sunburned frizz that stood straight up and I liked it that way. Whenever Mami put ribbons in my hair, they ended up on the floor, or stuffed between the couch cushions, or in one of Abuela's planters.

She led me into her kitchen, where her only table was a child-sized plastic one with two small red chairs. Jesenia sat there, a plate of chocolate chip cookies in front of her, getting crumbs all over her purple dress. Her pigtails were perfect, each plaited into a tight, long braid and secured with a ribbon. La vecina pulled out the other chair and set a small plate for me.

"Jesenia, say hello to Jaqui."

Jesenia barely looked at me. "Hola."

I nodded, took a cookie, and instead of playing with Jesenia, I answered more questions for la vecina.

"Where does your father work?"

"He goes to the university," I told her, even though I could not remember the last time my father took any classes.

"Really? What does he study?"

"Books," I said, which made her laugh.

Jesenia got up, pushed her chair aside, and left the room.

La vecina poured a cup of milk, set it on the table, then wiped her hands on her dress. "So what's your mother like?"

I studied her for a minute, not sure what she was asking.

La vecina was nothing like Mami. My mother would never wear a dress like my abuela's, would never smell like fried plátanos and pine oil, would never ask question after question before getting to the point. My mother was direct and she took no shit. She got right to it. We'd go to a party and right away she was dancing. She was small but scared of nothing, a foulmouthed chain-smoker with a hot temper, who drove a stick-shift Mazda RX-7, who never set foot outside without makeup, without her door-knocker earrings, or her heels. As petite as she was, my mother owned every room she walked into. She eclipsed the sun with her confidence, took the world by the throat and shook it until it gave up what was hers. You crossed her and she was ready to throw down on the spot, taking off earrings and heels and tying up her hair. She was curvy, with a swing in her hips, and everywhere we went she had admirers, leering men asking her name, asking for her phone number, calling after her, *Mira, mami!* But she didn't give any of them the time of day. My mother was utterly and completely in love with my father. Hers was the blazing, frenzied love of Puerto Rican novelas, the kind of love that drives you mad. She loved her children, the three of us, even more so. And she never let us forget it.

La vecina waited for me to respond. This woman, so different from my mother, I just couldn't picture her in red stilettos and a fishnet dress, dancing like Madonna in front of her TV.

"She's blond," I said finally, "with green eyes like my brother. And she likes Madonna."

Jesenia came back into the room, dropped a bunch of dolls on the table. "Do you like Barbies?" she asked.

"Sure," I said, which was not entirely true. I had Barbies, dolls Mami had given me for my birthday or Christmas, or that my titis had handed down to me. But I didn't exactly *like* them. They were like reminders of everything I wasn't—blond-haired, blue-eyed. They always made me feel ugly, the brown kid who would never look like her white mother. They'd end up on the floor, tossed aside, with their heads bald. Later, when I learned about sex, I started posing them strategically: Barbie and Barbie facing each other, kissing, their stiff arms sticking up, naked Barbie on top of naked Barbie.

"Do you want to take your father some lunch?" la vecina asked.

"Okay," I said.

She sent me home with a platter of arroz con pollo, some red beans on the side. It was so heavy I almost dropped it walking through our front door, but Abuela took it off my hands.

HOURS LATER, AFTER Abuela was already gone, Anthony watching TV, and Alaina in her crib, Mami walked through the door, tired from work. She sat at the kitchen table, rubbing her feet.

"Did you eat?" she asked. "I'll make you something."

"I already ate," I said. "Had some of la vecina's arroz con pollo."

"La vecina?" my mother asked.

"She sent a big platter of food for Papi."

Suddenly, my mother got up, slamming her fist on the table, shut her eyes tight, brought her hands to her face. Then she stomped out of the kitchen.

My father, again, denied everything. He followed my mother as she came back to the kitchen.

"It's not true, Jeannette," he said. "I don't know what she's talking about."

My mother opened the refrigerator, opened the freezer, the oven, lifted the lid to our trashcan. She inspected the dishes in the sink, opened and closed all the cabinets, searching and searching. She came over and took me by the arm.

"Show me," she said. "Where is it?"

I looked for la vecina's platter everywhere, opening cabinets and checking the fridge again, but nothing.

"I don't know," I said, tears starting to sting my eyes.

"I'm telling you," my father said, "it never happened."

I looked to my father, trying to understand, trying to look in his eyes. But there was nothing there that could clear things up. I burst into tears.

Mami looked back and forth from Papi to me then Papi again. She finally turned back to me, leaning down so her face met mine. "Are you lying?" she asked me.

I couldn't get any words out. My mother was mad as hell, standing there, breathing hard, the stink of her cigarette on my face.

"It never happened," Papi said again.

My mother did not move, did not say a word. She was waiting for me to break. I kept crying, looking at my father for answers. He looked at my mother, beads of sweat collecting at his temple. But he would not look at me.

"I don't know what she's talking about," my father said, looking down at his feet, at the floor, at the wall, at the stove, unable to meet my eyes. And then, finally, I understood.

That night, I would swipe Mami's sewing scissors, cut the hair off every single one of my Barbies, the ones that still had any hair, and flush it in bunches down the toilet. I would pull my father's favorite book off the shelf, Hugo Margenat's *Obras completas*, slide it under my mattress. And while my parents yelled at each other and my mother threw the rotating table fan across the room and threatened to leave, I would lay my head on my pillow and feel nothing but the sharp sting of my father's betrayal.

I would never return that book to him, would never let on that I knew where it went, even when Papi asked if I'd seen it, even as I saw him searching and searching the bookcase in Abuela's house, every closet in our apartment. Even after I am a grown woman with books of my own, after I recognize all the ways I am exactly like my father, a runaway, abandoning relationships, jobs, homes, when things get too complicated, or too intense, or too *anything*, after looking at him becomes like looking in a mirror, his face my face, his eyes my eyes, his life like a roadmap for my own. My father, loved by so many women, would never love them back the way they wanted, not even my mother, and I would spend my life trying to be exactly like him, moving from lover to lover, someone always reaching for me, someone always trying to please me, and me, wanting everything, taking everything, but giving little in return. My father, keeper of secrets, teller of tales, who passed down to me his love of words and music and stories—and running—who created worlds for me, who would sit me down at sixteen, when I was spending days and nights on the streets of Miami Beach, drinking and using and fighting, and say, *This is not the life I want for you*, and I'd look him in the eye, toss my notebook, toothbrush, a change of clothes into my backpack and take off, launch myself like a missile into the night.

. . .

Days later, me and Eggy walking back from Abuela's house, where we'd polished off a half-dozen mangoes by ourselves, our faces and forearms sticky with juice and pulp, we ran into a mob of people outside my building. Eggy's mom and his brothers, the guy who sold pinchos around the corner from the front gate, a bunch of street kids, some viejas who lived a couple buildings over, everybody rowdy, hollering, shoving each other.

I spotted Pito and Anthony and lost Eggy as I pushed through the crowd to get to them.

"What's going on?" I asked.

Pito pointed toward the middle of the group, his face sweaty and red. He elbowed one of the other kids out of the way and pulled me by the arm, trying to squeeze us both through the small space.

"Your mom!" he yelled.

Somebody rammed me right into Pito. I almost fell, but kept moving, struggling through the throng of people, bumping them with my shoulders.

Behind me, Anthony shoved me, yelling at the back of my head. "Move!"

"I'm trying!" I hollered back.

When a space opened up, Pito thrust us through it until we made it to the front and I saw them: Papi had Mami in his arms, trying to hold her back. Mami was kicking and slapping at him, trying to get free, her hair windblown and tangled.

Our upstairs neighbor, a six-foot-six basketball player everybody called Gigante, was holding la vecina, her curly hair pulled out of its ponytail and torn to shreds. La vecina swung both arms blindly, aiming for anything she could hit.

As Papi tried to carry Mami toward our front door, she slid down and got loose, and all the street kids exploded, Pito and Anthony and Eggy calling out, "Light her up! Knock her out! Préndela!" It was the same kind of shouting we heard in our living room during boxing matches, my father and his friends knocking back Medallas in front of the TV, everybody jumping to their feet when Macho Camacho started wailing on José Luis Ramírez, hollering, *Knock him out! Light him up! Préndelo!*

My mother tangled her hands in la vecina's hair, pulled her down out of Gigante's arms and onto the ground, and started kicking. My father got a hold of Mami again, picked her up in the air, my mother red-faced and shrieking, spit flying out of her mouth. He carried her inside.

Gigante helped la vecina get up. She had three long, bloody scratches over her nose and mouth, like claw marks.

Just then, as la vecina was getting to her feet, Mami burst through the front door, a steak knife in her hand. The crowd moved back, opening up more space between themselves and my mother, and everything seemed to slow down, Pito and Anthony and Eggy, all of them, disappearing until it was just me and my mother and my mother's knife, the three of us echoing through the years, propelled forward in time. And because I am my mother's daughter more than I have ever been my father's, it will be this moment I think of when I'm a fourteen-year-old hoodlum tucking razorblades into the sides of my Jordans, brass knuckles and Master combination locks and pocketknives in my backpack, when I am fifteen and getting jumped by five girls at the bus stop, when I am sixteen and trying to decide how to deal with a friend who has betrayed me, when I am seventeen and fighting with my brother. How I would always come back to this, my mother and her knife and all that rage, la vecina leaping back out of her way. And then my father, my father's face, my father's hands, my father's voice, *Jeannette, let go of the knife*, how he took both of her hands into his, saying it over and over, *Suelta el cuchillo, suelta el cuchillo, suelta el cuchillo.*

But my mother would not let it go. Instead, Papi lifted her hands above her head, trying to pry it from her fingers, and Mami bit his shoulder, kicked him. He leaned her up against the doorway, pressing his body against hers until she couldn't move, subduing her, and when he was finally able to get the knife, some of the onlookers rushed to help. It took three grown men to get Mami, kicking and slapping and hurling insults at them, back inside our apartment.

Outside, as the crowd split—while la vecina was still fixing her hair and clothes, limping around looking for her chancletas—I saw Jesenia. She saw me, too. Standing on the front lawn, outside the crowd's perimeter, Jesenia in one of her Jesenia dresses, a white one with big yellow flowers, her hair parted down the middle, braided. How she stood there, alone, her face stained with tears, how nobody else seemed to see her, how nobody stopped as they headed back to their apartments or the basketball courts or la plaza, how nobody asked if she was okay, if she needed help, anything. I'd like to say that when I saw her, Jesenia looking back at me, yellow ribbons in her hair, that we had a moment. That as we looked into each other's eyes, we both understood that we had been lost, that we had been lucky to find each other in a crowd, and we both thought, *Here is a girl who sees me. Here is a girl who understands.*

The truth is we did have a moment, Jesenia and I, seeing each other, knowing each other, and it was clear: We were the same. I hated her and she hated me. Because we were our mothers' daughters. Because we could not turn back time to the days when our mothers were just girls, or forward, when we would finally break free of them. Because back then we could not see what either of us would become.

Home Is a Place

There was a time, before my mother's illness, before my parents divorced, before we left Puerto Rico for Miami Beach, when we were happy. It was after Alaina was born, after Mami had gone back to work in the factory, after I'd started school and learned to read. I spent countless hours poring over books, reading them to Alaina, who was three years old by then. Books about sharks and dolphins and coral reefs, stories about El Pirata Cofresí, Puerto Rico's infamous honorable pirate, mythologized for his marauding, but also for his sense of justice.

On weekends, or whenever we didn't have school, Anthony slept over at Abuela's house. Alaina and I spent entire days in our parents' bedroom, sitting up in their bed, eating Popsicles and watching *The Wizard of Oz* or *Alice in Wonderland* or *The NeverEnding Story* or Jacques Cousteau films about underwater worlds. At night, I'd lie in my own bed, imagining myself in those movies, writing revisions of them that included characters like me. I'd fill composition books with these stories, except in my versions the hero was always an eight- or nine-year-old curly-haired Puerto

Rican girl traveling through time, flying Falkor the luckdragon, exploring the ocean floor, trying to find her way home.

During that period of happiness, Papi couldn't sit still. He wanted to see Puerto Rico, to find another place for us. When Mami was off from work, we'd climb into Papi's old Honda Civic and hit the road, the radio loud, the windows down, the island's green mountains passing us by, palmas and giant ferns and flor de maga until we hit ocean.

Our family was from the east coast. Mami's side from Humacao, and Papi's side from Naguabo. We lived in Humacao, a beach city. There were two small uninhabited islands just off the coast of Humacao: Cayo Batata and Cayo Santiago, which some people called La Isla de los Monos because it was overrun with monkeys running wild. It was off-limits to people. I'd heard stories about the dozens of monkeys that ran free on the beach, how they'd attacked a group of teenagers that made it to the island on a dinghy. I imagined La Isla de Los Monos was kind of like the Haunted Forest in *The Wizard of Oz*, a small island teeming with flying monkeys, proof that there were places in the real world that were exactly like the movies, like books, like stories. But as much as I begged Papi to take us to Monkey Island, we'd always end up at the regular beach.

We drove all over Puerto Rico during those months, visiting swimming holes in Arecibo, El Yunque's rainforest waterfalls, Fajardo's bioluminescent bay, seaside restaurants in Naguabo, rivers and chorros all over the island. And so I learned to swim, to dive headfirst into the ocean, to float on my back with my eyes closed, the sun on my face, arms extended. And I learned to love the road, to feel restless while standing still, always sensing that pull, the water calling, the ocean like a beacon.

IN SOME VERSIONS of the legend, El Pirata Cofresí is just a pirate, a thief who sails the Atlantic, deep into the Caribbean, with his crew of thieves aboard the *Ana*, stealing from the rich. He arrives at night, docks the *Ana* at the port near el Paseo de la Princesa in el Viejo San Juan, before descending on the sleeping pueblo.

In others, Cofresí is a child of the ocean, born and raised on the coast of Cabo Rojo, near the red salt flats on the southwest, where he sleeps with the waves crashing at his window, the sea pulsing like his own blood in his veins. A hero, he spreads his loot to the poor, gold and silk and rum, feeding the hungry, guiding the lost.

In my version, the pirate is an ordinary girl, an octopus tattooed on one shoulder, a seahorse on the forearm, wielding a golden cutlass. She is smart and fierce, captain of the *Aurora*, hunting phantom ships in the night. She imagines herself like Jacques Cousteau, diving among moray eels and spiny urchins and sea anemones, watching schools of fish dance underwater. She is looking for something. A place. Somewhere like home.

THREE YEARS AFTER Alaina was born, my father found a new place for us. We were getting out of the projects, moving away from El Caserío into a house. A real house.

We moved into the new place in Fajardo a few weeks after that, a big yellow house with five bedrooms, a large living room with fancy furniture, a brand new big screen television, a record player with a new salsa collection for Papi, a laundry room that was bigger than the old room I'd shared with Alaina and Anthony. But we didn't just get a new house—we got a completely new life. Mami's mom, Mercy, moved back from Miami, and overnight she was living ten minutes away with our titis. We also got new clothes and shoes, new wheels and a paintjob for Mami's RX-7, an Atari 2600 for Anthony, new bikes for me and Alaina. Mami didn't have to work at the factory anymore, and every couple of weeks Papi would show up with another new car: a BMW, a Ford pickup, a brand new El Camino.

Abuela got a new house, too. Papi had bought a building on a block in the city square in Fajardo. The first story, he turned into a liquor store with a warehouse in the back. On the second story, he built Abuela an apartment with two bedrooms, a large balcony in the front, a huge terrace in the back, and a view of the city square. Abuela's house—and Papi's store—were two blocks away from my new school, so after I walked home I spent whole afternoons with Abuela in her kitchen while she cooked.

Abuela, who had raised Papi and Tío David on her own, was the strongest woman I knew. A devout Catholic, she had two large portraits hanging in her living room—one of Jesus Christ, and one of Abuelo, who died of a brain hemorrhage when Papi was three. When my parents got married, they'd moved into the spare bedroom in Abuela's apartment in El Caserío until they were able to get a place of their own. It was Abuela who'd raised us, who took care of us while Mami was at work, or while Papi was running the liquor store.

Abuela was unapologetically Boricua, unapologetically black. She *owned* the word "negra." In Abuela's house, we were all negros, even if we had a white mother, even though Alaina and I looked brown, even though my blond-haired brother looked white. She called us "mi negrita" and "mi negrito," always as terms of endearment. She refused white people's standards of beauty, refused to perm her hair or use a hot comb. She wore her hair in an Afro, and when it grew long, she oiled it with TCB or Alberto VO5, parted it, twisted it, and rolled it into four moñitos.

Abuela was resourceful, believed in living modestly. She owned maybe nine dresses and one or two pairs of shoes, never wore pants. Nothing in her house was wasted. She made her own curtains, her own sofrito, cooked everything from scratch. Stale bread was saved for bread pudding. Leftover rice was fed to the chickens she raised in the terrace out back. She grew a garden in the front balcony, roses and amapolas, plantas curanderas, herbs for cooking and for teas. She had been raised in the country in Naguabo, where her own mother had taught her to keep house while her father and her five brothers cut cane in the cañaverales. Everybody worked, period. In those days, she told me, you grew your own food. You wanted meat? You went fishing. In Naguabo, they'd been poor, but happy. She went to school, and eventually became a nurse, got married, and moved to Humacao to be closer to her job at Ryder Memorial Hospital.

Abuela believed in treating people with kindness. She always made us feel loved, even with her deadpan humor. She had been a nurse for over thirty years, and even after she retired, she visited the homes of the elderly around the neighborhood, taking care of those who were sick, took them her asopao de pollo. Occasionally, someone would knock on her door with a fever, a rash, a bloody gash between their thumb and forefinger, and Abuela would take care of them, dousing kids in alcoholado to break fevers, boiling water for te de tilo y manzanilla, bandaging injuries. Every single person who set foot in her house was offered a place to sit, something to eat or drink. She ate almost every meal standing in her kitchen. She was always caring for others, and took breaks only to drink her café, black, no sugar—café puya, she called it—to chain-smoke on her balcony, and to watch her novelas: *Cuna de lobos*, *Cadenas de amor*, and *El extraño retorno de Diana Salazar*. Caffeine and menthol and melodrama—those were her only vices.

She was easy to love. She loved us all, but Anthony was her favorite. Abuela was old school. Anthony had been her first grandchild, and when he and I fought, which was often, she always took his side, no matter what. I always wondered why, if it was because he was the only boy, or that he was white, or that he'd almost died when he was born. Abuela had helped deliver him. He was born two months premature, was kept in an incubator in the NICU for months, and Abuela took care of him while Mami was in recovery.

When Anthony was seven, Mami started showing symptoms of schizophrenia, hearing voices. When she became violent, Anthony ran away from home and went to Abuela's house. Abuela agreed to take care of him to give Mami a break, and so my brother started living with her. He refused to come back to live with us, and Mami gave up trying to make him. And so, wherever Abuela went, Anthony went. The second bedroom in Abuela's house became his.

After school, I came home to Abuela's house, sat in the kitchen, and watched her cook while Alaina and Anthony plopped on the living room floor watching TV. Abuela stirred a caldero of white rice, red beans simmering in a large pot. Always in my abuela's kitchen: bags of red beans that had to be soaked overnight, a heavy sack of white rice on the bottom shelf of the pantry, adobo, sazón, bags of frozen gandules, three different kinds of café from Yauco, extra-virgin olive oil in a large green can, a jar of manzanilla olives stuffed with pimentos, calabaza, plátanos, ñame, aguacate, batatas, potatoes, yautía, pana. And in a large wooden basket on the counter, everything she needed to make sofrito: garlic bulbs, onions, recao, cilantro, green bell peppers, handfuls of ají dulce. Sometimes she made oxtail, or carne de res, but most often we ate lechón, the chickens she raised herself, or bacalao. On special occasions, she made my favorite: ensalada de pulpo with a side of tostones.

Almost every afternoon, while Alaina and Anthony were watching *ThunderCats*, I had Abuela to myself. I shadowed her, boiling water, peeling batatas, washing rice, fetching saucepans, learning how to sift flour, how to separate egg yolks from whites, how to pack la cafetera full of ground coffee, how to soak salted bacalao.

In my abuela's kitchen, with the aroma of sautéed garlic and frying chicharrón de pollo settling on my skin, I forgot about the long days in my new school, where nobody believed that Anthony and I were brother and sister because he was a beautiful golden boy with blue-green eyes that all the girls loved, and I was a gap-toothed sweaty girl with a lopsided Afro and a unibrow, the strange girl from El Caserío, a misfit from the projects who read above her grade level, always off in some corner with her nose in a book, while the other kids ran around the P.E. field during recess. In the kitchen, I forgot about how at night, Alaina and I lugged our backpacks into Mami's car. How we drove home alone, the three of us, to wait for Papi. How Papi was always working late nights at the liquor store, and how some nights he didn't come home at all, Mami pacing the big yellow house, talking to herself in the dark about all the women Papi was running around with, about the phone calls, about the pictures she'd found in Papi's office at the liquor store.

In Abuela's kitchen, I forgot how much I missed climbing the flamboyanes in El Caserío, shooting hoops in the middle of the afternoon, how much I missed Eggy.

OUR WHITE GRANDMOTHER, Mercy, hated that my hair was a tangle of dry frizzy curls like my father's. Bad hair, she called it.

The summer I turned six, Mercy had decided I needed a haircut so that I'd look like a decent young lady and not a street urchin. "Look at you," she said. "You look like you belong to a clan of bandoleros." And she knew hair, because she'd gone to cosmetology school. She'd also gone to school to become a phlebotomist and an EKG technician. Mercy collected certifications but never had a job. She collected other things, too: unemployment, food stamps, disability, welfare, Social Security, settlements from multiple slip-and-fall lawsuits. She collected eviction notices, moving twelve times in ten years. She collected husbands and daughters— seven daughters and twice as many husbands. And when the husbands all left, she sent the daughters away to be raised by a sister in Patagonia, an aunt in El Caserío.

The day before my sixth birthday, Mercy sat me down in my mother's kitchen and spread her beauty supplies on the table: combs and hairclips and scissors and hand mirrors and a hair pick. She draped a towel over my shoulders the way I'd seen stylists do to Mami.

Mercy spritzed my hair with water, and went to work with a fine-toothed comb. I flinched each time she yanked my hair, cried out as the comb got tangled in it. She smacked the top of my head with the comb, told me to stop flinching. It wasn't her fault I took after my father. Mercy never wasted a chance to complain about "those people." Her worst nightmare, she'd say, had been that her white daughters would end up marrying negros. So, of course, what had my mother done first chance she got? She married my father, un negro.

Mercy started cutting, back to front. The strands tickled my neck as they fell. She talked and snipped, and I sat quietly so I wouldn't get whacked again.

"Your brother got lucky," she said. "He turned out like me." But no matter how much Anthony looked like Mercy, he was *nothing* like her. My brother *adored* Abuela, could not stand Mercy, refused to be around her, even if she was Mami's mother.

After she finished combing and cutting, Mercy pulled the towel from my shoulders with a dramatic swoop and announced that she was done. I looked down at all the brown hair at my feet. She took my chin in her hand, lifted my face, and got a good look at me. Then she handed me a mirror.

My hair was gone. She'd cut off all my curls, leaving me with a close-cropped Afro like my father's. I ran a hand over my head, shocked. I was hideous.

It wasn't the haircut, she said, chuckling, it was my bad hair.

It would be that way my entire childhood. *Your father's fault. Your father and his black family. Your black grandmother. Your black uncle.* I would never look like my mother, or like Mercy, and she would never let me forget it.

At school, Anthony would laugh his ass off and introduce me to his friends: "Have you met my *brother*? His name is Jaquir-*o!*" It was the first time in my young life I actually wished I were more like a girl. Other girls wore their hair in ponytails or pigtails or braids, or let it fall loose so the wind could sweep it in front of their faces. Now I hated those girls. I thought about how good it would feel to cut off one of those pigtails, just one.

Now they came up to me and asked, "Why do you look like a boy?" I tried to ignore them, until one day in the cafeteria, Tammy—who had long blond hair and perfect bangs—called me a boy. I punched her in the stomach and said the worst thing I could think to say, something I'd seen scrawled on the window of my yellow school bus: "Fuck you, bitch."

Over the next few years, Mercy would cut my hair off many times, as if trying to teach me something about who I was, who I was supposed to be: my grandmother was the first person to ever call me nigger.

ABUELA COULD USUALLY sense when I was down. One afternoon, after a hard day at school, I got to her house and sat at the kitchen table silently, waiting for her to start dinner. When she saw that something was wrong, she called me over to help. She set a cutting board on the counter for me, then set a thick slice of cooking ham on it, and a small knife next to it.

"Wash your hands first," she said.

I washed my hands, dried them on the towel she kept hanging from a hook by the sink. I wasn't as tall as Abuela, so I had to get on my tiptoes to reach it.

While Abuela set the caldero on the stove, I picked up the knife.

"Be careful," she said. "Just take it slow."

I got to work cutting, slowly, just like Abuela had taught me. She watched me closely as I cut the ham into cubes, sliding them over on the board as I worked, exactly like I'd seen her do so many times.

Abuela poured a little oil into the caldero, and when it was hot enough, she set the heat to medium-low.

"Can I do it?" I asked.

She smiled. "Go 'head," she said, and watched me as I picked up the cutting board, then used the knife to slide the cubed ham into the caldero, just like Abuela always did.

We continued like this all afternoon, making arroz con gandules, reheating half of a pernil in the oven, shredding repollo, onions, and carrots for slaw, adding sugar, then drizzling it with olive oil and vinegar. Abuela let me do whatever I asked to do, trusting me with the heavy roasting pan as I slid it into the oven by myself, trusting me with the knife, letting me turn the rice when it was ready.

"You like to cook?" Abuela asked me.

I shrugged. "Yeah."

For Abuela, cooking had been like a balm. She had worked long hours as a nurse when Papi and Tío were kids, and hadn't had much time with them. Often she'd come home late at night, with just enough time to fry them some chicken and potatoes, and that would have to do. Because Abuelo had died when they were little, she'd had to work long hours just to keep a roof over their heads. She felt she'd missed most of their childhoods—they'd spent so many hours sitting in the hospital waiting room, doing their homework, while they waited for her to get off. She was determined to make that up with us, her grandchildren, and cooking for us, making these elaborate meals, was one way she knew she could take care of us. Even when we were poor, as long as we had some rice and beans, Abuela could perform miracles in her kitchen.

ONE NIGHT, AFTER closing up the liquor store, Papi came home with us. Mami's car had a flat, so we all climbed into Papi's truck. My father drove, Mami in the middle with Alaina on her lap, and I sat in the passenger side, my head resting against the window.

We pulled up to the big yellow house late that night, after all the other kids on the block had stopped riding their bikes on the street, after all the other families in the neighborhood had turned off their lights. Papi parked the truck in our driveway, and as soon as he got out, there was a man on him, pushing him toward the house, the driver's side door wide open.

Mami slid over, got out of the car, holding a sleeping Alaina against her, calling after him, "¡Cano! Dios mío. ¡Cano!" And on the passenger's side, my door swung open, and a man's hand was on my arm, pulling me out of the truck, my mother's screaming piercing the night.

My father and the man disappeared inside our house, my mother standing in front of me, my sister crying in her arms, a stranger's hand gripping my forearm, pulling me close, and suddenly, finally, my mother was silent.

Later, whenever Mami told this story, she would always start with the guns. A revolver, the man pressing it against the side of my head, another pistol aimed at my father, the stranger's hand trembling with its weight. How she had tried to reason with them, how she kept saying, *Don't do this. You can't do this.* How outside, standing by the truck with Alaina in her arms, she kept looking at that gun pressed against my head, the man's face, how he was just a kid, and where was my father, where, while this son of a bitch held his children at gunpoint, her babies, her little girls. How she had *told* my father this would happen, *told* him not to keep all that money in the house. How this man, this stranger, knew her name, her children's names. How they knew about the flat tire. They knew so much about our lives, she said.

She would describe the man that grabbed me, held me in front of her. *Look at your mother*, he said. *Don't look at me.*

I don't remember the gun, or how he didn't let me go until we were inside the house, the phones ripped from the walls, my father's guns pulled from his safe, deposited into a pillowcase. I remember my mother's face. Alaina in her arms. How we stood in our parents' bedroom, all of us watching as Papi handed over money, jewelry, car keys. How they walked us from room to room, opening drawers and turning over mattresses and searching closets. *Don't look at me.*

My mother kept looking, kept searching their faces, trying to figure out if she knew them, and if she did, *how.* And then his hand on my arm again, grabbing me as he said to my mother, *Stop. Don't look at me. Look at Jaqui.* But she couldn't stop looking, couldn't be still, no matter how much they told her to stop, stop fidgeting, stop talking, stop. And afterward, they walked us into the guest bathroom, Mami and Papi and Alaina and me, all of us sitting cross-legged on the floor, and even after they had closed the door behind us, his hand *still* on my skin, his voice locked in that room with us, *Don't look at me, look at Jaqui.* My name, in his voice, like a knife.

ON THE TELEVISION in my parents' bedroom, Glinda the Good Witch of the North gifts Dorothy her sister's ruby slippers. Later she will tell her, "Home is a place we all must find, child."

At sea, eyes on the North Star, the pirate girl decides: she'll be a pirate, but never a thief.

At sea, so far from home, she will lose her mother again and again.

WE WERE HAPPY once. But after the big yellow house, we were runaways. We took only the essentials—toothbrushes, some school uniforms in my backpack, a fistful of Alaina's clothes shoved in there with my own. Papi carried Alaina, Mami held my hand, and we took off into the night, walking a few houses down to a neighbor's, where Papi made a phone call.

And then we were back at Abuela's house, all of us sitting at her dining table, my father on the phone again, and Alaina, brave, so brave, telling Abuela the whole story. "They opened all of our drawers and threw our clothes on the floor," she said. "They had a gun," she said.

Abuela wrapped her arms around her, kissed the top of her head. "Se quedan aquí," she said. "You can sleep in the second bedroom. As long as you want." She gave Alaina another squeeze.

Sitting next to Papi, my mother cradled herself, her eyes somewhere else, already gone. "I need the phone," she told Papi.

Before daybreak, my grandma Mercy would arrive at Abuela's house. She would blame my father, demand that he take care of us, that he take care of *this.*

Abuela would boil water for manzanilla, tell Anthony to sleep in her bed.

We would stay in Abuela's house for the next week, until Papi found us another place. We would never go back to the big yellow house.

THAT YEAR, WE moved to Luquillo, to a small house on a hill a few minutes from the beach, where Alaina and I rode our bikes downhill to the candy store or the playground, or uphill to the Baptist church's parking lot, where we threw breadcrumbs at pigeons then rolled back down, hands on our handlebars, feet in the air. Mami brought home a brown Pekingese she called Peggy, a tiny dog who was all bark and even more bite, who we all thought needed an exorcism.

On Saturday mornings we hopped into Mami's RX-7, and she peeled out of our driveway, flew down the expressway with the radio blasting, racing other cars, Peggy yapping in the back, Alaina and I holding on for our lives, both our bodies squeezed into the single passenger seat, nobody wearing a seatbelt.

We woke up one morning to find the front door wide open, Peggy gone, no sign of her anywhere. We listened to Mami on the phone, telling a story about a man she'd been seeing in the backyard, in the front yard, waiting by her car, looking in our windows, and how he was probably the one who took Peggy. We rode our bikes all over the neighborhood, flagging down other kids to ask if they'd seen our crazy brown dog, rode to the park, the candy store, the church, looked down into ditches and potholes, calling her name into the night.

That year, when our titis and primos came to visit from Miami, we climbed a ladder onto the roof, then sat on the edge watching our feet dangle, sucking on lollipops and singing Menudo songs, me and Alaina and Tanisha, Mami's youngest sister. Tanisha was only four years older than me, and she was brown, with black hair as straight as Mami's that she let grow all the way down to her butt. She had a wicked sense of humor and lived for breaking rules and I adored her. We climbed that ladder every day, took Popsicles and popcorn up there, took cans of Cola Champagne and Coco Rico up there, and when we were done with them, we crushed them and flung them off the roof like grenades. We watched the blue sky turn dark on that rooftop, day after day, and every night I asked when Papi would be coming home.

That year, we moved from the house on the hill back to Fajardo, to an oceanfront high-rise apartment complex, Dos Marinas. From our balcony overlooking the marina, we watched dozens of moored boats, thieving gaviotas hovering above them, wings extended, their angled bodies tilting in flight, plunge-diving for prey.

We spent entire days in the pool, our bodies browner than they'd ever been, our curls getting lighter, dried out by the sun and salt and chlorine. We morphed into mermaid creatures—part dolphin, part ordinary girl—fins and tails covered in scales, prepared to live out our lives in some underwater reef world, surfacing only to sun ourselves on the rocks along the sea wall.

We begged and begged Mami for another dog, not a crazy one this time, promised we'd take care of her, but Mami would not budge. We locked ourselves in our room when Mami insisted that there was a man at the door, the same man she'd seen at our house in Luquillo. When Tanisha and Xiomara came over, we told them about the man, and we looked over our shoulders as we walked down the hallway to the elevator, as we walked from the pool to the tennis courts, from the tennis courts to the docks, as we played Ms. Pac-Man in the game room. On the swings, our feet bare, me and Tanisha and Alaina kicking up sand, we listened to Mami telling Titi Xiomara about Papi's new life, his new penthouse apartment, his new girlfriend, the divorce papers, and instead of asking questions, we swung higher, wind in our faces, bodies flying flying flying through the air.

Titi Xiomara was a year younger than Mami, but she knew something about love. She had been married to our uncle Junior since she was seventeen.

"Forget him," Xiomara told Mami. "You have your whole life ahead of you, and as long as he keeps taking care of the kids, you'll be okay. Enjoy your life!"

Weeks later, Mami announced that we were moving again, and we packed our clothes and books and toys, went back to the house in Luquillo as if we'd never left.

THAT YEAR, BACK in the house on the hill, we stopped asking when Papi would come home. We sat around on beach chairs in the living room, our furniture left behind in Dos Marinas, lit candles to San Judas Tadeo, the patron saint of lost causes. We listened to Mercy as she told stories about aliens and their spaceships landing in El Yunque, about men who had seen ghost women, hitchhikers, dragging their long skirts along the side of the road in the pitch black of night. We listened and listened as her stories turned darker: How black people like Abuela were known to be brujas. How everybody knew they sacrificed animals, and lord knows if that's what happened to poor Peggy. How we needed to be watchful, say our prayers before going to sleep, because now that Mami and Papi were not together anymore, we could be in danger.

That year, in that house on the hill, I prayed and prayed for our parents to get back together, I prayed to be back in Abuela's kitchen, the two of us grating canela for tembleque, I prayed for the man who was terrorizing Mami to go away, I prayed for Peggy to come home, and every hour and every minute in every room in that house, I was afraid.

Then one day in the middle of the afternoon, as Alaina and I tossed around a Frisbee out front, there she was. Dirty, her long hair matted, and—we'd find out later—pregnant. Peggy, waddling up the hill toward our house.

LATER THAT YEAR, in the summer, Mami and Alaina and I would see El Caserío one last time before moving to Miami Beach. We would park Mami's RX-7 right in front of our old building, and Mami would visit our extended family, all her old friends, stopping by each apartment to say goodbye. We were moving to Miami, she would tell them, sparing them none of the details.

We would run around our old neighborhood for hours. Alaina and I would play hopscotch, and I'd sit on our old front steps, waiting for Eggy to come around, riding his bike up the street or dribbling a basketball on the sidewalk. Other kids would walk by on their way to the candy store. Kids I knew. They'd take one look at us, then keep walking, like they didn't even see us, like we didn't belong there anymore. I would want to call out after them, make them see me. But I wouldn't have the words.

I would wait, and wait, and wait. Until the sun went down, until the other street kids picked up their skateboards and headed home, until our titis and neighbors and Mami's friends hugged us goodbye, wiping tears from their eyes, until my mother called out to me from the car where Alaina was already sitting in the passenger seat, waiting for me. But Eggy would never turn up. I wouldn't be able to recall the last time we saw each other, but I knew, as I opened the door and slid into the passenger seat next to my little sister: we would move to some foreign place, learn a foreign language, go to school with strangers, and Eggy would be here. Eggy would always be here.

We would never see each other again.

WE LEFT PUERTO Rico that summer, after Papi came back home one night, and both he and Mami acted as if he'd never left. We still didn't know everything we would lose—the ceibas, the flamboyanes, the morivivi, the coquis singing us to sleep at night—everything we'd already lost. We wouldn't know until it was too late.

We arrived in Miami Beach, Papi, Mami, Abuela, Anthony, Alaina, and me, our parents back together for the last time. We stayed in a hotel in South Beach until we found an apartment on West Avenue.

Anthony and I started a new school, where we would be stripped of our language, where we wouldn't be allowed a hall pass to the bathroom unless we could ask in English, where boys ignored me and I ignored boys, where girls asked, like I knew they would, *Why do you look like a boy?* We walked the nine or ten blocks home from school alone, cutting through Flamingo Park, where I sometimes stopped to sit in the swings or watch the high school guys play ball.

We would move like six times that first year, and our parents would not stop fighting, and every new apartment would be smaller than the last. Eventually, we would run out of money, and Papi would work two jobs seven days a week to make ends meet, barely managing to support our family. Papi would leave Mami again, after one of their screaming matches turned into a fight, a fight that ended with Mami knocking him unconscious. We would get evicted after that, and Mami would take us to live with Mercy for a while, until her diagnosis, and then we'd finally have a name for the demons, for the people sending messages through the TV, for the man who had been following us around all these years. Mami would be in and out of hospitals, and Anthony, Alaina, and I would move in with Papi and Abuela.

The five of us were the kind of poor you could feel in your bones, in your teeth, in your stomach. Empty-refrigerator poor. Sleeping-on-the-floor-until-somebody-threw-out-a-sofabed poor. Stirring-sugar-into-water-and-calling-it-lemonade poor. And then we'd take off again, like runaways. One apartment, and then another, and then another, never staying long enough to put up a picture, leaving while the place still smelled like the people who lived there before us.

It wouldn't occur to me until my teens—when I'm a hood rat running around Miami Beach, riding in cars with gun-toting gangsters, stealing vans from parking lots, joyriding down to Key Largo, sleeping in somebody's truck bed. When I'm standing on another rooftop, passing a Dutch to a boy who doesn't even know my real name, when I'm stepping up onto the ledge, when I'm looking down at the two stories below, when a two-story fall is not enough to kill me, when the boy is not a boy, but a man—that Abuela's kitchen, that house in Fajardo, was the last place I ever felt safe. That maybe home *is* a place. That maybe my mother would never find her way back. That maybe I wouldn't either.

PART TWO

Monstruo

Monster Story

I.

It was the year they found a dead toddler in the bushes, head bashed in, bite marks and cigarette burns all over his body. He was wearing a T-shirt with lollipops across the front. It was November 1990. Police detectives were all over the news, searching for the baby's parents, for some clue about his identity, but no one had come forward. My mother was homeless that year. Sometimes she crashed on Mercy and Tanisha's couch, but she spent most nights on the streets with Pedro, one of her scutterhead boyfriends. I'd get a phone call in the middle of the night—Mami calling collect from Dade County Jail, begging me to convince Papi to bail her out. She'd promise to pay him back, promise me she'd change, stop using.

Until one day Pedro vanished, and Mami was left with nothing but her habit to keep her company. That's when she decided she needed her kids back.

I was eleven.

AFTER OUR PARENTS' divorce, a couple of years after we arrived in Miami Beach, Anthony, Alaina, and I moved with Papi and

Abuela into a small apartment across the street from Flamingo Park. Papi was never home. He'd brought us from Puerto Rico in search of a better life, had left behind his life as a hustler, his penthouse apartment, his cars and properties, to work two jobs. One at a factory in North Miami, and one as a security guard at a high-rise apartment complex in Miami Beach.

Papi worked all the time, so it was Abuela who took us to school, dropped me off in front of Ida M. Fisher Elementary, walked Alaina across the courtyard to her second-grade classroom at Leroy D. Feinberg Elementary, where the little kids went. It was Abuela who ironed Anthony's clothes for school, who helped with our homework, who hiked all the way to school when we forgot sweaters or science projects, who came calling for us when we were late for dinner. Sometimes she'd let us play in the alley out back so she could keep an eye on us from the kitchen window. That's where we were the afternoon after the news about the dead toddler broke.

We were playing stickball with the other street kids and my best friend, Sara, who wasn't really from the streets. Sara and I were complete opposites. I always ran wild around the neighborhood, sometimes with Alaina in tow, even though Abuela insisted that we stay on the block. Sara and her little brother Steven never even crossed the street without permission. I was abrasive, foulmouthed, and got suspended from school for fighting. Sara always said *please* and *thank you* and answered all of her mother's questions with *yes, ma'am* or *no, ma'am*. She had silky blond hair and wore new clothes and clean sneakers. I had a tangled mess of curls, was constantly sunburned and dirty, and wore Tanisha's handme-downs. Sara went to church every Sunday. I spent Sundays in the park shooting hoops with boys from the neighborhood. I had a thick Spanish accent, and Sara spoke perfect gringo English, but she never made fun of me or called me "Spanish girl" like some of the boys on my street. Sara's mom, a single mother and school-teacher, sometimes invited Alaina and me over for dinner. The only thing Sara and I had in common was that both our families lived in the ratty, bug-ridden, art-deco slums of South Beach.

During our game of stickball, I was on first base, and Sara was at bat, about to strike out, when Frankie showed up uninvited.

"What's up, mamacitas?" he called.

Frankie was a high school kid who came around once in a while, always bugging us girls to play spin the bottle or seven min-utes in heaven, which meant he wanted to feel you up behind the possum-infested dumpster. He walked around sucking his thumb, and sometimes, when you weren't looking, he'd stick a spit-cov-ered finger in your ear and yell, "Wet Willie!"

Some kids said Frankie was slow, that he was harmless, but I had my doubts. He was older than Anthony, and I'd heard he got kicked out of school for sneaking into the girls' locker room and pulling out his dick.

Even though Alaina was pretty tough, and had more sense than most second-graders, I warned her to stay the hell away from him.

"Can I play?" he asked.

I rolled my eyes.

Alaina crossed her arms. "I don't think so."

Sara lowered her broomstick bat and shook her head. "No way!"

I took Sara's bat, held it out in front of me, threateningly. "Go home, pervert."

"Come on," Frankie said. "If you let me play, I'll show you where there's a dead body."

The other kids groaned and huffed and rolled their eyes, but I asked, "What do you mean 'a dead body'?"

"I found a dead boy in the bushes."

I didn't buy it. It was the cops who'd found the baby, or so I thought. And they'd probably taken him away to the morgue or the police station or wherever it was they took murder victims. What were the chances that there'd be another body in the bushes? Still, I considered it. The prospect of seeing a real dead body seemed too good to pass up.

"Show us," I said.

Frankie laughed, his thumb stuck in his mouth.

"You're such a liar," I said.

Sara stepped forward. "Get out of here, pervert."

"Yeah," I said.

Someone threw a tennis ball at him, but he ducked.

"Fuck you," he said, throwing up his middle finger, and turned to run.

We chased him down the alley, throwing tennis balls and rocks. And me, waving my stick in the air like I was out for blood.

THE MEDIA AND the cops called the toddler "Baby Lollipops" because of the design on his shirt. The police had determined that he was about three years old, that he had been starved and tortured over the course of several weeks, maybe months. His two front teeth had been knocked out and his skull fractured by a blunt object. When they found him under the cherry hedge outside a bayfront home in Miami Beach, he weighed only eighteen pounds.

At first it was just a story on the six o'clock news—police detectives holding press conferences, offering a $1,000 reward, trying to learn the identity of the baby John Doe. But as the days turned to weeks and Baby Lollipops remained unclaimed, it became part of our daily lives. We followed the news on Channel 7, on Univision, on Telemundo. We picked up the early edition of the *Miami Herald* or *El Nuevo Herald*, our days sustained by the promise of more details, more story. Maybe it was because the dead baby had been found so close to our neighborhood, or maybe because we had cherry hedges right on our street, where we rode our bikes after school and egged each other on Halloween and break-danced on flattened cardboard boxes spread out on the sidewalk.

Every TV station was broadcasting reports about Baby Lollipops: Who was he? Where did he come from? Why hadn't anyone claimed him? What kind of monster would torture such a precious little angel? They aired shows about child abuse and child trafficking and child labor and homeless children and the children of immigrants who had washed up on our shores on makeshift rafts. Before the discovery of the body, the news had been dominated by the infamous Miami drug wars, but now it sounded like it was more dangerous to be a child than a drug dealer.

News vans with reporters and camera crews pulled up to our playgrounds and softball fields and interviewed anyone who would speak to them, even though no one could really tell them anything. The story even made *America's Most Wanted*.

Boy Scout volunteers took to the streets with flyers and questions: *Do you know the parents of this baby? Do you know his name?*

That picture, it was everywhere. All over the pages of the *Miami Herald*, strewn about Miami Beach supermarkets and parking lots, and taped to light posts in front of Fisher Elementary. The little bruised face, the lollipop T-shirt, the small eyes, closed as if he were sleeping, looking so innocent I could see how everyone called him an angel.

That picture. It was everywhere. Always with the same caption: "Toddler (unidentified)."

ONE NIGHT, SEVERAL weeks after they found the body, I couldn't sleep. We were lying on the sofa bed, Alaina snoring while I lay awake listening to Miami Beach's late-night traffic: car horns blaring, taxicab doors slamming, tires screeching. Around midnight I heard a knock on the door.

It was my mother. She'd often show up late at night with gifts for Alaina and me: an embroidered sweater, a leopard-print blouse, a used Barbie with matted hair. She'd say she'd bought them from some fancy boutique on Lincoln Road, but her gifts always smelled like dumpster.

I let her in, shutting the door quietly so I wouldn't wake Papi, Anthony, Alaina, or Abuela. Mami's hair was platinum blond, her darker roots showing. She wore a black lace top with no bra and jeans cut so short her ass cheeks hung out. This had become my mother's way. She was twenty-seven but dressed and acted like a teenager, flaunting her curves, using her body to get what she wanted from men—rides, cigarettes, scutter. She'd take us to the beach and sunbathe topless, and Alaina and I would spend the day trying to drive away the losers who offered her a light or a beer or told her how striking her eyes were, though we knew they just wanted a closer look at her tits. Once, when on a whim my mother insisted on walking me to school, I refused. I wouldn't tell her why, didn't want to hurt her feelings, but she kept nagging me and nagging me until I spilled it: "You look like a prostitute." I regretted saying it the moment the words came out, thought of how she'd always taught us to love our bodies. She looked hurt at first, her eyebrows crinkling like she might burst into tears. Then she slapped me hard on the mouth. I could tell she did it not to discipline me but out of anger, to get back at me. That was also my mother's way.

Mami sat next to Alaina on the sofa bed and shook her awake. "Get up," she said, "we're leaving."

"What do you mean, 'We're leaving'?" I asked.

She picked up my sneakers and thrust them into my hands. "Put these on."

Alaina sat up, looking confused. "Where we going?"

"Just get your shoes on," Mami said.

I tried to think of a way to get this idea out of her head. We couldn't just leave with her in the middle of the night. I asked if we could say goodbye to Papi and Abuela.

"We'll call them in the morning."

"But what if they wake up and we're gone? They'll be worried."

"I'm your mother and I can take you wherever the hell I want. I don't need permission."

And so Mami took us. Pulled the front door shut and blocked it so we couldn't get back inside. I thought about running or calling out for my father, but Mami was unpredictable. Once, she'd chased me down that same hallway, pulled off her chancleta, and beat me with it because I refused to get a haircut. When I went to Papi and complained about having to cut my hair, he said I'd better just do it to avoid problems. He worried my mother's screaming would get us evicted.

Alaina and I wore pajamas, sneakers, no socks. We walked with Mami past the piss-soaked handball courts in Flamingo

Park, past Ida M. Fisher Elementary, past the closed swim shops and jewelry stores on Lincoln Road. I held Alaina's hand and searched the night for a police officer, a stranger, anyone I could walk up to and say, "Help! We're being kidnapped." But the cops never appeared, and when we did pass a stranger, he just stared at my mother's tits.

Mami took us to a mildewy motel on Collins Avenue, across the street from the beach, one of those places people liked to call "boutique hotels" even though everybody knew they were the kind you could get for a few dollars an hour. Alaina and I got into one bed, and I spent most of the night thinking about Papi and Abuela, wondering how worried they'd be when they didn't find us in the morning, and Anthony, who wouldn't miss us at all. I thought of Sara, safe in her own bed, in the tiny bedroom she shared with Steven because their mom couldn't afford a bigger apartment on her teacher's salary. And I thought of ways Alaina and I could sneak out of the room without waking Mami. But I knew that if she caught us sneaking out, I would catch a beat-down.

When the sun started to seep in through the blinds, I turned on the TV. Every station was reporting on the new developments in the Baby Lollipops case. Police had finally identified him as three-year-old Lázaro Figueroa. According to the news, they'd found Ana María Cardona living somewhere in central Florida with her two other kids and Olivia González, who they called "her lover." The two women had dumped his body under the bushes outside a house on North Bay Road, and once they saw on the news that he'd been found, they headed north. They were arrested in Orlando and brought back to Miami Beach, where they were charged with aggravated child abuse and first-degree murder.

The medical examiner had determined that it had taken Lázaro
up to three days to die from his injuries. For three days he was
under that cherry hedge, body swollen, brain damaged. People all
over the city were outraged, told reporters that they were praying
for Lázaro, how they hoped the two bitches who killed him got
fried. I couldn't get the thought out of my head: It was his mother
who'd done it. His own mother.

When Mami got up to use the bathroom, she took her purse
in there with her. I knew her morning routine: snort a couple of
lines of scutter, smoke a cigarette, then brush her teeth. I'd seen
her do this since I was nine. As soon as she closed the door, I
shook Alaina awake, took her by the hand, grabbed our sneakers.
Together, we ran out of the motel.

We ran down toward the beach, sneakers in our hands, Alaina's
curls bouncing. When we got to the beach, there were hundreds of
jellyfish washed up on the shore, translucent blue bubbles, tenta-
cles coiled in the sand. I didn't notice that Alaina had stopped running until I heard her cry out. She was holding her wrist with one
hand, forehead scrunched up with pain, gasping. She'd reached
down and picked up one of the blue bubbles.

Behind her, headed right for us from the direction of the motel,
was Mami. She was barefoot, her blond hair tangled, black mascara smeared beneath her eyes. I measured the distance between
her and us. If I just grabbed Alaina's hand and ran, how long
would it be before one of us tripped and fell face down in the sand?
Would Mami keep running after us? Would she give up?

I remember when Mami and Papi were still together, how
they'd scream at each other in their bedroom until Anthony,
Alaina, and I burst in and made them stop fighting. Once, right

before Papi left her for the last time, Mami grabbed me and Alaina, held us out in front of him. "Take a good look at them," she told Papi, "because once you leave, you will never see them again."

We're supposed to love our mothers. We're supposed to trust them and need them and miss them when they're gone. But what if that same person, the one who's supposed to love you more than anyone else in the world, the one who's supposed to protect you, is also the one who hurts you the most?

That morning on the beach, when our eyes met, I knew that Mami would catch us. I saw it in her face. She knew it, too. And she would never let us go.

YEARS BEFORE THEY'D found the baby, before the drugs, when we still lived in Puerto Rico, Mami took us to Castillo San Felipe del Morro in el Viejo San Juan, and we spent the whole day at the fortress by the sea. Anthony had stayed home with Abuela, and Papi was at work in the liquor store. But the three of us spent the day together, Mami and Alaina and me. Mami held my hand and I held Alaina's hand, and we walked along the stone walkway behind other families and tourists. Mami snapped Polaroid pictures with her instant camera, of Alaina and I feeding the sea gulls, of the stray cats by the seawall. She bought a red kite from a vendor and taught us how to fly it on the lawn. Alaina and I took turns unspooling it, tossing it up until it caught the rush of wind and took flight, getting higher and higher. How small it looked after a while.

After a whole day out in the sun, Mami was exhausted. She sunbathed, lying on the grass while we flew the kite, ran around after each other, tumbling and laughing and calling out to her,

Mami look at me, look at me. She was tired but happy, her face turned up to the sun, her golden hair pulled back, beads of sweat collecting at her hairline.

This is how I want to remember my mother. These are the memories I want to keep: my mother, exhausted but happy, how carefree she was, how beautiful. How for those moments, before we knew that she was sick, the whole world seemed possible. How when I looked at her, I hoped that one day, I would be exactly like her.

AFTER THE LIFEGUARDS treated Alaina for a Portuguese man-of-war sting, Mami took us back to the motel. For days we wore the same pajamas, hand-washed our underwear in the shower. We ate dry Frosted Flakes and bologna sandwiches. When we ran out of cereal and bologna, we ate mayonnaise sandwiches. Then one morning the housekeeper knocked on our door and told us we needed to check out.

Mami shut the door in her face and sat on one of the beds for several minutes, as if in a trance. Alaina watched *Scooby-Doo* while I waited for Mami to tell us that we were finally going home. But when she spoke, she didn't even look at us.

"Your father," she said, "this is all his fault." Then she got up and locked herself in the bathroom.

After a few minutes I heard her voice. I turned down the volume on the TV, pressed my ear against the bathroom door. Mami was having a conversation, laughing.

Alaina tiptoed over, whispered, "Who's she talking to?"

"I don't know."

After a while, Mami stopped talking, just laughed and laughed. Alaina and I sat on the floor and waited. Although we looked a bit alike, when you looked closer, you'd see how different we really were. Alaina was darker, shorter. She had loose, thick, black curls. Alaina was the brave one, the kind of kid who didn't need hand-holding. She was even-tempered, had a strong sense of justice, cared deeply about animals, and about doing the right thing, always. I was the loud, angry one, the one who always got into fights, fought over anything, everything. I cared about books and music and monsters and not much of anything else.

I could tell Alaina was confused. It had been confusing for me, too, when it first started, and afterward, when I realized what it meant. Papi had just left Mami for the last time, in a dramatic scene that spilled out into the street, Mami following Papi down the street as he hailed a cab, Anthony, Alaina, and me running after them. As he got in the backseat he promised to come back for us. Mami promised she'd find out where he was staying and set him on fire in his sleep.

After that, Mami started seeing the man again. He followed her to the bus stop, to the laundromat, to her job as a housekeeper at the Deauville Hotel, to the grocery store. She told me how he stood outside her bedroom window and pressed his face to the glass, always looking for her, always watching her. He'd send her messages through the radio, through the TV. She couldn't shake him. One night, as she was getting out of the shower, she slid back the shower curtain and found him sitting on the toilet. When I told her I hadn't seen any man, she exploded, eyes bulging. "I've given you everything!" she said. "Everything! And now I have nothing left."

At the motel, Alaina and I waited on Mami.

"What's wrong with her?" Alaina asked. "Who's she talking to?"

I sat on the bed, considering what to tell her. How many times had I asked Papi the same question? He'd always avoided the details, saying simply, "Your mother is sick." He'd let me discover her drug use on my own. I didn't know whether my mother's madness had caused her addiction, or if her addiction had led to her madness. At eleven years old, I preferred to think that the drugs had driven her crazy. Maybe the thought that my mother had done this to herself was less frightening than the idea that madness was something that could just happen to you, as it had to my mother, as it had to Mercy before her, as it had to Mercy's father, who my mother had called Abuelo, before I was born. Because if that was the case, then it could also happen to me.

When Mami came out of the bathroom, her hair all messed up like she'd been pulling it, she gathered the few things she'd brought with her.

"Get your shoes on," she said. "We gotta go."

On the walk back, I gave her the silent treatment. Since we were going home, it was finally okay to hate her for what she'd done. And for what she was. It seemed easier than hating my father for never standing up for us, or myself for letting her take us, or God for letting her be crazy.

Every time we passed a cherry hedge, Alaina and I picked the fruit and speculated about whether or not it was the same bush where they'd found Baby Lollipops. Mami was having a conversation with herself about the pains of giving birth, and how once your children are expelled from your body, they begin to turn against you. They begin to look like their father. She stopped in the middle of the sidewalk, lit a cigarette, then kept walking.

"Who were you talking to?" Alaina asked her.

She studied Alaina's face, her eyes narrowing. "What do you mean?"

"Like two minutes ago, and in the hotel bathroom."

She took a long drag off her cigarette, then exhaled the smoke. "I was talking to Pedro."

Alaina and I looked at each other. But we said nothing.

WHEN WE GOT home, Papi kissed us each on the forehead and stepped into the hallway to talk to Mami while Alaina and I went into the kitchen with Abuela.

Anthony, who was on the couch watching TV, barely looked up when we walked past him.

Abuela pulled us close, squeezed us tight. "Are you hungry?"

"Starving!" I said.

She pulled two bowls from the cupboard, then started serving me rice and beans. Alaina took her bowl and started serving herself.

"Where were you?" Abuela asked. "Your mother called your father at work, but didn't say where you were staying."

"We were in some ratty motel close to the beach," I said. "Anthony's lucky Mami didn't take him, too."

When Papi came back inside our apartment, he didn't wrap his arms around us or pick us up or twirl us in the middle of the living room like I'd imagined he would. He just went to the bathroom to get ready for work. I wanted to shake and shake him. Did he know how scared we'd been? How many times had Mami threatened to take us away, to keep us from him? Why hadn't he tried to find us?

I didn't say anything, though. I knew Papi—he avoided conflict. Even when they were still married, no matter how many times I'd shown him the bruises from one of Mami's beatings, he never said a word to her. I realized then that if my mother wanted to take me and Alaina, she could have us, and there was nothing my father would do about it.

WHILE LÁZARO'S MOTHER and her partner sat in jail, their stories kept changing. They blamed a babysitter, then the drugs, then they told police they'd left the baby with a rich woman in a restaurant who took a liking to him. It must have been her, they said.

Then they turned on each other. Witnesses came forward with stories about how they'd called the police or the Department of Children and Families countless times. Family services had taken away three older children, had even taken away Lázaro, only to give him back. His torture and death could've been prevented, neighbors said, if only someone had listened.

One day after school, I stood in line at the bodega around the corner from my elementary school, listening to the cashier and a stock boy.

The cashier, a middle-aged woman, dusted the shelves behind the register. "That baby would still be alive," she said, "if only they'd kept him away from those lesbians."

The stock boy was refilling the candy bar boxes under the register counter.

"What kind of mother sleeps with another woman, then lets her abuse her baby?" the cashier said.

"I hope they kill those fucking dykes," the stock boy said. "I'd do it myself if they'd let me."

I paid for my candy, kept my head down, and left the store. It wasn't the first time I'd heard people say this, and it wouldn't be the last. It was all over the neighborhood, how the women needed to be put to death, especially the mother, who was supposed to be the one to protect him, but instead had let some lesbian abuse her son.

People on TV sometimes called her "the lesbian mother," or talked about her "lesbian lover." I heard this so often, in so many different ways, sometimes implied, sometimes deliberate, that after a while it seemed as though being a lesbian was part of the crime, something a mother could also be charged with.

AFTER SCHOOL LET out for winter break, the neighborhood kids hung out at the Flamingo Park pool. Sara and I would test the water to make sure it was cold as balls, then pick an unsuspecting boy and push him in. Occasionally, one of them would grab me, then jump into the deep end with me, letting me go as soon as we hit the water. We played chicken, sitting on each other's shoulders. We raced, freestyling from the shallow end to the deep end and back. We tossed a quarter into the middle of the pool and dove for it, showing off how long we could hold our breaths underwater.

Frankie showed up at the pool one afternoon, sucking his thumb and checking out the girls. I was glad Alaina had stayed home with Anthony and Abuela—the thought of him undressing my little sister with his eyes made me sick.

In the afternoon, when the pool was about to close, I headed downstairs to the girls' locker room. I was the last one there—all the other girls had gone home. After a quick shower, I wrapped a towel around my naked body, put gel in my hair, put on deodorant. I'd just pulled my panties on underneath the towel when I turned around and saw Frankie.

I jumped, wrapped the towel tighter around my torso. "What are you doing in here? Get out, pervert!"

He stood there sucking his thumb, rubbing the back of his head with the other hand. "Whatcha doing?" he asked.

"What the hell do you think I'm doing?"

"Taking a shower."

"Get out!" I scrambled to get my T-shirt in the mess I'd left in my locker.

"Show me your tits."

I reached for my tube of hair gel and flung it at him.

He started laughing. "Come on, just flash 'em real quick."

"My dad's gonna kick your ass!" I said.

"Girl, please." He pulled his thumb out of his mouth and mocked my accent: "'My dad's ganna keek your ess.'" He chuckled. "Come on, just one time."

Maybe it was because Alaina wasn't around to keep me strong. Or that at eleven, I was already wearing a bra, a B-cup, larger than most of the other girls in my grade, and that it always made me feel self-conscious, especially when boys looked at me, or when they made comments about my breasts, which was often. Or maybe it was the way he said it, like he wasn't just laughing at my anger or my accent but at what I'd actually said, that my father would kick his ass, and maybe even Frankie could tell it was an empty threat. He probably knew all about me and my crazy ass mother who lived on the streets half the time and talked to herself and insisted there was a man who followed her everywhere and that my father was ruining her life. My mother, who had told me so many times that I should love my body, but then turned around and said the worst thing she could ever imagine was having a daughter who was a puta. Maybe it was the thought of my mother that broke me, made me believe there was no use fighting it.

I opened my towel. Blinked once. Closed it again. "Get out."

WEEKS LATER MAMI came knocking in the middle of the afternoon. She had a new place, she told us, and Alaina and I could come live with her now. As she started tossing our things into a black garbage bag, we cried and clung to Papi. We didn't want to go, we told him. What if this new apartment wasn't even real? What if she never brought us back this time, and we never saw him or Abuela again? And how come Anthony didn't have to go?

Papi just stood there.

I thought about running to Abuela, who was in the kitchen making dinner. She was the one who took care of us anyway—Papi was almost never home. But I knew if I did, my mother would blow up. Anytime we'd ask Abuela's permission for anything in front of her, Mami would turn bright red, say, "That vieja is not your mother!" This would lead to me screaming at my mother that she needed to respect my abuela's house, which would lead to my mother slapping me, which would lead to me bursting into tears and threatening to call the cops on her, which would lead to her slapping me again while Abuela watched helplessly, being no match for my mother, which would lead to my father sitting me down when he got home from work and lecturing me on not starting trouble.

Mami tossed the bag at my feet. "Start packing."

"But we don't want to live with you," I said.

She looked me up and down, then stared my father in the eye. "Tell them. Tell them this was only supposed to be temporary."

I looked at my father, waited for him to admit that he had promised us to our mother.

"Don't make this harder than it has to be," he said.

Alaina burst into tears, then ran to the kitchen to bury herself in Abuela's arms.

I stared at my father hard in the face. How easily he had just given us away. I started crying, too. There comes a time when we realize that our parents cannot protect us, as much as we want them to, or need them to. There comes a time when we realize that we must save ourselves.

I picked up the bag, and without taking my eyes off my father, said, "I will never forgive you." Then I packed some of our clothes and schoolbooks and walked out.

I tossed the bag down the building's front steps and stood on the stoop with my arms crossed, waiting for my mother. I was wiping tears off my face when I spotted Sara, Steven, and their mom coming out of their building. Sara and her mom wore identical floral dresses with yellow sunflowers on them, and Sara's hair had been curled. Steven wore a short-sleeve button-down shirt and a pair of khaki shorts. I sat down on the top step, trying to make myself invisible as they hustled into their Ford Taurus, which was parked in front of our building. As the car pulled away from the curb, Sara rolled down her window and waved. Steven did, too. Even their mom stuck her hand in the air. I put on a fake smile and waved back as if it weren't the last time I'd ever see them. Sara, with her perfect mom, who took the kids out to dinner just because, who invited me to winter festivals and Easter pageants at their church.

I missed her already.

THEY BURIED LÁZARO that December, after a funeral service at St. Patrick's Catholic Church on Miami Beach. The children from St. Patrick's school filled the pews, and the children's choir sang "On Eagle's Wings." Small memorials popped up all over Miami Beach: Teddy bears and prayers written on poster boards and crosses and images of baby Jesus. And lollipops. An entire city mourning the loss of a boy no one knew. We carried him with us. And even though he belonged to no one, he belonged to us all.

II.

The spring after they found the body, Mami stashed us in a one bedroom in South Beach, a small place on Bay Road with a mattress on the floor and the stained rattan sectional Mami got in the divorce. We thought it was the same street that had been all over the news, North Bay Road, and for days it was all Alaina and I could talk about: how Mami had taken us against our will, how she'd brought us to live in a place where dead bodies were dumped.

It had happened one morning in early November. Two Florida Power & Light employees were working outside a house on 54th and North Bay Road when one of them discovered the body. It was the beginning of the dry season, and most of the Beach was still recovering from one of its legendary Lincoln Road Halloween street parties: the entire pedestrian mall transformed, every block between Alton Road and Washington Avenue overcrowded, stages with live music, haunted houses, floats with demons and vampires waving at us from the rafters. And everywhere we looked, Freddy Kruegers with their razor gloves, Jasons in their hockey masks, knife-wielding Michael Myerses. Serial killers were the most popular monsters that year.

When Craig Kriminger and Stewart Silver parked their FPL van in front of the house on North Bay Road to do some repair work on a utility pole, most of the neighborhood kids were already in school. The mourning doves sang as the two men worked, the smell of cat piss all around the block, and something else. Something stronger.

At around 8:30 a.m., Kriminger and Silver made the discovery: under the cherry hedge between the house's driveway and the garden wall, lying in a pile of grass and leaves, the dead body of the little boy.

In El Caserío Padre Rivera, parents summoned La Llorona, the mythical monster that kept kids from misbehaving. I was obsessed with monsters. I watched novelas about demons and exorcisms, movies about witches who came back from the dead to kill the townspeople who'd burned them at the stake. I loved zombies, werewolves, Frankenstein's monster, Dracula. I was fascinated by the possibility of killer alligators living in the sewers, a real-life Jaws stalking swimmers in la playa de Humacao, knife-wielding leprechauns running around town looking for their pots of gold.

La Llorona was a boogeywoman, sometimes a pumpkin-headed demon in a tattered wedding dress, sometimes a woman with a goat's head. She roamed the streets mostly unseen, unless you were so bad that La Llorona was hunting you.

Our titis always had La Llorona's phone number. Our fathers, if they came home from work to disobedient children, would be sure to get their hands on those digits. Our mothers sang us La Llorona lullabies, which were really horror stories about how she would come for you in the night. And when she finally found you, ripped you from the arms of your parents, or took you from your bed while you slept, what awaited you was a fate worse than death: La Llorona ate kids for breakfast.

If you were a troublemaker, if you got into fights, if you didn't eat what your abuela made for dinner, if you refused to sleep come bedtime, La Llorona rose from the darkness to make you hers.

THAT YEAR, BEFORE Mami took us, we'd been living with Papi, Abuela, and Anthony in an apartment across from Flamingo Park, a small place with paint peeling off the walls, rusty hinges on the doors, a family of mice living in a hole behind our ancient refrigerator.

We'd find the mice in our shoes, in the kitchen cabinets, under the bathroom vanity, fast little fuckers that darted across the lino-leum while Alaina and I screamed and ran for our lives, Anthony laughing his ass off.

Anthony was thirteen that November and thought he was our watchdog, so he beat us up when we didn't listen, or when we gave him lip, or when he was pissed at something we did or didn't do. He'd terrorize us with stories about mice building nests in our curly hair, chewing off the tips of our fingers while we slept, suck-ing the liquid out of our eyeballs. One day he got Abuela's cast iron skillet and whacked one, brain and blood and guts splattered on the kitchen floor, picked it up by the tail and flung it at us, me and Alaina ducking out of the way, screaming, *Oh my God, what is* wrong *with you?*

It would be months before a boy down the street threw a rock that sent Alaina to the hospital with a bloody eye, before I ran away from home, went joyriding in a stolen van, and took off for the Florida Keys with some older boys, before I swallowed my mother's pills, the first time, the second. Would be years before Anthony started using steroids, before he tried to strangle me, before I stabbed him with a steak knife. These were the days before juvie hall, before blunts laced with scutter and bottles of Cisco and quarts of Olde English, before school counselors and teachers and friends' parents and juvenile probation officers tried to save me, pulling me aside and looking into my eyes, saying, *Don't you know how dangerous this is? Don't you know?*

Before all that, there was a second mouse, a third, a fourth. And then it was the dead ones that started showing up in our shoes, our backpacks.

ONCE, WHILE WE waited for a hurricane to land on Miami Beach, the rain pelting our windows like pebbles, Anthony punched me so hard in the ear that he sent me tumbling across the bedroom we shared, my whole head ringing. Later, an audiologist would show me the results of my hearing test, look into my eyes, say, *It's pretty bad.*

Once, while running wild through the cañaverales behind El Caserío, Anthony pushed me face-first into the sugarcane, sliced a gash down my left thumb almost to the bone. Sometimes the scar itches. Sometimes, I can make out the sweet-brown burnt sugar smell of those summer mornings.

Once, that same summer, I watched my titi Tanisha take a sharp blade to the inside of her forearm. She was still a child herself—just four years older than me. Three years before, Anthony had slammed a door on her hand so hard it severed her pinky. They weren't able to reattach it.

In our family, the story of the severed pinky became the stuff of family legend, like a monster story. Told over drunken New Year's Eve parties and barbecues, each one of us claiming to remember it like it happened yesterday—the rush to the hospital, the severed pinky in a cup of ice. All that blood. All that screaming. All those years of resentment.

EVEN AFTER THEY buried him, people in Miami Beach still told the story. The diaper wrapped in packing tape, the lollipop T-shirt. The severed limb of an entire community.

As the years passed, we could all remember where we'd been when we heard the news, how old we were when they found him. How we watched it all unfold, how we waited each day for developments, how we speculated about the parents, passed strangers in the park and wondered, *Is it her? Is it him or him or him?* And then later, how we learned his name, his mother's, that he did belong to someone. That he had not been, as we'd come to think of him, ours.

ANTHONY DIDN'T GO with us to the apartment on Bay Road. He simply refused, and Mami didn't bother trying to make him. He stayed behind with Papi and Abuela. Alaina and I had to survive living with Mami on our own. She'd just been diagnosed with paranoid schizophrenia and was on a cocktail of antipsychotics, anxiety pills, sleeping pills. Sometimes she snorted lines of scutter off our kitchen counter, off a hand mirror on her nightstand, off the cover of a *Cosmopolitan*. Other times she smoked crack from makeshift pipes made from tinfoil, a soda can. Sometimes she used an actual pipe. She'd be passed out on the couch for sixteen hours one day, and the next, she'd be manic, running around the apartment talking to herself, throwing things, laughing at nothing, at everything.

Papi came by a couple times a week, gave us a couple dollars apiece, and we'd stash it away for days when there was no food, keeping it a secret from Mami so she wouldn't steal it. When we were hungry, we'd hoof it to 7-Eleven for ninety-nine-cent hotdogs.

Alaina and I spent most weekends plotting our escape, resenting Papi because he let Mami take us, resenting Anthony because he had it so good not having to deal with Mami and eating actual meals made by Abuela.

Living with Mami meant we could never have friends over, could never have birthday parties or sleepovers like all those normal, ordinary girls. We were afraid our friends would find out about her madness, her drug use, her violent outbursts. So we kept it to ourselves, our secret shame, hiding bruises from teachers and classmates.

Sometimes we snuck out of the apartment on Bay Road, made a run for it, tried to make it to Papi's place before Mami caught up with us. But when our mother was high on coke, fast-talking and paranoid and enraged, she was like an Olympic runner. She'd take off after us in the night, barefoot and wide-eyed and angry, and she always caught us. Always.

Alaina and I didn't believe in monsters, not really. We weren't scared of the dark, or Freddy Krueger, or Pennywise the clown in Stephen King's *It*. And even though she was the youngest, Alaina was always the bravest. Nothing scared her. But I was a different story. My greatest fear, the thing that scared me the most in the world, was my mother. It wasn't the drugs, or her threats that one day she'd take us so far away we'd never see Papi or Abuela again, or even her violent streaks. I was afraid that, eventually, I would turn out just like her.

THE FIRST MOUSE was the hardest: the chaos in the kitchen, Anthony shoving me out of the way. How he trapped it, garbage can on one side, Papi's toolbox on the other. How he closed it in with a cardboard box. How, out of nowhere, he handed me the skillet. How afterward, I would lie, say it wasn't me who did it, but my brother. How in a different apartment years later, my brother coming after me and all I can do is breathe, brace myself, chest rising, falling, I open a drawer, pull out a steak knife.

ONE SATURDAY AT the beach, the summer after she took us to the apartment on Bay Road, Mami met a man. He was younger than her, maybe twenty, and looked like he couldn't care less, with dirt under his fingernails, his sun-bleached T-shirt sporting a quarter-sized hole on the shoulder. He'd walked up to her while Alaina and I were swimming, struck up a conversation.

When we got out of the water, I found him lying on my towel, smoking a joint and getting sand all over my sneakers.

We looked at him hard.

"That's my towel," I said, my mouth a fist.

He smiled, ignoring me, and handed my mother the joint. "Your kids are tough."

By then, Mami had already schooled us in the ways of men: what they wanted, what they needed, how they let you down, abandoned you, made promises they'd never keep, how they hurt you then made you think you deserved it. Men were not to be trusted, not even our father. And especially not men you'd just met. But she decided to take this guy home anyway.

When we were ready to leave, Alaina and I wrapped in our towels, our curls frizzy from the saltwater, Mami announced that he was coming home with us. Just for a little while, she said.

During our walk home, Alaina and I argued with her, told her that we didn't even know this guy who could turn out to be some monster, a murderer or rapist looking for single mothers with girls. We told the guy straight up that we didn't want him in our apartment and there was no way in hell he was going there and that we would call our father and then our uncles and then the cops. But we didn't have a phone, and our threats didn't bother Mami. "Just ignore them," she told the guy. And he did.

When we got to the apartment on Bay Road, Mami and the man locked us out of the bedroom, left us in the living room, waiting. I thought about taking Alaina to the payphone at the Chevron station two blocks away, or walking over to Papi's job, but I couldn't leave my mother alone with some guy who could still turn out to be a murderer.

We sat out there most of the night—Alaina on one side of the rattan sectional, me on the other, both of us still in our bathing suits. Alaina in her purple one-piece with a ruffle skirt, red hearts on the bodice, her skinny arms dark brown, her cheeks and nose a reddish copper-brown. My little sister looked like me, except she was smaller, browner, with darker hair. If I stayed out of the sun, I got pale. But Alaina always looked brown.

I knocked on the bedroom door several times, reminding Mami that we needed showers, that we needed dinner. We were anxious to wash the saltwater off our bodies, condition and detangle our hair. We wanted to get to our secret cash—we'd stashed enough for two hotdogs and a Slurpee, maybe a bag of chips. We fell asleep waiting.

Later, every time I told this story, I'd say I was not afraid, just angry. I was mad at my mother for locking herself in the bedroom and leaving us to fend for ourselves with no food, for bringing some stranger into our apartment, into our lives. I would say that this is when it happened, in the middle of the night, when I woke to the sound of my little sister's snoring, asleep on an empty stomach, and decided that we didn't need a mother, that we could take care of each other. I would not say that when I woke, wearing nothing but my pink and black bikini with the zipper on the front, handed down to me by Tanisha, the man my mother brought home was standing in front of me in the middle of the living room, naked, holding his dick. How when I opened my eyes and saw him standing there, I pretended I was not surprised, pretended I was not scared, and said something like, *Get away from me, you asshole*, even though what I really wanted was to scream for my mother. Or how he laughed at the sound of my voice. Or how afterward, when we were finally allowed back into our bedroom, Alaina and I found our secret stash of money gone, how Mami admitted that he hadn't stolen it, that she'd let him have it. Because, she said, he needed cab fare.

IT WAS HIS mother who killed him. Or that's what everybody said, every news station broadcasting the story, every day her picture in the papers, even after the case had been closed.

Once, months later, eating cereal in front of the TV, I watched the news on Channel 10, turned up the volume when they showed how the two women were transferred from the Miami Beach Police Station to Dade County Jail. I balanced the cereal bowl on my lap as the two handcuffed women were escorted by Miami Beach Police detectives, a crowd of locals, reporters, photographers, and camera crews waiting.

I put down my spoon, my frosted flakes getting soggy as each woman was walked past the crowd toward the police cruiser, the onlookers erupting, spitting at them, calling them "asesinas," "baby killers," "monsters."

AFTER WE GOT kicked out of the apartment on Bay Road, one of the many times we got evicted, Mami took us to stay with Mercy. We showed up at her one-bedroom apartment on a Saturday afternoon, all our clothes and shoes spilling out of black garbage bags. Alaina and I hadn't had anything to eat since our school lunches the day before. I'd stopped talking to Mami since she'd gotten us evicted, and because she wouldn't let us go back home with Papi, Abuela, and Anthony, where Alaina and I wanted to be.

Mercy opened the door, and my mother explained that we needed a place to stay for a while.

"Why isn't their father taking care of you?" Mercy asked. "Doesn't he know that his children are in the streets like stray dogs?"

My mother dropped her bags on the floor. "He doesn't care if his kids starve," she said. "He spends all his money on women."

"That's a lie!" I blurted out. "Papi brings us money every week." Then, on purpose, I spilled all my mother's secrets: how my father paid child support, but Mami spent it all on cocaine and beer; how we never had food in the house unless my father bought us groceries; how Alaina and I had to hide money from Mami so we could buy hotdogs at 7-Eleven; how she lied and told Papi that someone broke into our apartment and stole the rent money, when she'd spent it on a three-day binge with some scutterhead from the neighborhood; how they'd locked themselves in the bedroom, and when the guy finally took off, he left behind *dozens* of empty cans of Budweiser.

My mother slapped me in the face, told me to shut up.

Alaina got between me and Mami, even if it meant that Mami would slap her, too. We spent most of our childhood that way, me and Alaina, dodging chancletas and belts, always feeling like all we had was each other.

Mercy didn't pay me or Alaina any mind. "You need to be out in a week," she said. "And I'm not taking care of any kids. I already raised my girls."

My face was on fire. I was on fire. I hated my mother, hated Mercy, and I wanted to punish them. I looked Mercy dead in the eye, recalling all the times she'd talked about Abuela, called her "negra," made up stories about how she was doing voodoo in her kitchen to ruin my mother's life. How she always blamed my father for my mother's illness, saying my father drove my mother crazy, my father made her do drugs, my father, ese negro, who ruined her life.

I took a breath, said, "You didn't even raise your kids. You gave them away."

And then Mercy slapped me, too.

IN 1994, FOUR years after they found Lázaro's body, a tearful South Carolina mother, Susan Smith, would get on TV with a fake story about an armed black man, a carjacking, a kidnapping. She would look into the cameras, beg the so-called carjacker to return her sons safely. Her two little boys, three-year-old Michael and one-year-old Alexander, would be found shortly after, inside their mother's car, still strapped to their car seats, drowned at the bottom of John D. Long Lake.

After Smith's confession, after she admitted she had made up the story, had made up the armed black man and the carjacking and the kidnapping, she gave police all the details about dressing her children, strapping them to their car seats, driving the car to the lake, and parking it on the boat ramp. How she released the emergency brake, stepped out of the car. How she let the car roll into the lake, let it take her children.

Two years after police pulled their bodies from the lake, seven people—four of them children—accidentally drowned while visiting the memorial erected there for Michael and Alexander. They had been driving one night, parked their SUV on the same ramp, letting their headlights shine on the two marble stone pieces.

They had been drawn there, people said, wanting to see the place where it had all happened.

The lake, they said, had become like a legend, attracting visitors from all over the world. A mythical place.

In El Caserío, I spent hours awake in bed, listening for the sounds of La Llorona. I waited for crying, wailing, a woman's voice in the distance calling for her children—one boy, one girl—whose names I didn't know.

The stories say that La Llorona killed her children after being rejected by a lover. She had taken her two babies from their beds one night, had walked with them through the woods down to the river, held their bodies underwater until they both drowned. Then, when she realized what she'd done, with their lifeless bodies in her arms, she walked into the river and let it take her, too.

And so, the legend says, La Llorona wails in the dead of night, haunting rivers and beaches and lakes where children swim, parks and playgrounds where they play, calling out for her ghost children.

FIVE YEARS AFTER they found Lázaro's body, when I was sixteen, I sat in a holding cell at the Miami Beach Police Station. It was my sixth or seventh arrest, this time for stabbing my brother. The fight had started weeks earlier, after Álaina and I moved back with Papi, me and Anthony screaming at each other like our parents used to.

"You ain't my father," I said. "You ain't shit!"

"Count your fucking blessings," my brother said. "I woulda sent your ass away a long time ago."

He'd snitched to Papi about how I'd walked in stumbling drunk at 3:00 a.m., and I'd snitched about how I'd found syringes and vials of Depo-Testosterone in his backpack, both of us desperate for our father's attention. Anthony was already eighteen, and by then Papi was too tired or too busy or too high to be bothered.

"What kind of girl . . . " my brother often said, pulling out pages he'd read and then ripped out of my diary, holding them up for scrutiny, hard evidence of the monster I was, definitely not the girl I was supposed to be, the girl Abuela had tried to raise. "What kind of girl *are* you?"

That afternoon, the fighting had escalated to us wanting to kill each other: during one of Anthony's 'roid rages, after I'd flung his T-shirts, sneakers, and duffel bag off our eighth-floor balcony, after he'd slapped me and I'd slapped him back, he landed a punch on the side of my head that knocked me face-down on the floor. When I got back up, he tried to strangle me. Somehow, Alaina got him off me.

Then I went to the kitchen for the knife.

And when they arrested me, the knife on the living room floor, someone on the phone, Alaina crying and crying, the cops asking, *Was it a stabbing motion or a slicing motion? How was she holding the knife?* How my father, his forehead beaded with sweat, his eyes red-rimmed and puffy, kept asking, *Que hiciste? Que hiciste? What did you do?*

ONCE, WHEN WE still lived in El Caserío, the two of us running wild with the other street kids, I pushed Anthony off the front steps of our building. The night before he had pulled out my hair in handfuls.

The sound of his head cracking on the concrete steps was terrifying, exhilarating.

My brother and I, we were the same: part monster, part mouse.

AT THE POLICE station, every cop stopped by my holding cell, wanting to get a look at the kid who'd tried to kill her own brother.

"Jesus, I *know* you," one of them said, then turned to the others, "I've picked her up before."

I looked him up and down and said nothing. I was a runaway, a high school dropout, a hoodlum. I had been picked up so many times, for aggravated battery, for assault, for battery on a police officer.

I was questioned by two detectives without a parent or lawyer in the room.

The cop who said he knew me sat across the table, asking again and again, *Why did you stab him? Were you angry? Did you want him dead?*

"Yes, I was angry," I said.

"Yes, I wanted him dead," I said.

I didn't ask, "Where is my father?" and I didn't ask, "How is my sister?" and I didn't tell them that for years, after every black eye, every bloody lip, every fistful of hair yanked from the roots, I had imagined the weight of that knife in my hand.

And after I was fingerprinted and photographed and hand-cuffed and escorted into and out of the elevator and past the lobby and out the back door and into a squad car, after I was dropped off at the juvenile detention center where I would be held overnight to await my hearing with other girls who maybe stabbed their brothers and maybe didn't, I imagined that these cops who thought they knew me talked about me, that they called me "juvenile" and "delinquent" and "offender"—words they thought were a good fit for a girl like me.

WHAT DOES IT mean to rupture an eardrum? To scrape a dead mouse off the floor, save it for later. To pick up a knife, point it, thrust it. To sever a finger.

What is a finger without a child's body attached?

What good is a pinky anyway?

IT WAS ALMOST midnight when we arrived at the juvenile detention center, me and two other girls, all the cells in the girls' wing

closed, all the other inmates asleep on floor mats. The juvenile corrections officer walked us to the showers, where we undressed as
she watched, a juvie strip search, the three of us lifting our breasts
and spreading our legs and opening our mouths. How none of us
said a word as the guard poured lice shampoo into our cupped
hands. Not a word as she told us to lather up our heads, armpits,
pubic hair, or when she said and kept saying, *Let me see, let me
see, let me see.*

Once we were in our orange jumpsuits, we had to braid our
hair, she told us, or they would cut it off. So I braided my hair
in front of the mirror while avoiding the other girls' questions.
Where do you live? Where do you go to school? What did you do?

What did you do? People would always ask that question. But
I wouldn't say, not for years, not after I got out of juvie, or after I
turned eighteen and my record was expunged, or after I got my
GED, started taking classes at Miami Dade College, thinking that
it would change me, that it would get me off the streets and I'd be
able to look my father in the face again, finally know what it felt
like to have someone be proud of me.

After I braided my hair, they took me into one of the cells,
handed me a mat and blanket for the floor, locked the door behind
me. The room was empty, freezing, and once I was on the floor,
shivering through the night, I thought, I've finally been put in my
place.

I woke up the next morning to a new roommate. She was lying
on her mat, crying, wiping her nose on her sleeve.

"Don't eat the grits," she said. "They put something in them to
make you shit."

. . .

THE SCARIEST PART was not that La Llorona was a monster, or that she came when you called her name three times in the dark, or that she could come into your room at night and take you from your bed like she'd done with her own babies. It was that once she'd been a person, a woman, a mother. And then a moment, an instant, a split second later, she was a monster.

IN A FEW years, after leaving my mother's house for the last time, after my brother has become a grown man with a wife and a baby and a house of his own, after Ana María Cardona has been tried and convicted and sentenced to death, I would write to her in prison:

> Dear Ms. Cardona,
> I would like to hear your story. Not what the papers said or what people said or what was on the news, but the truth.

And she would write back:

> Dear Ms. Jaquira Díaz,
> This is not a story. This is my life.

Candy Girl

It was the fall after Hurricane Andrew, when we were still kids and Miami Beach still belonged to us, not to the movie producers or the modeling agencies or the real estate investors. It was 1992, three years before I'd stab my brother with a steak knife, before the prosecutors and police officers and public defenders stopped talking to me and started talking *about* me, before they'd decided to send me on a tour of Miami-Dade County Jail, as part of some Scared Straight deal, an intervention program for at-risk youth.

After my third or fourth arrest that year, when I got released from the Miami police station where I'd spent hours in a holding cell, I found my mother waiting in the lobby. Mami was pacing the waiting area, an unlit cigarette dangling from her lip. She wore a white tank top, cutoff jeans, dirty chancletas, her hair a tangle of blond, her red toenail polish chipped, mascara running. As I approached, she just looked me over and didn't say a word, didn't even hold out her arms for a hug, though I hadn't seen her in several weeks. I'd been bouncing from my father's place to my

mother's for months, and then one day, after a fight with Mami,
I ran away, tossed some clothes into a backpack and took off in
the middle of the night. I'd spent the last two weeks sleeping at
friends' houses or on the lifeguard stands out on the beach, skipping all my eighth-grade classes. Until the cops picked me up after
a brawl with some girls outside the Omni mall.

Mami unclipped her visitor's pass from her shirt, dropped it on
the counter in front of the police officer working the front desk, a
small, older woman all the other cops had called Ms. Olga.

Ms. Olga picked up the pass, took one look at me, and frowned.
"I need you to sign a personal property receipt," she said to my
mother.

"I can sign," I said. I'd done this so many times already I was
used to the drill. Besides, Mami had stopped signing shit for me
a long time ago.

My mother turned on her heel before I'd picked up the pen,
walked through the glass doors, and once outside, lit her cigarette.

Ms. Olga put a paper bag on the counter, opened it, and looked
inside. Then she passed it across the desk to me. She did the same
with my backpack, empty and unzipped.

"This all you got?" she asked.

I checked. One pair of gold hoops, six dollars, one apartment
key, one Bob Marley T-shirt, one hair pick, three blue Bic ballpoint
pens, one composition book, one Revlon's Toast of New York lipstick. I gave her a half-smile. "Yeah."

She slid her clipboard toward me. "Sign at the bottom."

I scribbled my name.

"Don't come back here, Miss Thang," she said.

Outside, my mother took a long drag off her cigarette.

"I won't," I said.

"I mean it. I don't want to see your face 'round here again."

I walked through the double doors and found Mami waiting for me with Benny, one of her boyfriends. He was twice her age, in his sixties maybe, mostly bald, wearing brown slacks, a short-sleeved guayabera, and a newsboy cap. The last time I'd seen him, he'd bragged about how he'd been some sort of boxing legend when he was younger, trying to impress me even though we both knew Mami only kept him around in case she needed a favor. My mother was a hustler. She got men to buy her cigarettes, or scutter, or food. She got them to give her money for clothes and shoes. She got them to drive her around, and in this case, to take her across the bridge to pick up her thirteen-year-old daughter from the Miami police station.

Outside, Mami threw her arms around me. She smelled like cigarette smoke and dirty laundry.

"I missed you so much," she said, loud enough that half the block could hear. Nowadays all she did was smoke and party with her scutterhead friends. If I ever saw her, it was only during moments like this, when I called her for a favor, promised to spot her twenty dollars if she picked me up. Or when I was staying at Papi's house and she came knocking, asking to borrow money, too strung out to remember it was Christmas, or the day of my piano recital, or my birthday. I remembered how back in the day, she was proud, well-dressed, and her blond hair fell down her back in heavy layers that she sometimes let me brush or braid or curl. And even though she wasn't perfect, she'd walked us to school, always made sure there were presents under the Christmas tree.

"You missed me? That's a fucking lie."

She pulled back, her hands on my shoulders, the sunlight washing out her bleached hair. "Why would you say something like that?"

I brushed her hands away. I didn't tell her how scared I'd been, spending hours in that cell by myself while the cops talked about me like I wasn't even there, how they said that if my parents didn't come for me, they'd have to process me, then drop me off at the juvenile detention center, where I'd spend the next month or so until my trial. Or how I had shrugged when one cop and then another stopped as they passed my cell and asked, "Where are your parents?" and I didn't even bother correcting either of them, even though I was thinking, *Mother. Where is your mother?* Or how I hadn't called Papi because he was already so fed up with me. How I'd thought maybe she wouldn't even show up, that she was probably in jail herself. I wanted to tell her what it felt like to be the girl whose parents had stopped showing up, but I didn't think she'd hear me.

"You hungry?" she asked, changing the subject. That's when I realized what this was: my mother putting on a show for her man, pretending she actually took care of her kids, using me as a prop to impress some has-been boxer who was probably going to leave her anyway when he realized what he got himself into.

"Starving," I said.

Benny had parked his rusty old Chevy Nova at a meter across the street. He opened the passenger door for my mother, and when he got the back door for me, he didn't look me in the face. The leather seats were torn and stained and they smelled like moldy cheese and old man sweat. As we pulled out of the spot, our eyes met in the rearview mirror.

"I'm saving for a new car," he said.

Usually I hated my mother's boyfriends. But I felt bad for Benny, embarrassed even, that he was apologizing for not having a better car. I couldn't remember the last time one of these men had apologized for anything, let alone looked at me like I was my mother's daughter instead of just some dumb kid, or worse, some jailbait piece of ass.

WE DROVE ACROSS the 112 toward Miami Beach until it turned into Arthur Godfrey Road. Benny put the windows down so my mother could smoke, the wind whipping stray curls in my face. We pulled into the Burger King drive-thru as I was tightening up my ponytail.

My mother leaned back to get a look at me, smiling. "Do you know what you want?"

I stuck my head out the window and talked to the microphone box. "Can I get a Whopper with cheese and a large chocolate shake?"

A girl's voice responded. "Whopper with cheese, large chocolate shake. Anything else?"

"Hang on." I stuck my head back in the car. "Y'all want anything?"

Benny leaned toward the window and ordered for them both. He didn't even bother asking what she wanted, and when they passed him the bags, he just handed them over like they did this shit on the regular. After I got my shake and food, I went back to ignoring them. Benny drove one-handed while taking huge bites of his Double Whopper, and every once in a while, he'd glance at me through the rearview like he was going to say something.

After a while, my mother turned to me again. "So," she said, "you must be happy to come back home."

I wanted to remind her that her apartment had never felt like home, that it was the reason I'd spent the last three years running away. "I don't know, Jeannette," I said, enunciating every syllable in her name so she'd know I was no longer calling her *Mami*. "How was it for *you*, all those times *you* were in jail?"

She turned around, back to her food.

I didn't check for Benny's eyes in the rearview, but I caught how he put his hand over hers, how he tried to comfort her. Was he for real? And how was it that my mother, who usually lost her shit for scutterhead assholes, had found Benny, some regular guy. I wondered how long it would take him to snap out of it, how long it would be before he woke up in my mother's bed at 3:00 a.m.—his wallet missing, his pockets and his dignity turned inside out—and ran like hell.

BENNY STOPPED THE car in front of our building, and I got out quickly, strapping on my backpack and shutting the door behind me. But my mother didn't get out, or wouldn't. I stood on the sidewalk, holding my bag of half-eaten Burger King, my milkshake almost gone, watching them. Benny tried to talk to her, pointing at our building, at his watch, like he needed to be somewhere. I hoped she wouldn't ask me for the twenty dollars I'd promised on the phone.

But then, Benny turned the car around, tires screeching as he and Mami sped away.

My mother lived a block away from Normandy Park, in Section 8 housing, in one of two motel-style two-story Art Deco buildings with multiple layers of paint peeling off in three different pastel colors. Christmas lights were still up in July, August, September. No matter what day of the week, my mother's building always looked like the hangover after an all-night block party, the parking lot and stairs cluttered with random shit that never made it into the trash: crushed beer cans, cigarette butts, candy wrappers. You could always tell who the Section 8 kids were—the ones still riding their bikes in the street after midnight, who knocked on the neighbors' doors to make phone calls since we almost never had phones, whose mothers sent them to the corner store to buy cigarettes with food stamps. We came from broken homes, broken English, and broke-ass parents.

I stepped into our apartment, closing the door behind me, setting my backpack down on the worn carpet and my food on the coffee table. Alaina was at Papi's house, and Anthony hadn't lived with Mami in years, so I had the apartment to myself. All we had in the living room was my mother's old stained sectional, a thirteen-inch television the neighbors had left behind when they moved out, a mahogany table we used as a TV stand, and a rickety glass-top coffee table. There were empty beer cans all over the place, on the floor, where they'd been left standing next to the sofa, on top of the TV, on the kitchen counter, on the windowsill. Oh, and ashtrays. Ashtrays everywhere, all of them full. My mother collected cigarette butts. When she was out of cigarettes, she'd just search her ashtrays and find a butt with some smoke left in it. Once in a while, I'd find half a white boy and it'd be like Christmas.

Sometimes, when Mami and I weren't fighting, when she was on her meds, when she'd stop using and having scutterheads over for weeks at a time, we had good days. We'd get in the kitchen and fry up some chicken, sit around in the living room watching novelas on the scrambled TV. It was during those days that I could ask her anything, when my mother and I could have a conversation.

What do they sound like? I asked once. *The voices?*

She took one long, slow drag off her cigarette, thought about it a while, exhaled. *They sound angry. There's so many of them. But sometimes, it's just Pedro.*

On those good days, I'd have her to myself, almost like I had her back. I'd watch her light cigarette after cigarette, chain-smoking until the entire living room blurred. I'd gather the ashtrays, empty them into the trash in the kitchen, think about how unfair it was that my mother had lost her mind, how unfair that I had lost my mother.

I HADN'T EVEN made it to my bedroom yet, when I heard a knock on the door. I peeked out the living room window.

It was my friend Chris, who I hadn't seen since I ran away. I got the door quickly. "Hey!" I said.

"Long time, stranger." He looked tired, his curly hair longer than I'd ever seen it, and paler than usual. Chris was a light-skinned Afro-Boricua, but I'd never seen him look so pallid. I guessed he'd been working a lot.

"You look like shit," I said.

"Just the way you like me, nena." He gave me a crushing hug, then pulled back. "Where the fuck you been?"

Chris worked at the gas station bodega around the corner, which was just three aisles, a couple of coolers, and the register. Most people in our neighborhood went there to get Phillies and cigarettes and beer when they didn't want to hoof it sixteen blocks to Normandy Supermarket. Chris was there working the register most afternoons. He was older than me, already twenty-one, but he'd been flirting with me since we met a year before. I used to go in there to buy candy, Now & Laters and Airheads and Tootsie Pops, and eventually, he just let me have it all for free. "It's on me, candy girl," he'd say. I'd roll my eyes but take it anyway, and he'd say something like, "Why you gotta be so mean?"

Once we became friends, Chris took care of me. He took me out to eat, bought me clothes and shoes, let me drive his car. He'd stop by with cigarettes and candy, bags of Ring Pops and Charms Blow Pops, packets of Nerds and Sour Patch Kids, Snickers bars and Reese's Peanut Butter Cups. Every day with Chris was Halloween, except without the monsters lurking around the corner—at least none that I could see. He'd park his beat-up Toyota in front of our building, and we'd sit inside, listening to New Edition with our cigarettes and our candy and our lust.

He wasn't exactly my boyfriend, and I didn't love him, but I loved the way he loved me. He talked about us like we had a future, like we had so much to look forward to, saying things like, "Someday, when you're older, I'm a buy you a house," or "When you're sixteen, I'm a take you to Disney World." He pulled bills from his wallet, handed them over and said, "Here you go, candy girl," without me even asking.

Candy girl, that's what he always called me, breaking into song while we waited in line at the movies, or while we skated around the roller rink on Collins Avenue. "Candy girl, you are my world," he'd sing, pretending he was Ralph or Ricky, so willing to be my man even though I wasn't even in high school yet.

While I was away, I hadn't thought of him at all. I had affection for Chris, but mostly, I only thought of him when he was

around, when I was staying at my mom's house. He was someone
who took me and my friends out, someone I called to come get me
when I was bored, or when there was a movie I wanted to see, or
when I wanted new sneakers, or weed, or Wendy's. I knew there
was something off about him being older, but I liked the idea of an
older guy being in love with me, buying me things.

Chris and I went and sat inside his car listening to music,
smoking his Newports. I reclined the seat and just listened: there
was TKA's "Louder than Love," but also the sounds of cars and
buses driving by, a boy on a bike calling out to someone across
the street, viejas out on their balconies yelling at their grandkids.

It had been right in that little Toyota Tercel that Chris had first
confessed that he loved me one Friday night. We'd been drinking
St. Ides. After he said it, he leaned over to kiss me, and suddenly,
I threw up. Yellow vomit, straight down the front of his hoodie.

He'd yelled, "Fuck!" Then he stripped off his hoodie, turned it
inside out, and used it to wipe up the rest of the vomit. "Fuck!" he
kept saying. "Fuck, fuck, fuck!"

I was embarrassed, and drunk. "It's *your* fault!" I said. "You
brought the liquor."

He made a gagging sound. "Fuck!"

Now, even though it had been just a couple of months, it
seemed like that was a million years ago. So much had happened
since then. So many fights with Mami, so many nights out on the
beach.

"When was the last time you cut your hair?" I asked.

"Don't remember," he said, laughing.

We'd hung out in his car for a while, talking and making fun
of each other, when Benny's car pulled into the parking lot. My

mother got out, and walked up to Chris's car as Benny drove away.

Chris rolled down his window. "What's up, Mami," he said.

My mother smiled the way she always smiled at my friends when she was about to bum a cigarette. "Hola, Chris."

Chris rifled through his pockets, like he knew what she was about to say. He gave her a couple Newports and a five-dollar bill.

"Gracias," she said. "You think I can borrow five more?"

"Mami!" I snapped, then turned to Chris. "Don't you fucking give her any more cash."

"You know I'm gonna pay you back," my mother said, then winked at him.

He pulled out a ten-dollar bill and handed it to her, just like that.

"Gracias," she said, then headed inside.

She was always like this, learning my friends' names, getting familiar enough to ask for money, or cigarettes, or drugs. It would be this way into my late teens, when I'm grown, when I'm a woman. It was like I was the only one getting older, changing. But Mami, she was frozen in time as that twenty-year-old who listened to Madonna and thought my father was running around on her, still haunted by those same monsters, and even years after we'd left Puerto Rico, she believed we still owned the house in Luquillo, the liquor store, that we would go back there, pick up right where we left off. That it would all be waiting for us to get back.

"You know you ain't never gonna see that money, right?" I told Chris.

He looked at me, then turned the engine. "See you tomorrow, candy girl. And fix your damn hair."

I reached for the door handle. "Get a fucking haircut."

WHEN I GOT up the next morning, I listened for signs of my mother. She went out partying almost every night, and I hadn't heard her come in. When she wasn't gone for days at a time, she'd be locked away in her room with some asshole, blasting Madonna on the radio, smoking and doing lines of scutter. Alaina and I would be locked in our room—me on the bottom bunk, Alaina on the top—trying to tune it all out. Sometimes I could hear her through the walls, laughing and laughing. If a frustrated next-door neighbor knocked on the door at two in the morning, she'd turn up the volume on her radio, until the cops showed up and broke up the party, which meant her boyfriend would jump out the bedroom window with her stash, and Mami stayed behind talking to the cops.

Living with Mami had become so unpredictable that Alaina and I started sleeping in our clothes—T-shirts and shorts, even jeans sometimes, sneakers and socks always ready in case we had to grab them and jump out the window. We were always in survival mode, always on the lookout in case somebody called the cops on Mami, in case Mami was having a 2 a.m. breakdown, in case one of her drunk boyfriends tried to come into our room in the middle of the night.

I slipped on my chancletas and went out into the hallway. In the living room, I found a mess: half-empty beer bottles, a pizza box left on the coffee table, the couch cushions on the floor, men's clothes tossed all over the place. A pair of faded blue jeans, a white T-shirt, white Nikes, balled-up tube socks.

As I headed back toward the bathroom, I heard the toilet flush, then the door swung open and there he was, in the hallway between the bathroom and my bedroom, standing right in front of me in nothing but boxer shorts. It wasn't Benny.

It was J.R., a kid I went to school with. A kid who'd tortured me since we were sixth graders at Fisher. He'd tried to kiss me once while we stood in line at the bumper cars on a field trip to the Miami Youth Fair, and I'd thrown my frozen lemonade at his head, and a week later he started a rumor that I was the one who'd tried to kiss him, and a week after that he tried to trip me as I was getting off the school bus.

J.R. beamed when he saw me, didn't say a word as he stood there, in my house, almost naked. He looked me up and down, and suddenly I was the one who felt almost naked, in my Bob Marley T-shirt and cutoff shorts, no bra. I crossed my arms across my chest.

J.R. chuckled, then marched past me toward my mother's bedroom like he knew the way. I leaned back against the wall, almost fell over.

He went to school with me.

What the hell was he doing partying with my mother?

And he didn't even wash his hands.

When he got to my mother's door, he knocked three times. "I gotta go, dog," he said to whoever was in my mom's room. "I'm out in five." He strutted back toward me, and I couldn't think of a single thing to say. I stood there almost frozen as he walked past.

In the living room, J.R. was throwing on his clothes when my mother's bedroom door opened and out walked a guy I didn't know. He was older than J.R., maybe in his twenties, in a white undershirt and paint-stained cargo pants, like he'd come straight over from work. I'd never seen him around the neighborhood. He nodded as he walked past.

And then the two of them, leaving the mess behind in the living room, walked out the front door.

ONCE I GOT to school, I stomped through the hallways in my baggy jeans, combat boots, and a Malcolm X T-shirt Chris had bought me at Flea Market USA. I ignored the boys, their stupid braces, their baseball jerseys, the girls with their ponytails bouncing as they pranced down to PE or Civics. Everywhere I looked, I saw new faces. Hurricane Andrew had hit us so hard that the school was overcrowded with kids from Homestead, kids who'd moved up to Miami Beach because their families had lost their homes, their schools closed. When I got to my Honors Language Arts class, my classmates straggling in and filling all the desks around me, I found some empty seats in the back. I kept my eyes on my notebook, doodling in the margins, trying to make myself invisible, until my friends Boogie and China walked in. And then, for a while at least, everything was okay.

Boogie, China, and I were best friends, like sisters. We'd known each other since we were in Ida M. Fisher Elementary, and they were the only ones who knew where I went when I ran away. Sometimes I slept over at one of their houses. Sometimes we took off together and stayed at a boyfriend's house.

China sat in the seat next to me, and Boogie sat in front of me. Before the bell, I told them about getting arrested, about spending hours in the police station before my mom picked me up.

"Stay over at my house if you want," China said. Out of the three of us, she was the only one who lived in a two-parent household.

Her parents owned and managed a restaurant on South Beach, and she worked there after school almost every day. We'd often stop by for free milkshakes and burgers. Even though her parents worked at the restaurant every single day, from morning until night, worked their asses off just to stay afloat, China never seemed poor because she was so generous with everything she had. If you were hungry, she'd make sure you knew you had a standing invitation to eat with her family. If you didn't have a place to stay, she'd make sure you knew you could crash at her house, sleep in her bedroom. She took care of us all, always thinking more about others than herself.

We'd been friends since fourth grade. Two years later, Boogie came into our lives, the new girl, who all the boys started crushing on the second she walked through the door of Ms. Bregman's sixth-grade classroom.

Boogie pulled a bag of Doritos from her backpack, then turned to me. "Want some?"

I picked up a couple and started crunching. We weren't allowed to eat in class, but Boogie usually did whatever she wanted. We both loved to break the rules, except *I* was the one always in trouble. Boogie was loud, with a hot temper and a smart mouth, but she could sweet-talk her way out of anything. I was the girl who flung pre-algebra textbooks across the classroom at the teacher, the girl who climbed onto the table in the cafeteria and threw creamed corn in order to start a food fight, the girl who dove headfirst into a giant water barrel when we were supposed to be bobbing for apples during Field Day, the girl who got into a fistfight with a boy at the top of the bleachers in the gym, then tumbled all the way down with the boy in a headlock. There was no sweet-talking my way out of any of that shit, so I didn't even bother trying. In our group, China was known as the shy one, the one who was quiet but tough when she needed to be. Boogie was the flirt. And I was the wild girl, the one who had fought half the girls, and some of the boys, in our school.

My friends would often throw down with me, if I was getting jumped, if there was more than one girl, if it was a brawl. But I never expected them to. Fighting was my thing and we all knew it. Sometimes they'd see it coming, the way I mean-mugged girls at the bus stop, in the mall, on the boardwalk, the way I refused to move out of the way when somebody was trying to get by in the crowded hallway on their way to class, just itching for a fight, begging for it. The open palm to the face, the two of us crashing against the lockers, the searing pain as we stumbled and my knee hit metal, and the rage, that unstoppable force, all those years of beat-downs barreling against me, the adrenaline rush as all the other kids gathered around us to watch, the confidence that I would win, even when I wouldn't, even if in the end I'd wind up slumped over in the locker room, or on the PE field, or on the dance floor. Then, at least, there would be the certainty that I'd gotten exactly what I deserved. Years later, after I'm a grown woman, after I've stopped throwing down, when I can't remember the last time I actually hit someone, a friend would ask, "Do you need it, all that shit, in order to write, in order to be who you are?" He would mean the fighting, the chaos, the rage. I would say no. And of course that would be a lie. And of course he would not believe me, because even all those years later, as much as I tried to hide it, he could see it, my whole body clenched like a fist.

China leaned over, and between the three of us, we polished off the Doritos.

"Chris came over yesterday," I told them.

China gave me a look, raised one eyebrow. "*That* guy?" she said. "What?"

"Don't you think he's too old?" China didn't like Chris—she thought it was creepy that his little brother went to school with us, and that Chris sometimes picked him up from school, according to her, *just* so he could check out the girls.

"He's not my boyfriend," I said. "We're just friends."

Boogie laughed. "Yeah, okay," she said. Boogie had her own opinions. Most of her boyfriends had been older, with their own cars, jobs, even if they lived with their moms. She wasn't worried about me—she knew I could handle myself, and she was also not interested in any boys our age.

China was worried though, I could tell. She loved her friends, and kept us all close. Her quinces was coming up in a few months, and her family was planning a huge birthday party, an old-school quinceañera with puffy ball gowns, fifteen couples dancing to Chayanne's "Tiempo de Vals," a DJ, a three-tier birthday cake. China's mom and tías were into this whole big production because they wanted to keep us all busy, off the streets, spending time with boys our age, where they could keep their eyes on us. Two days a week, we all went to China's house for rehearsals, all of us part-nered off according to height, and I tried not to die of humiliation as one of her cousins twirled me around in the yard, as he placed his hand on my back, dipped me, and looked into my eyes like he was trying to be Antonio Banderas. I was dreading the idea of wearing a dress. I was always in baggy jeans, baggy T-shirts, and sneakers or combat boots. And now I was supposed to wear a magenta bustier-topped monstrosity with a giant ruffled skirt.

It was some Rican Cinderella shit, all of us prancing around like La Cenicienta.

After the bell rang, Mr. Williamson closed the door behind him and started talking about Hurricane Andrew, which didn't seem like whatever we were supposed to be talking about in our Honors Language Arts class. Usually, it had to do with Greek mythology or *The Legend of Sleepy Hollow* or Edgar Allan Poe. But we stopped paying attention. Instead, we passed around a compact mirror and fixed our hair, our makeup, checked for orange Doritos in our teeth. China admired her hair—like always, it was perfect. She had thick brown ringlets, like my sister's, almond-shaped eyes, and plump, heart-shaped lips that she filled in with dark lipstick. I would spend half my life crushing on her, and hating every dude she ever dated. None of them would ever be good enough.

Boogie had straight brown hair that she always colored either auburn or honey brown, depending on her mood or whatever she found at the drugstore. She was smart as hell, and could sing her ass off. I was madly in love with her then, but would never, ever tell her. I didn't know what it was about her, but there was *something*. The way she always smelled like Violeta body spray, the way she was brave like I could never be, the way she loved her curvy body, always wearing skintight Brazilian jeans or miniskirts, how she was fiercely independent, even at thirteen, all the ways she was strong, but also vulnerable. Her parents let her do whatever she wanted, stay out late, date older guys, and didn't really pay attention to her. She wanted, more than anything else, to be loved. And I wanted, more than anything else, to be the one who got to do it.

"Do you understand?" Mr. Williamson asked. When I glanced up, he was standing right in front of my desk, looking at me. Not Boogie, not China, not anybody else. Me.

"What?" I said. Everyone laughed.

"That's what I thought," he said. "If you're having trouble listening, maybe you'd like to sit up front, next to me."

The dunce seat. An empty seat next to Mr. Williamson's large desk, facing the whole class, where everybody would be looking at me like I was some kind of idiot. Hell. No.

"I'm okay," I said, then quickly picked up my pen and pretended to write, not looking up to meet his gaze.

Mr. Williamson turned and walked to his desk, picked up a stack of papers, and started passing them out. It was a homework assignment. We were supposed to write an essay about Hurricane Andrew: our experience, how our families planned for it, how we survived it, and the aftermath of the storm. Mr. Williamson explained the assignment in depth, and then walked over toward my desk again.

"Do you have any questions?" he asked the class.

"No," everyone said in unison.

"Jaqui?" He waited.

"No," I said.

"Good."

When the bell rang, I threw the paper, my notebook, my pen, everything into my backpack, determined to slip out fast, but he caught me. "Jaqui," he said sternly as I headed for the door.

I stepped up to his desk. "Yeah?"

He stood with his arms crossed, and I noticed that his lip was quivering a little, like he was more nervous than I was. "I expect you'll have your homework assignment when it's due. Tomorrow. Not the next day, or the day after that."

"Yeah," I said. Boogie and China waited for me by the door, listening in.

"What happened to you this past week? You weren't in school."

"I was sick," I said.

He looked at me, sighed. "I hope you're feeling better. I'm looking forward to reading your essay." He pointed to the door. "See you tomorrow."

AFTER MR. WILLIAMSON's class, we split to our separate electives. Boogie and China took off down the hall, and I headed toward the music room. As I passed the girls' bathroom and the water fountain, I bumped into Chanty, another old friend from Fisher. We hadn't talked in a while, and she looked messier than usual, wearing a baggy T-shirt half tucked into her tight jeans, her brown hair pulled back in a messy ponytail. She came right up to me, gave me a peck on the cheek and a quick hug.

"Hey nena, long time," she said.

That was normal for us at Nautilus Middle School. A quick kiss hello, a hug. It was how we said *what's up* to our friends, all the other kids we'd known most of our lives, who'd lived down the street for years, who we ran into at the grocery store or the pharmacy or while walking along the boardwalk. Miami Beach was like a small town that way—everybody knew each other, and everybody knew everybody else's business. But Chanty and I, we weren't friends anymore. Not really. We hadn't been for a while, not since her mom decided that I was trouble, a no-good hoodlum from the streets who was bound to end up pregnant, who would spend her life on welfare, or in jail, and that was not the life she wanted for her daughter.

It happened after Chanty got caught skipping, months before. Chanty and I had left school early, went to the beach with her boyfriend, Andre, and his boy Devin, this beautiful, quiet Jamaican boy from some other school in North Miami. We went to the park on the North Shore, and Andre lit a blunt, smoked us all out. We were there for hours, the four of us lying in the sand, finding shapes in the clouds, exploding with laughter when somebody found a cheeseburger or an elephant or an alligator.

"Hey," Chanty said after a while, all serious, "I have to pee."

"So pee," Andre said, not taking his eyes off the clouds.

She got up, slowly, trying to steady herself. She was fucked up. I shook my head at Andre. "Go with her, you asshole."

When Chanty and Andre left, Devin and I stayed behind. We sat on the sand, side by side, leaning against each other.

"You wanna climb one of those trees?" he said, pointing at the tallest sea grapes.

I laughed. "No."

He was quiet for a while, like I'd shut him down, and I could tell he was shy. But he was cuter than most of the boys who went to Nautilus.

"You wanna kiss me?" I asked.

He smiled, but didn't say anything. He turned to me, leaned over slowly, and I pulled him by his shirt's collar, pressed my lips against his. I waited, but he didn't do anything, just kept his mouth there, awkwardly, with his eyes closed. It could've been the first time he ever kissed a girl, from the way he was frozen there, but he was mad fine, so I stuck my tongue in his mouth. We kissed, softly, for a while, and then I pulled away.

"What's your name again?" I asked.

He shook his head, laughed. "Devin."

We kissed for a long time, the waves crashing in the distance, the wind blowing my curls in his face, and when I stuck my hand down his pants, he pulled his face away slightly, opened his eyes like he was shocked, then smiled. I didn't exactly know what I was doing, but I did it anyway. I was curious, and a lot of my friends were already having sex, and I was dying to get rid of my virginity, like it was a burden, and anyway by then I was masturbating so much I was sure I was ready. So I kissed him and I slid my hand inside his underwear and grabbed his dick and stroked it for about three seconds before he let out a single long sound, part grunt, part moan, and came in his pants.

"Shit," I said.

"Damn," he said, and wouldn't look at me, or couldn't. He kissed me again, then tugged on my jeans. "Take these off."

I slid off my jeans and underwear, and right there on the beach he went down on me, put his whole face in my pussy, and it didn't take long at all, and I squeezed my legs around his head and dug my fingers into the sand and moaned and moaned and didn't fucking care who heard or who was watching, and maybe it even excited me a little, knowing that other people could hear me. For a second I worried that maybe Andre and Chanty could hear us, that they would see us as they were walking back from the bathrooms, but then I decided I didn't care. After I came, Devin kissed me like he finally realized what kissing was, his tongue in my mouth, and I could taste myself, the salt, the cigarette he'd smoked minutes before going down on me, and I felt free, at least for a while. Later, after I'd forgotten the way he tasted, the way his finger felt inside me, all I felt was sadness.

When Chanty got home that night, after skipping most of the school day, her mother had already gotten a call from school, and when she asked Chanty where she'd been, who she'd been with, instead of saying she'd been with Andre, she said she'd been with me. Just me. And her mom, who already thought I was bad news, banned me from her life. Chanty was allowed to hang out with all our other friends, Boogie and China and even Chuckie, the skater kid who sold weed in the cafeteria. But not me. Chanty came right up to me and said hi whenever she saw me, but we barely hung out anymore. I avoided talking about it, just so I didn't have to remember that I was somebody her mom hated. A loser.

I told Boogie and China, and they both agreed it was fucked up, and that Chanty shouldn't have snitched to her mom about skipping school with me.

That's how it was with us, how it was supposed to be. We kept each other's secrets, wiped each other's tears, protected each other. We passed notes during class, we told each other everything, our fantasies and our crushes, the latest argument with our parents, the TLC concert we'd been saving up for, the guy who confessed his love while we rode the bus together on a Friday after school. We sat together in the cafeteria, found each other in the hallways. We harmonized to Shai's "If I Ever Fall in Love" or En Vogue's "Hold On" while we waited for the bell to ring. We went on missions together, cutting class and catching the bus to the mall, or the flea market, or the beach, singing Whitney in the back of the bus. We snuck out to salsa music festivals at Bayfront Park on the weekends, turning each other to Andy Montañez's "Casi Te Envidio" and Frankie Ruiz's "Mi Libertad" until the park closed. We went to birthday parties at Hot Wheels, where we strapped on rented roller skates and cruised around la pista with the disco lights, shaking it to 2 Live Crew.

We wore short shorts and crop tops, baggy jeans and basketball jerseys, big hoop earrings. And no matter what, everybody had opinions about how we dressed, called us tomboys or hood rats or fast girls. Our shorts were too short, our jeans too tight, too baggy, our voices too loud. Everybody wanted to control what we wore, what we did, who we did it with. We were not the girls they wanted us to be. We were not allowed to talk like this, to want like this, were not supposed to feel the kind of desire you feel at thirteen, at fourteen. *What kind of girl*, they loved to say. *What kind of girl*, even as they took what we gave, took what we tried to hold on to. Our voices. Our bodies. We were trying to live, but the world was doing its best to kill us.

We would have boyfriends that didn't last the year, the month, the week, older guys who didn't go to school, who drove Broncos and Camaros and Cutlass Supremes. We would hide them from our parents, our friends' parents. When we got tired of them, we would break it off, but sometimes they wouldn't go, and instead they'd show up at the pool or the movie theater or the roller skating rink uninvited, asking to talk to us just one last time. We were thirteen, fourteen, fifteen, and they were men, in their twenties, and no matter how we said no, they would keep coming back. Until we had babies, or abortions, and then they *would* leave.

We were girls, but we'd spend the rest of our days together if we could. Until one day we realized that without meaning to, we grew up, grew apart, broke each other's hearts.

I WENT TO my two music classes, the only two periods I felt bad about missing. As soon as I walked into the orchestra room, Ms. Seoane, in her sweet and encouraging way, gave me a talking-to: I was supposed to be practicing for a big concert at the end of the year, where we'd play together with our jazz band and all the Miami Beach High musical ensembles, strings and brass sharing the stage. I was Nautilus' only advanced bassist, and they needed me. I couldn't keep skipping school.

I apologized, promised to make up for all my missed practices.

Two periods later, in Piano, I plugged my headphones into one of the Yamaha electronic keyboards in the back of the room. Instead of practicing Bach's "Minuet in G minor" from my assigned sheet music, I spent the whole hour trying to figure out the music for "Candy Girl." I'd play a few notes, then write them down, filling in a sheet of blank staff paper. I wanted to surprise Chris one day, and I'd spent hours combing the racks for the sheet music at Spec's and Camelot Music, but I'd never found it. I played "Candy Girl" until the bell rang, then packed my things and strapped on my backpack. Before I left the room, Ms. Seoane handed me a folder with sheet music for our concert, James Swearingen's "Majestia."

"Don't forget about practice," she said in a singsong voice.

The rest of the day, I kept my head down, avoiding eye contact, taking notes and pretending to work out math problems, going from class to class without slowing down long enough to notice what everyone else was looking at: me. I didn't realize it until school let out, until I was at my locker turning the wheel on my Master Lock, struggling with the combination. I'd been gone at least a week, but it had been much longer since I'd even seen my locker. After a second try, I leaned against the red metal door, told myself to *breathe, just breathe.* I straightened myself out, ready to try again, checking out the long, crowded hallway, and that's when I saw that everyone was staring at me, every face turned in my direction, not one person even trying to fake it. All eyes on me.

Halfway across the hall, J.R. leaned against his own locker, arms crossed. I scanned the crowd, from one face to the next, and then back to J.R. He'd told them. I was sure of it. They'd all been talking about me. He'd probably given them all kinds of details about what our apartment looked like, about how we didn't have any food in the fridge, about my mother and some guy I didn't even know. I wanted the world to crack wide open and swallow me.

I held my algebra textbook against my chest, my face and ears and all my insides burning. Across the hall, J.R. was still smiling at me. He wanted me to see him. He wanted me to know that he'd told them all. I imagined chucking the book across the hall at him, how good it would feel to send it flying and knock his ass out with seven hundred pages of math problems. But I thought about Ms. Olga back at the Miami Police station; Alaina, who looked up to me, and who was probably dealing with her own problems at Treasure Island Elementary; and Paula, my court-appointed counselor, who I was supposed to see every week, and whose favorite line was, *Jaqui, you're all out of second chances.* But J.R. kept staring at me, that stupid smirk on his face.

Finally, I stood up straight and yelled across the hall. "What the fuck you looking at?"

And then, as if he'd been waiting for this exact reaction, he blew me an air kiss, which made them all explode with laughter, the preppy boys with their piercing white smiles, the headbangers in their dog collars and hair dyed jet-black, three or four rich girls who never talked to me shaking their heads as they shadowed their boyfriends down the corridor, even the one pregnant girl who tried to hide her belly under oversized hoodies, like she was fooling anybody. J.R. laughed, too, like I was some kind of show. When he finally stopped laughing, he pursed his lips, brought his fists to his eyes, wiping off imaginary tears, then he slowly mouthed the words, "Don't cry."

I didn't cry. I made a choice, right there in that hallway: this would not be my life. I was not, and would never be, the kind of person who got bullied or made fun of, because I'd grown up with an older brother who'd whooped my ass since I was in diapers, with a mother who handed out beat-downs like they were life lessons, and if they'd taught me anything, it was how to fight. So no, I didn't fucking cry. Instead, I dropped my backpack and made a beeline for him, past the stoners and the surfers and the skaters and the wannabe rappers, all of them cackling and snickering and watching me as I gripped my textbook tight with both hands, all seven hundred pages of it, as I swung it at him, as I caught him square in the jaw. He crashed sideways against his locker, slid down onto the floor, arms splayed about, one leg tucked underneath. And everyone went quiet.

WHEN I GOT to my building that afternoon, kicking stones out of my path and giving people dirty looks as I walked past them, Chris was waiting for me in the parking lot. He was sitting in his car, my mother leaning against the driver's side, talking to him. When she saw me, she said hi, and quickly went inside.

"Did you give her money?" I asked.

He laughed, shaking his head. "Just a cigarette," he said. "Wanna go for a ride?"

"You're such a fucking liar," I said.

"What's with the attitude?"

"Why are you giving my mother money?"

Chris's expression changed, eyes narrowed. "What's going on? You okay?"

And then, even though I knew our upstairs neighbors were probably all listening, I blew up. "What are you even doing here?!" I yelled. "You're not my boyfriend! You'll never be my boyfriend! You ain't shit!"

We were there for a long time after that, the two of us in that parking lot, just looking at each other. I stood there, my backpack strapped on tight, the sun on my face, my armpits all sweaty, staining the shirt he'd bought me as a gift, staring him down. I could hear the boys in the park across the street dribbling the basketball during their afternoon pickup game, a car horn blaring somewhere in the distance. He didn't say anything. Maybe he didn't know what to say. Years later, I'd think about this moment, how I'd meant to hurt him, how I'd said those words only because I knew he wouldn't hurt me back.

There were things I'd never told Chris about my life, about all the ways I'd tried to make that life bearable. That I wrote songs I belted out in the shower, that my friends and I sang while we rode the free trolley up and down Lincoln Road, that in my dreams, I saw myself playing in some piano bar, or some jazz club, my bass's pizzicato vibrating through time and space, that I spent most of my days pretending I could sing, dreaming of going on the road with Whitney or Mariah. Or how I filled spiral notebooks with stories about monsters, stole books from the library, skipped entire school days so I could spend sunny afternoons lying out on the beach, reading, and that every time I picked up one of those lollipops he brought me, I thought about that toddler, Baby Lollipops, how they'd found his body, and how I'd written down all the details I could remember, filled pages and pages, and I didn't even know why.

Finally, Chris turned the key in the ignition. He watched me for another second, then slowly, he put on his dark shades, backed his Tercel out of the parking space, and without another word, he drove away.

THAT NIGHT, I actually did my homework. I read Mr. Williamson's handout, then got to work, writing feverishly, one page, two pages, three, four. I kept writing, even though it seemed much longer than any homework assignment I'd ever attempted, and when my pen ran out of ink, I picked up another one and kept at it until I finished.

Afterward, I lay in bed with my eyes closed, my whole body vibrating, exhausted like I'd just sprinted across the park. I could hear my mother in the living room, alone, laughing. Usually, around that time, she was getting ready for a night out, heading to South Beach, where she went to score, where she'd been arrested a few times for possession. In the living room, I could hear her talking to herself, then laughing and laughing and laughing.

I remember the first time I'd heard my mother laugh like this, for no reason. It was years before, only a few months after we moved from Puerto Rico. I was eight. We'd just moved to a small apartment on South Beach, a few blocks from Fisher. She'd been making sandwiches when the phone rang. She picked up and talked for a few minutes, then she set the receiver down, stood in the kitchen, and cried silently.

It was a call from Puerto Rico, she told me. Her titi Meri had just died.

She was my mother's aunt, but had been like a second mother. I had never met her, this woman my mother had loved so much, although I'd answered the phone when she called a few times, and she'd known my name, Anthony's name, Alaina's. I'd only seen her in a photograph, her salt and pepper hair pinned into a loose bun on top of her head, face pale and caked with powder, lips painted some unnatural shade of red. I had no stories of her as a live person, no memories of her brushing my hair or giving me terrible handmade sweaters as birthday presents or making Sunday dinner for us. I didn't even know how she'd died, if she'd had a heart attack or some incurable disease, if she'd been struck by lightning or hit by a car.

Mami had left the sandwiches on the kitchen counter and I'd snatched mine up, watched as my mother held the receiver to her ear, as she set it down and stumbled to the kitchen table, as she pulled out one of the chairs and sat. She had pulled me onto her lap, wrapped her arms around me, and cried into my neck. I was hungry, but I didn't eat my sandwich. I held it carefully, and worried that I would drop it or crush it as my mother was squeezing me with all that need. I'd held my tongue when it occurred to me to ask if there were other family members that belonged to us, like this aunt I'd never met, out there in the world. The thought of these nameless faceless people, and my mother, breathing my air, her body against mine, needing me so much, made my chest ache. But there was nothing I could give her. So I fed her my sandwich, held it up to her mouth, and she took one bite, chewed it slowly, swallowed with her eyes closed.

Then, a shift in the air. Mami sitting at that table, having just lost a mother, crying softly, silently, into her hands, and suddenly the laughter shattering the silence like a spear. She cupped her mouth, laughing and laughing and laughing.

We'd moved to Miami Beach only months before, and I barely spoke English, but I knew the word "orphan." I'd watched *Annie* about a dozen times, and found the idea of being a child with no parents terrifying and thrilling. It had been like a terrible fantasy, something I longed for, something I feared. And years later, this would be exactly how I understood love: thrilling and terrifying, tears and laughter and then tears again. Love, I learned, could destroy you. Love drove my mother mad.

A FEW DAYS later, I caught the bus to Downtown Miami, and then the Metrorail to the Mailman Center for Child Development for my appointment with Paula. It was the first time I'd be seeing her in her office—every time I'd seen her, we'd met at the courthouse or the police station or in an office at my school's library.

"Have a seat," Paula said as I stepped into her fourth-floor office. I plopped down on the love seat, and she sat across from me in her swivel chair. She wore slacks and a short-sleeved blouse, except she was barefoot, with a toe ring and tattooed forearms, her brown curls messy and frizzy. The whole office thing didn't agree with her, like her clothes were some kind of costume to hide the real Paula, the tattooed white woman with moonstone and turquoise jewelry and wild hair who probably played the drums in some therapist garage band.

Paula's office was like a children's playroom, with small plastic tables and chairs like the ones in a kindergarten classroom. Toys littered the floor: Barbies, Legos, blocks. Board games stacked on short bookcases. There was a set of beanbags by the window, and hanging on the walls were colorful crayon drawings of stick-figure families and houses with yellow suns hanging over them.

"How are you?" she asked after I sat down.

"Fine."

"Fine?"

"Yeah." I told her I was back in my mother's house, skipped over the part about running away, and skipping school, and getting arrested. As far as she knew, I'd been in my father's house the whole time.

"How was it? Seeing your mom again?"

"Fine."

"Jaqui." She pursed her lips, waited.

And waited.

I avoided eye contact, checking out the board games stacked on the shelves. Was that what they paid her for, to play with little kids in her office?

"It was fine," I insisted. I talked about school, about my music classes, about Alaina, who was staying with Papi for a while, although she mostly lived with Mami and didn't bounce back and forth from Mami's apartment in Normandy Isle to Papi's place in South Beach like I did. We talked about Anthony, who I was in a constant battle with, always fighting, how I sometimes felt helpless around him, and how my father didn't even care.

She swiveled her chair over to the side table, picked up a box of tissues, and offered them to me. "Is that why you always run away?"

"I'm not gonna cry," I said, rolling my eyes. "It's just not fair. Anthony has never lived with Mami. He doesn't know what me and Alaina have to deal with."

She studied me for a while, then put the box of tissues on the armrest next to me.

"Can you tell me more about that? What you had to deal with?" It occurred to me that the few times I'd seen Paula, I'd never told her the whole truth about my mother, never mentioned the drugs or the drinking, or how things had been much worse for Alaina because she never ran away. As far as Paula knew, my mother had a mental illness and she was taking her medication.

I tried to change the subject, told her all about Benny, how he bought me Burger King and drove me home, about how I'd be playing bass in a big end-of-year concert. I talked for a long time. Paula just watched me.

"What made you go back to your mom's house?" she asked after a while.

"I do what I want," I snapped.

This made her sit up. "So you want to be treated like an adult?"

"Yeah. I can take care of myself."

"Then why don't you start behaving like one?"

I looked down at my sneakers, shrugged.

She picked up the small trashcan under the side table, and held it out in front of me. "And get rid of those cigarettes."

"What cigarettes?"

"Hand 'em over!"

I pulled the pack of Newports out of my jeans pocket, dropped them in the trash reluctantly, which hurt when I thought about how much another pack would cost. "How did you know?"

"You *stink*," she said.

I sniffed myself, but didn't notice any smell.

"I keep telling you, you don't have to live your life this way. And I mean that. Some things are out of your control, but Jaqui," she inched closer, put her hand on mine, "some things are not."

"Like what?"

"Like the stealing, fighting, smoking." She waited for my reaction, then continued. "Like going to class." She rolled her chair back toward her desk, put on her reading glasses, picked up a pen, and started scribbling something in a yellow legal pad. When she was done, she ripped out the page. "I have something for you." She wheeled back over and handed me the sheet.

It was a list of questions. Things like *What makes you sad?* and *What are you afraid of?* and *What is your happiest memory?* and *Where do you feel safe?* and *If you could travel anywhere, where would you go?*

"So I'm supposed to answer these?" I said.

"For next week's session. Think of it as an exploration."

"You mean *homework*?"

She sighed. "Jaqui."

WHEN I GOT home later that afternoon, I could hear Madonna's "This Used to Be My Playground" coming from Mami's bedroom, the hallways foggy with cigarette smoke. As I walked into my bedroom, I heard laughter, Mami's first, then a man's. My mother, laughing and laughing, and then, over the cacophony of the song ending and DJ Laz on Power 96, Chris. My Chris. His voice in my mother's bedroom.

I dropped my backpack on the floor and stepped out into the hallway. Had I imagined it? Would Chris do this? Would *Mami*? I made my way slowly toward my mother's door, then stood there, waiting, listening, waiting. And then, there it was again. Chris and my mother, laughing together, their voices familiar with each other. They had done this before.

Suddenly, without thinking, I turned the knob, threw the door open, the two naked bodies scrambling to cover themselves, my mother with her bedsheets wrapped around her, and I wanted to scream but all I could manage was an exhale, a long, drawn-out breath like all the air was being squeezed out of me. *How could you?*, I wanted to say. But then, the smoke beginning to clear, the naked man in my mother's bedroom pulled his pants on, and they were not Chris's pants but Benny's, and it was Benny standing there, avoiding my eyes. Benny bending to pick up his shirt from the floor. Benny's voice. Benny's laughter.

"Jaquira!" my mother yelled. Not *Jaqui* but "Jaquira." Not *Please close the door* but "Who the fuck do you think you are?!"

I pulled the door closed again, not sure why it had been so easy to imagine Chris with my mother, to hear the sound of his voice in my mother's bedroom, his laughter. I'd felt betrayed not because I loved him, but because I thought I'd lost him. It would be years before I could see it clearly: I was a thirteen-year-old girl. Chris was twenty-one. A man. Maybe I thought of him the same way Mami thought of Benny. I was, after all, my mother's daughter. My mother, who was thirty at the time, who'd had me when she was just seventeen. Maybe, back then, she'd been exactly like me. An ordinary girl.

It was a morning like any other when I got the news. I'd missed school the day before, and I hadn't been expecting it. It was Chanty who told me. She was waiting for me in front of my homeroom when I got to school, five minutes before the first bell.

"Nena, have you seen it?" she said as soon as she saw me. She looked skinnier than the last time I'd seen her, small and pale, her hair in that sad ponytail that had become her go-to style. She grabbed my arm, pulling me along the hallway toward the front office.

"Seen what?" I asked.

She started laughing, hopping around on the balls of her feet. It had been so long since we'd had a real conversation, and I hadn't realized how much I'd missed her until this moment, how much she'd changed. When had she lost so much weight? When did she start wearing her boyfriend's ratty T-shirts, three sizes too big? Was this the same girl I'd sat next to during all of fourth grade? The same girl who ran around Flamingo Park with me all summer? I realized I didn't even know what to say to her, or how to say it. We stopped right in front of the office, and she pointed to the bulletin board where they posted announcements and photographs. Canned food drives, awards ceremonies, jazz band recitals, intramural sports teams . . .

"You weren't here yesterday when they made the announcement," she said. "You were skipping, you fucking nerd!"

I hadn't been expecting this. I'd just turned in my homework and then forgot about it. But there it was, my essay, printed on a page of the *Miami Herald*, thumbtacked to the bulletin board, my words for all to see.

Chanty explained that Mr. Williamson submitted it to some writing contest for South Florida students, that the *Herald* was collecting stories about Hurricane Andrew, and mine was selected from all the students in Nautilus.

I almost cried right there in that hallway, almost cried as I took off, leaving Chanty standing there, as I sprinted to my class when the bell rang. And later, almost cried as we all sat in Mr. Williamson's classroom and he congratulated me, handed me a copy of the paper, and told the class all about it. China sitting next to me, smiling, Boogie in front of me, her body half turned to me as she joked, "Girl, I didn't even know you could read, let alone write!" and everybody laughed, including me. I pretended everybody else laughed because of the obvious—I was in an Honors Language Arts class, so of course I could read and write. But I knew the truth: nobody thought I belonged there.

Everybody was surprised, including me. I was not *that* girl. I was the girl who kept getting arrested, who missed school and got suspended, the girl Chanty's mother didn't want around her daughter.

I looked at the paper again, right there in my hands. It was proof of something, I didn't know what. That I would be a writer someday, that I would be *something*, somebody who mattered.

CHRIS WAS BACK a few days later, like I knew he would be, with a bag of Twizzlers and a two-liter Pepsi. I let him in because I was hungry and bored and alone. We hung out in my room for a while, listening to Power 96, whacking each other on the head with Twizzlers and sipping soda from a big plastic cup. Then, out of nowhere, he got all serious. He put the half-empty cup down on the carpet by the bed, took my hand. "You know I really care about you, right?"

"Sure."

"I mean like for real. I really care about you. I love you, and I want you to be my girl."

I took a deep breath. "Ok."

And that was that. He was my boyfriend. And less than an hour later we were undressing, the Twizzlers on the floor, the apartment empty except for the two of us. He pulled off my jeans and T-shirt and when my panties didn't slide down fast enough he ripped them off, tossed them aside.

"What the fuck!" I said.

He pulled his shirt up over his shoulders and tossed that aside, too, and for the first time I noticed the hair on his chest, a skull tattooed over his heart, a Puerto Rican flag that wrapped around his shoulder and upper arm. He was muscular and sweaty and smelled like cologne and cigarettes and I could not think of a single thing I actually liked about him. Not one.

Once he was naked, his dick hard and pressing against my thigh, I said, "Let's just get this done."

"Ok, mami, whatever you say."

I closed my eyes and thought about Boogie, the girl who sat next to me in homeroom, that first girl who kissed me, that beautiful boy, Devin, who went down on me but didn't fuck me. As Chris tried to push himself inside me, I kept thinking of Devin. Why couldn't this be *him*? And then I changed my mind.

"Wait," I said. "Stop."

Later, in my thirties, telling the story during a late-night drinking game with friends, I would leave out the parts about how I said no, how I pushed him, sliding sideways and backward trying to get him off me, how I banged my head against the top bunk as

I was trying to get away, his hand yanking my hair, and then, his lips against my ear, how he kept saying, *It only hurts for a second*, and then telling me to shut up shut up shut up. I would leave out all the blood, a large smear that covered almost half the bed. Or how a couple of years after that night, in high school, I ran into him while walking into Burdines on South Beach. How he smiled, like he knew something about me the rest of the world couldn't see, and that smile was so disarming it turned my stomach and I almost threw up right there by the women's shoes, and then when he said, *Damn, girl. You just gonna walk by your first love and not say hi?* how his voice took me right back to that night, the moonlight filtering in through the mini-blinds, the wooden beam of the top bunk almost splitting my head open, his breath sour against my face, how I kept thinking, It's almost over, almost over. How after he was gone, I ripped the bloody sheets and the mattress cover off the bed, rolled them up, tossed them into the dumpster out back. How Mami came home the next day, found me sleeping on the bare mattress, asked what was wrong, and when I said I felt sick, she brought me water, sat on the edge of the bed and watched me drink. How she put her hand to my forehead, brushed the hair from my face, and when she looked into my eyes, I could tell she was looking for something. But whatever that something had been, I knew, it was already gone.

MONTHS AFTER THAT night with Chris, after I'd left my mother's house, on my way home from Paula's office, I would take the Metrorail, sit by the window, check out the commuters during rush hour. Doctors and nurses leaving the university hospital buildings, the courthouse staff headed to their cars, the Miami-Dade County

corrections officers in their uniforms, all of them crowding the
parking lots and Metrorail platforms. When most of the passengers had gotten off, I'd lean all the way back, put my feet up on
the rear-facing seat in front of me. I'd get off at the Government
Center stop, transfer to the bus headed to Miami Beach, to Papi's
house. Downtown Miami would be jam-packed with people, like
it always was in the afternoons, with all the tourists shopping in
the boutiques or headed toward Bayside Marketplace, the Miami
Dade Community College students headed to their jobs. After
dark, Downtown Miami would be dead, except for the packs of
squatters, the homeless lining up for beds in front of Camillus
House, scutterheads and tweakers panhandling under the bridges.
And then, somewhere in all that darkness, my mother. She would
be there, night after night, her whole life spilling out of a single
backpack, her glass pipe tucked in the outer pocket.

At sixteen, after the depression got to be too much, after dropping out of school and getting my GED, after I stopped talking to
Chanty for good, after I stopped taking music lessons, stopped
playing the piano and the bass, after I forgot what J.R. and Benny
and Paula looked like, I would try to forget the sound of Chris's
voice when he sang New Edition. *Candy girl, you are my world.*
And after I turned eighteen, after the playground equipment in
Normandy Park was replaced, the blacktop resurfaced, after all
the people who'd lived in the neighborhood ten, twenty years were
gone, I would leave Normandy Isle for the last time. Alaina would
be in high school, and Anthony would be a bartender at a nightclub
on South Beach, and I would work nights as a pharmacy technician at a drug store and come home to an empty studio apartment
and I would think of my mother, adrift in that city, alone. How she

descended into madness, sometimes sleeping on the steps of the Miami Beach Post Office, sometimes in the hallway of a friend's building. I would remember how she detached herself from me, piece by piece. How I lost her, slowly, until one day she just didn't come home.

Ordinary Girls

We started talking about dying long before the first woman jumped. What our parents would do once we were gone. What Mr. Nuñez, the assistant principal at Nautilus Middle School, would say about us on the morning announcements. How many of our friends would cry right there on the spot. The songs they would dedicate to us on Power 96, so that all of Miami Beach could mourn us—Boyz II Men's "It's So Hard to Say Goodbye to Yesterday," DRS's "Gangsta Lean." Who would go to our funerals—boys who'd broken our hearts, boys whose hearts we'd broken.

She was a French woman, the first jumper, that's what people said. She didn't live in Southgate Towers—Papi's high-rise apartment complex, where he also worked as a security guard—but her boyfriend did. According to the boyfriend's neighbors, they'd been having problems—she drank a lot, he drank a lot, they fought. That night, the neighbors told Papi, she'd been banging on the door for a while, calling the boyfriend's name when he wouldn't open it. My father was in the security booth outside the lobby when he started getting calls from some of the Southgate residents. They thought they'd heard a crash, something falling from the sky, the air conditioning unit on the roof maybe. Or maybe someone had flung something heavy off their balcony. Nobody had expected it to be a person, least of all my father.

OUR PLANNING STARTED way before the French woman jumped, during a four-month stint living with my mother in Normandy Isle. For a few weeks, Alaina spent the weekends with Papi and Abuela, or next door at Titi Xiomara's, while Anthony was living lovely with Abuela cooking for him, cleaning up after him, and doing his laundry.

One day after school, Boogie and I were on the swings, rocking back and forth, digging our sneakers into the dirt and kicking off. We talked about how we'd do it, imagined we could make it look like a tragic accident. We'd get hit by a Metrobus while crossing the street, which would be easy since nobody expected a girl to just step in front of a bus in the middle of the afternoon. The park would be alive with people—ballers on the courts, kids on the merry-go-round, boys riding their bikes on the sidewalk, hood rats on the corner waiting for who knows what. We'd smoke one last stolen cigarette, flick the butt before we jumped the fence out of the park. Then we'd take care of it, the business of dying.

Some girls took sleeping pills and then called 911, or slit their wrists the wrong way and waited to be found in the bathtub. But we didn't want to be like those ordinary girls. We wanted to be throttled, mangled, thrown. We wanted the violence. We wanted something we could never come back from.

Ordinary girls didn't drive their parents' cars off the Fifth Street Bridge into Biscayne Bay, or jump off the back of a pickup in the middle of I-95, or set themselves on fire. Ordinary girls didn't fall from the sky.

We spent most afternoons that way, in the park, smoking my mother's cigarettes, drinking her beer. Sometimes we paid the neighborhood tecatos to get us bottles of Cisco or Mad Dog 20/20 or St. Ides Special Brew. Occasionally Kilo, my boyfriend, and his cousin Papo, would show up with a bag of Krypto and smoke us out. We'd lie on the bunk beds, listen to DJ Laz's power mix, and laugh our asses off. Until the effect wore off and we were ourselves again—reckless, and unafraid, and pissed off at our parents for not caring that we spent most of our time on the streets or drunk or high, for being deadbeats and scutterheads. But it wasn't just our parents. We were pissed off at the whole fucking world. Our teachers, the principal, the school security, the D.A.R.E. cop. All those people, they just didn't get that there was no way in hell we could care about homework, or getting to school on time—or at all— when our parents were on drugs or getting stabbed, and we were getting arrested or jumped or worse. Only three months before, Mikey, Kilo's best friend, had been killed in a drive-by shooting.

ONE SATURDAY MORNING, after a long night of drinking and smoking out on the beach, the four of us walked back to Normandy Isle in a haze. It was so early the sky was still gray and the Metrobuses had just started running. The sidewalk along Normandy Drive was secluded except for the four of us. For a while we just walked, sand in our sneakers, our mouths dry, my hair frizzy from the beach air, Kilo holding my hand, Papo and Boogie holding hands in front of us, the four of us marching down Normandy Drive, laughing and fucking up all the lyrics to

Slick Rick and Doug E. Fresh's "La Di Da Di." It was our thing—
pretending we were beach bums, that nothing could touch us, that
life would always be like this. Carefree and limitless and full of
music. We still didn't know that Miami Beach wouldn't always
be ours. Or that even in a few years when we were all gone, we
would still lay claim to it always, that we would never truly belong
anywhere else.

We had just gotten to Normandy Park when we spotted this
kid riding his bike across the street. He was dark-skinned, with
hair shaved close to the scalp, wearing a wife beater and baggy
jean shorts. I knew him from the neighborhood. Everybody called
him Bambi. He was older than us, out of high school already, but
he looked young.

Papo had put his arm around Boogie, pulled her close, and I
hated him then, even though we were friends. She smiled, brushing her overgrown bangs out of her face, and kept singing. She
had just dyed her long, straight hair auburn, and had a slight tan
from our days on the beach. Papo had beady little eyes and an
overgrown bush of messy, shapeless curls, and I couldn't see why
she was attracted to him and not me. I was only thirteen, but I was
already wearing a C-cup, and I masturbated so much I was sure I
could bring another girl to orgasm, no problem.

When I glanced at Kilo, he had grown quiet, and his face had
changed, turned the color of paper. His lips were pressed together,
and I could see the vein in his temple throbbing like it did when he
was fighting with his mom, or when he was about to throw down.
We all stopped in the middle of the sidewalk, and Kilo let go of my
hand, pulled out his pack of Newports and lit one. He took a long
drag, then rubbed at his eye with the back of his hand.

"Y'all know that guy?" Kilo asked.

"That's Bambi," I said.

"Doesn't he look just like Mikey?" Kilo asked, but nobody said a word.

Back in my room, the four of us piled up on the bunk beds. Kilo and I sat side by side on the bottom bunk, our backs against the wall, and Boogie and Papo fell asleep on the top. She breathed softly, Papo snoring.

Kilo leaned over and lay his head on my lap, the vein in his temple still throbbing. I put my hand on his head, listened to him breathing, and after a while I noticed he had tears in his eyes. I wiped them away with my thumb, but they kept coming. He wrapped his arms around my waist awkwardly, like he needed to hold on to something but didn't know how. This was not the Kilo I knew.

The Kilo I knew threw up gang signs and wore baggy jeans and wife beaters and high-top Air Jordans. He was tattooed and foulmouthed and crazy. He looked at people hard, laughed loudly, talked back to everybody, played street ball and dunked on half the guys in Normandy Park. The Kilo I knew smoked blunts, drank Olde English 800 by the quart, talked dirty, cracked his knuckles, sucker punched a guy twice his size for calling me a bitch, tagged all over the back of the Metrobus, got kicked out of school.

We were like that for a long time, Kilo crying into my lap, holding me, and me, not able to say a single word. While I hated seeing him that way, the truth is it also made dying seem like more of an option. And I realized that that was exactly what I wanted—a love like that. I wanted somebody who loved me so much my death would break her.

THE FIRST TIME I was eleven.

I was living with Mami in South Beach. She'd been diagnosed with paranoid schizophrenia three years before, and was on a cocktail of antipsychotics and anxiety medications. She was also using cocaine. Our nights together were unpredictable. Sometimes my mother slept for sixteen hours straight. Sometimes she paced around the apartment talking to herself, laughing, screaming at me for doing God-knows-what. Sometimes she threw plates across the room, or threatened to burn me with a hot iron, or gave me a full-blown ass-whooping. I was five-foot-six by the time I was eleven, four inches taller than my mother, something she loved to remind me of as she was kicking my ass—the bigger I got, the bigger my beat-down had to be. Eventually I started hitting her back. We came to blows regularly.

That weekend I was alone with my mother. She was manic, talking to herself, screaming at me, insisting that I'd stolen a pair of her heels. She searched the entire apartment, turning over cushions, upending tables, emptying all the drawers onto the floor, pulling hangers out of the closets. When she didn't find her shoes, she made me search, standing behind me as I opened and closed and opened and closed drawers, as I turned over mattresses and emptied out the bathroom cabinets. I did this over and over, and every time I didn't find the pair of heels, she'd slap the back of my head, harder each time. Until I refused to search anymore.

I knew what it would mean, to defy my mother, but I did it anyway. I turned to her, balled my hands into fists, took a step back, and said, "I didn't take your God. Damned. Shoes." I turned to leave, and that's when I felt the whack on the back of my head— hard, much harder than before—and then a shower of blows.

She beat me until I fell, and after I fell, and stopped only when she was good and ready.

Afterward she put on multiple layers of makeup, slipped into a slinky silver dress, found a substitute pair of heels, and announced that she was going dancing.

I was still on the floor when she walked out the door, couldn't have gotten up even if I'd wanted to.

I got up a few hours later and took my mother's pills, all of them—antipsychotics, sleeping pills, anxiety pills. I washed them down with half a bottle of Dawn dishwashing liquid. I'd heard the stories about toddlers who'd gotten poisoned with Drano, or detergent, or bleach, but all we had was Dawn. If we'd had any Drano or bleach, I would've downed that, too. I was determined to die.

I sat in the living room, waited for my mother to come home.

WHEN SHE FOUND me, I was on my knees on the kitchen floor, throwing up blue.

I don't remember falling asleep, or making my way from the living room to the kitchen, or being on my knees.

There is the faint memory of riding in the ambulance, sitting up on the stretcher, someone's hand pressing hard against my chest, shaking me, bringing me back from wherever I was.

There is a woman's voice: *What is your name? Open your eyes. What did you take? Don't fall asleep.*

There I am sinking, sinking. Then I'm gagging, a tube up my nostril, down my throat. *Don't fight it. Don't cough. Swallow.*

There is chaos, the shuffle of people all around me, moving me, prodding me, holding me up until I'm throwing up charcoal into a plastic container.

There I am: stomach thrusting against the back of my throat until my eyeballs are almost bursting, until there's charcoal vomit splattered down the front of my T-shirt, until there's nothing left inside me and I realize I'm in a hospital and I'm in a hospital bed and there is my mother and there is my father and there I am: I am eleven and I am alive.

I USED TO imagine that the French woman knew something about pain, about planning. That she had tried before, as a child, as a teenager. That she sat in her bedroom and listened to whatever was on the radio, wrote poems about darkness, dreamed of jumping off bridges and arsenic cocktails and death by electrocution. Because she was no ordinary girl.

I'd like to think that someone loved her—before she jumped, and after—even if she didn't know it.

Or maybe she did.

ON HALLOWEEN, WE decided to throw a party. We'd spent the night at Kilo's house, slept on his two twin beds and woke up around 2:00 p.m., crusty-eyed and cotton-mouthed and ready for trouble. I called up Tanisha, who lived a short walk from Kilo's neighborhood—and smoked weed all day every day—and told her we needed a place for a party. An hour later we were at her apartment on Harding Avenue, smoking her Krypto and listening to her '80s freestyle. We called everybody we knew with the details. Bring your own weed, we told them, and wear a costume.

Whenever somebody's mom would ask about a chaperone, we put Tanisha on the phone. She gave them her address and phone number, said *please* and *thank you*, laughed easily. She was every teenage hoodlum's dream, my aunt. Like an older best friend who would cover for you, go to court with you when you didn't want your parents to find out you got caught stealing at Woolworth's or the bodega around the corner, who acted like a kid even though she was older. She partied with us, smoked us out, then took us to the movies or skinny dipping on South Beach. She taught us not just how to fight, but how to fight *dirty*, to use anything as a weapon.

That night, China couldn't make it because she had to take her brothers and sister trick-or-treating, and Chanty never showed up. But Boogie and I dressed up as toddlers, parting our hair into pig-tails, dotting our faces with eyeliner freckles, baby blue pacifiers hanging from the gold chains around our necks. We wore Mickey Mouse and Pooh Bear pajamas, sucked on Charms Blow Pops, drank malt liquor out of baby bottles. The apartment filled up with our friends from Nautilus, Kilo's friends from the barrio, Tanisha's weedhead friends. We sat in a circle on the living room floor and passed around a Dutch, blasting House of Pain on Tanisha's stereo, until Kilo and I got bored of watching everybody jump around, and stole a dozen eggs from her kitchen.

Outside, we climbed onto the hood of somebody's old Chevy Caprice and flung eggs at trick-or-treaters, some old scutter-head stumbling down the street, a guy in a pickup. Afterward, when all the eggs were splattered down Seventy-Seventh and Harding, we jumped off the car, Kilo all sweaty, the malt liquor in my baby bottle already warm. Kilo lit two cigarettes, handed me one. I slurred a faded version of Lil Suzy's "Take Me in Your Arms," and we started slow dancing right there on the sidewalk, Kilo breathing smoke into my neck. Danced in the yard next to

Tanisha's apartment building, and collapsed onto the grass. Then we lay there, side by side, laughing and laughing at nothing, at everything.

Everybody else seemed so far away, even though we lay there listening to them coming and going, the building's front door opening, closing, footsteps scurrying across the lawn, our friends coming over to say, "You got grass all up in your pigtails," and "I think they passed out," and "The hell you doing down there?"

When Boogie and Papo came over, one of them kicked my sneaker. Then Papo said, "Think they'll notice if I piss in their mouths?"

"I'll fuck you up," Kilo said.

"You dead?" Boogie asked, giggling.

"My eyes are open," I said.

"Don't mean you can't be dead," Boogie said.

I didn't look over at Kilo, but I could hear him breathing beside me. He wasn't laughing like the rest of us. I wouldn't realize it until much later, after the Krypto and the Olde English had worn off, after that miserable fall with my mother, after going back to my father's house, after Kilo had cheated with a girl from the barrio and gotten her pregnant and named the baby Mikey, like he hoped this Mikey would be the one to save him. After hating her for stealing him from me, after stealing him back years later, even if only for a little while, after the two of us, trying to be those same two kids we'd been, got drunk on the beach on a Saturday night, snorted an eight ball in just a couple hours, after he watched me take one bump of scutter after another and told me to *Slow down, ma*, and *Watch out, baby girl, go easy, that's how motherfuckers OD*, and I told him that that was exactly how I wanted to go and that it would be the best way to die and that nobody would miss me anyway, after he snatched the baggie from me, took my face in his hands, his breath rank like stale cigarettes and Hennessy, and said *Don't ever let me hear you say that shit again* and *I don't wanna lose you* and after I let him hug me and thought about the two of us lying in the grass that Halloween when we were only thirteen and fourteen, how we were just kids but seemed so much older, already so tired, so damn tired it was like we'd been fighting a war. That's when it would hit me, that maybe Kilo wasn't that different from me, that maybe back then he'd also been dreaming about dying. Maybe it was seeing his homeboy shot down right in front of him, and having to look in the mirror every day, accept that he was still here, still alive, Mikey's memory like a ghost that was always calling.

But that Halloween, the two of us on the grass, all I knew was that I felt nothing and everything all at once. Boogie and Papo lingered for a while, joking, smoking, laughing, and I didn't even notice when they snuck back to the party. I couldn't tell how long we lay there—could've been minutes, could've been hours—but I sat up when we almost got trampled by a pack of kids running wild though the yard toward Tanisha's building. There were like six or seven of them, boys and girls we went to school with, sprinting, pushing each other out of the way, calling out, "Move!" and "Run!" and "Go-go-go-go-go!"

Later, in the middle of Tanisha's living room, with the music turned down and their eyes wide, everybody listening and holding their breaths, they would tell a story about how they'd been hanging on the corner of Seventy-Seventh and Harding. How a couple of them had been sitting on the hood of a car, while Kilo and I were passed out in the yard or pretending to be dead or whatever it was we were doing. How some guys in a pickup had pulled up right next to them, how the passenger had rolled down the window, pulled out a gun, and asked which one of them had thrown the eggs. And while I stood there, the spinning in my head already fading, the dancing and the laughing and Kilo's face against my neck already like a dream I was sure to forget, I wouldn't feel guilty for egging those guys, and I wouldn't feel bad that my friends almost got shot because of us. I would resent them for being that close to death. I would imagine, like something out of a movie, the truck pulling up, the slow opening of the tinted window, the moonlight reflecting on the glass, then the barrel of the gun, like a promise.

I WALKED INTO the school counselor's office one afternoon, on a whim. It had been months since I'd been to see Paula, my court-appointed counselor, and it wasn't like I missed her or anything. I told myself it was because I had a math test during fifth period that I hadn't bothered to study for, that I didn't want to see Ms. Jones' face in front of the class as she handed out the test, how she'd be staring at me as I took one and passed it back. Truth was I couldn't care less. Every time Ms. Jones called me to her desk and asked, her voice almost a whisper, why I hadn't turned in any homework that week or the week before that, or why I never brought books to school, I just shrugged, rolled my eyes. The last three times, she'd threatened to send me to the principal's office if it happened again. Next day, same shit. I'd walk up to her desk, again, cross my arms, say, "My bad," and act like it was the first time in my life I'd ever heard of books or homework.

I didn't know what I'd say when I walked into Ms. Gold's office. That it was hard seeing Chanty sitting in the front of the classroom with all her new friends when we barely spoke anymore, thanks to her mom? That China was planning a huge birthday party for her quinces, with ball gowns and tuxedoes and a DJ, and that we were so poor there was no way I'd be able to come up with the money for the gown? That every time I went back home to Papi's, I'd end up fighting with Anthony, and he ended up pounding on me until he got tired, and that no matter what, Abuela always took his side?

Ms. Gold was known in most cliques as the counselor for the losers, druggies, troublemakers, kids who got suspended, kids who fought or brought knives to school, kids who flunked so much they were already too old for Nautilus, kids whose parents were drunks or junkies, or whose parents beat them, homeless kids, bullied kids, kids with eating disorders, or brain disorders, or anger problems. So naturally, when I showed up at her door, she knew *exactly* who I was.

"Come on in, Jaqui," she said, her voice hoarse, like she smoked a few packs a day. "Have a seat." She ran her hand through her long mane of orange hair, and I noticed her fingernails were long as hell and painted gold. She dressed like she was a young woman—ivory pencil skirt, short sleeved blouse, black high heels—and smelled like floral perfume. She was an attractive woman, and wore lots of makeup, but up close, you could tell how old she really was. Older than my mother. Probably a grandmother. This made me like her right away.

I stepped inside the small office and sat in the nearest seat. It was bigger than I'd imagined, with a few chairs set up in a circle.

I wondered how she knew my name, and if there would be other people coming.

"I've been wondering when you'd show up," she said, sitting at her desk chair. She leaned over and opened a drawer, rummaged through some files, then pulled one out. "I was going to get you out of class if you didn't make it over to me soon."

I tried not to look surprised. "For real?"

She smiled at me a long time, looking me over, studying me. Then, finally, she said, "I know all about you."

I doubted that she knew *all* about me, but at the same time, I was afraid of what she did know, and how. "Like what?"

She opened the file and put on her reading glasses, flipped through the pages quickly. "Well," she said, "I know you've been suspended quite a few times." She observed me from behind her reading glasses.

"Okay," I said, not surprised to find that everything she thought she knew she'd read from my school records.

She kept going, not taking her eyes off me. "I know you've been in a number of fights, in and out of school, that you ran away from home a year ago and the police picked you up two weeks later, that you were arrested last month for aggravated battery, and you have a hearing coming up." She took her glasses off and waited.

I took a deep breath but said nothing.

"I know you're *angry*," she said, really emphasizing the word *angry*, "but what I don't know is why."

I shrugged and looked down at my sneakers, suddenly feeling like I'd made a mistake, like I'd rather be faking my way through Ms. Jones' math test than sitting there being questioned.

"So why don't you tell me," she said, closing the file without even looking at it.

"I don't know," I said.

She nodded. "Why don't you tell me about your situation at home?"

I had no idea what she meant by "situation," but I just shrugged again, rolled my eyes like I'd done so many times with Ms. Jones. "What do you wanna know?"

"Let's start with what brought you here."

I considered telling her that I'd just wanted to get out of class, but somehow I didn't think she'd like that. I crossed my legs, uncrossed them. "Sometimes I live with my father," I said, "and sometimes I live with my mother."

"So they share custody."

I shook my head no. "I just go whenever I want."

"Where are you living now?"

"Mostly with my mother. But sometimes I don't sleep there."

"So where do you sleep?"

"Friends' houses, boyfriend's house, the beach."

"The beach?!" she said, raising her eyebrows.

It could've been her expression, the way her face contorted into something I read as disbelief, then anger, then pity, even though she was supposed to be the counselor for all the school's fuckups, so she was supposed to be the woman who'd heard it all seen it all. Or it could've been something else—that I'd admitted this for the first time, confessed it to someone other than my delinquent friends, even though it wasn't really anything, nothing compared to what still needed confessing. That once, last year, I stood in front of the mirror in my father's bathroom with a box cutter, determined to slit my wrists, but then couldn't do it, and instead I carved up my upper arm so deep it left a scar. That sometimes I saw myself climbing up on the concrete balcony in my father's high rise building, saw myself sitting on the edge, leaning forward, letting the pull of gravity take me. That even though I didn't like to think about it, I found myself catching feelings for girls, that sometimes when I was around Boogie the swelling in my chest and throat was like a bomb that was ready to explode.

But I couldn't say any of this. I didn't know why. And right then, sitting in Ms. Gold's office, the last place I'd expected to be even an hour before, I started to cry.

THE SECOND TIME was that winter. Holiday break. My mother was off her meds, and we'd been fighting for three days straight. We screamed at each other because there was no food in the house. Because my music was too loud. Because, my mother claimed, there had been a woman in the apartment going through her things and I'd been the one to let her in. Mami always had these stories—a woman who came into our living room and moved all the furniture while we slept, a man who kept looking in our windows at 2 a.m., people sending her messages through the television or the radio, a guy who came in and ate all our food while my mother stood in the kitchen, paralyzed with fear.

That morning my mother woke me before sunrise as she paced around the apartment talking to herself, refusing to take her pills or let me sleep. I covered my head with my pillow, and she pulled it off, started shaking me. I needed to get up, she said, help her check all the windows so nobody could get in the house. I turned over, my back to her.

She shook me again, yelled, "I said get up!"

"Fine!" I said. "I'm up." I'd already learned that when my mother was like this, I had no choice but to do what she ordered. So I ran around the apartment checking all the windows—the living room, her bedroom, my bedroom. I made sure the deadbolt on the front door was locked, then got back in bed.

Ten minutes later, my mother burst in, again, insisting that I'd left the windows open, again. But this time I didn't get up. I was awake, but refused. She yelled. I yelled back. She threatened. I threatened back. Then she left.

She came back with a steak knife, pointed it at me like a sword. "Who are you?" she asked.

I jerked up and hit my head on the wooden beam of the top bunk. "What the fuck are you doing?" I jumped out of bed, grabbed my pillow, the closest thing I could use as a shield.

"Tell me who you are," she said, "because you are not my daughter."

I should've cried, begged her to stop, put the knife down. I should've apologized and told her I loved her. But instead, before I could stop myself, I started screaming. "Are you serious?! I never wanted to be your daughter! You're not my mother! You're a crazy fucking crackhead!"

She stood there for a while without saying a word.

I kept my eye on the knife, gripping the pillow with both hands.

"You are small," she said finally, "like a fly. You are so small I could squash you. You are nobody. You are nothing."

I didn't believe what my mother said—not at first. I took it the same way I always took her rambling—everything she said was nonsense. But after she turned back for her room, left me standing there with the pillow in my hands, everything quiet except for the sound of my own breathing, something changed. It was like a switch that got flipped, and everything that happened after was mechanical.

Dropping the pillow on the bed, the beeline for the kitchen for a glass of water from the tap, a car horn blaring across the street somewhere.

My mother rushing to the living room window, peeking through the blinds.

The bottles of my mother's prescriptions on the counter, untouched for weeks.

My mother running back into her bedroom, slamming the door shut.

The first pill, a drink of water. The second pill, another drink. The third, fourth, fifth, another drink.

My mother coming back out of her bedroom, pacing back and forth. Bedroom, living room, bedroom.

Another pill, another drink. Bedroom, living room. Another pill and another and another.

The car horn again.

The way my mother walked past me so many times but never once turned to look at me, to see me killing myself again and again.

The wanting, more than anything else, to sleep.

My mother saying, "You are small."

My mother saying, "You are nobody."

My mother saying, "You are nothing."

THE FRENCH WOMAN. She was there before I swallowed the first pill. And she would be there always. But all I really knew about her was that she jumped.

Later, it would hit me: I'd been thinking of her as a myth, a legend, a story. But she was not any of those things.

THE SECOND TIME, I swallowed all my mother's pills, locked myself in my room, didn't sit to wait until she found me. The second time, I slid a dresser in front of the bedroom door to keep my mother out. The second time, I woke sick to my stomach, stumbled out of bed, but couldn't get the dresser out of the way in time to make it to the bathroom, so I threw up all over the carpet in my bedroom. The second time, I woke to find that, again, I had not died.

In my bedroom, spewing a foul white foam which I assumed was my mother's pills, and then the Kentucky Fried Chicken that Kilo had brought over late last night, blowing chunks of chicken and mashed potatoes and macaroni and cheese, I was sure that if I didn't die of a prescription drug overdose, then the retching would kill me. Bent over the mess on the carpet, the vomiting turned to dry heaving. It took me a few minutes to straighten up, to push the dresser out of the way, to wash my face and brush my teeth, to get my sneakers on and my hair in a ponytail, to stuff some of my things in my backpack and go.

I walked past Normandy Park, feeling jittery and weak, headed toward the Circle K, where I bought a small bottle of Gatorade and got some change for the payphone. Outside, I sipped some of the Gatorade, then picked up the phone, my hands shaking. And then I threw up again, just liquid this time, left the receiver dangling and bent over right there on the spot.

Again, it took me a minute to get myself together. Then I finally made the call. I put two quarters in the phone and dialed my father. The line rang four or five times before Papi picked up.

"Hello," he said, but not like a question, more like he was annoyed at whoever was calling. I was surprised by the sound of his voice, which I hadn't heard in months—not since I ran away to my mother's house. His voice stirred something inside me, and I couldn't believe how much I missed him, how much I *needed* him. I wanted to ask him for help. I wanted to tell him everything that happened since I left, ask him to come and get me, take me home. But he'd let me down so many times, and I'd let *him* down so many times, I was sure it was the only thing we would ever do—let each other down.

"Hello?" he said again.

But I couldn't do it. So I hung up.

I stood there for a long time, feeling tired and weak and so sick. I considered just going back to my mother's, getting back in bed, letting myself drift off. But I wasn't sure if the pills could still work, if my body had absorbed some of them before I threw up, if there was still a chance I could die.

I picked up the receiver again, but this time I called Kilo.

TWENTY MINUTES LATER, Kilo's dad picked me up in front of my mom's building. He was driving his station wagon, Papo riding shotgun, and Kilo in the back. I got in, dropped my backpack on the floor, and thanked them for picking me up.

"Where to?" Kilo's dad asked.

I gave him my father's address in South Beach, and he made a right out of my mom's complex.

In the backseat, Kilo held my hand. I hadn't told him that my mother had pulled a knife on me, or that just hours before, I'd swallowed her pills and went to bed, that I woke up vomiting, surprised to still be alive. All I'd said on the phone was that I was sick and needed a ride to my father's.

I leaned my head on his shoulder, and he put his arm around me. In the front, Papo and Kilo's dad were talking about the Miami Dolphins, Joe Robbie Stadium, what they planned to do this winter. When I called Kilo for a ride, I knew that I'd be leaving Normandy Isle for good, that there was no way in hell I'd ever go back with my mother, not if I could help it. I knew that my leaving would mean I wouldn't see Kilo, Boogie, and Papo every day, and maybe I wouldn't be able to stay out all night or hang in the streets whenever I wanted, that we could easily drift apart. But I was so tired.

Kilo leaned over, kissed me on the cheek, then whispered something in my ear that I couldn't make out. I told myself that he said, "I love you," even though I knew it wasn't true, but at that moment I needed it to be.

I spent most of the ride to South Beach thinking of our time as if it were already in the past. How Kilo and I had danced at the Nautilus Middle School Halloween dance, all sweaty and breathless and crazy. How once, Papo had introduced me to his neighbor as his sister-in-law, and afterward he always called me *sis*. How we had walked all over the place—the four of us shooting the shit from Seventy-First and Collins to Normandy Isle to Bay Harbor, even at three, four in the morning. How Boogie and I sat on a bench by the courts in Normandy Park, knocking back a quart, pretending we were grown, and watching the pickup game. How Kilo and Papo acted like they were super-fly street-ballers when really they were just okay. How in Kilo's room, the walls were all tagged up with spray paint and Sharpie, covered in bad graffiti, his homeboys' names, their neighborhoods, and on the bedroom door, the largest piece: *R.I.P. Mikey.* How once, I got so pissed that my name wasn't written anywhere, I took his Sharpie and wrote *Jaqui n Boogie* on the wall next to his bed, then drew a heart around it. How he came when I called. How maybe he saved my life and didn't even know it.

By January, we would barely see each other. By Valentine's Day, Kilo would already be with the girl who'd become the mother of his baby.

When I got out of the car in front of Southgate Towers, the air was too warm for winter. Even for December in Miami Beach. I strapped on my backpack, watched the station wagon as it drove off, headed north. They would drive past North Beach, past Seventy-First and Collins, then make a left toward Crespi Park. I would go into the lobby of the south tower, take the elevator up to my father's apartment on the eighth floor, where my abuela would greet me with a hot meal and café con leche, always ready to forgive me for stealing her cigarettes, for running away, for getting arrested so many times.

A few days after going back home, I would have a dream. I'd be on the roof of the north tower, standing close to the edge, my arms extended like wings. I would be looking down at Biscayne Bay, and across at the Venetian Islands, and then I would jump, and before I hit the ground, I would be flying, flying. The dream came back every couple of months, and, always, I would fly before hitting concrete.

A couple of years after the French woman jumped, another woman—Papi's friend—would fling herself off one of the balconies. The south tower this time. She would hit the side of the building, then the roof of the pool maintenance storage shed, then the ground. She would fall fifteen stories. And she would live.

Fourteen,
or How to Be a Juvenile Delinquent

You remember that first game of chess you played with your father: You, sitting across from him at the table, thinking, *Who does this old man think he's playing with?* He enjoys that stunned look on your face as he captures your last knight and lectures you on who knows what, trying to make life lessons out of stories.

You think you're playing. He thinks he's teaching.

You're determined to do the opposite of everything your father says. He's determined to stop you in your tracks. This is what passes for *I love you* these days.

You learn that day that you will always remember your one bad move, that moment when you could've made one choice but made another, and what follows is your whole game falling apart, piece by piece, check, cross-check, and suddenly, when you're fourteen, checkmate.

AT FOURTEEN, I walked into the Miami Dade County Children's Courthouse alone, not my first time in there by myself. Papi had stopped coming after my fourth or fifth time in front of the judge. Tanisha had given me a ride in her boyfriend's car, but dropped me off out front while she found a parking spot.

On the second floor, on the bulletin board where all the cases were listed, I found my name next to courtroom number 2-1. They always sent my cases to the same judge. At fourteen, I didn't think much about this, but looking back now, I'm sure that the prosecutor was sick of seeing my face, of reading my name and my multiple case numbers, all my charges, hoping the judge would finally come to his senses and lock me up for good.

As I approached the benches outside of 2-1, Tanisha walked up, found a spot and took a seat. Tanisha was eighteen, but looked around thirty-four. She'd gotten skinny and pale over the years, but her hair was the same, dark and thick, down to her waist. Looking older was a quality my mom and most of her sisters shared, but Tanisha was the most like my mother—smoking weed, mixing methamphetamines and prescription drugs, running over a boyfriend with another boyfriend's car, never backing down from a fight. Like my mother, Tanisha took no shit. When I turned eighteen—if I made it to eighteen— Tanisha was exactly who I wanted to be.

I didn't tell her why Papi didn't come to court with me, how when I'd tried to wake him up that morning, he opened his eyes, took one look at me, and went right back to sleep.

"But they'll lock me up if you're not there," I'd said, even though I was secretly hoping the judge would give me a few months. Every single time I'd been sentenced to house arrest or probation or some at-risk youth intervention program with court-mandated counseling, I'd been furious. I wanted to prove myself to all the other delinquents in my father's South Beach neighborhood, to be able to say I'd done some serious time and come out of juvie with stories. But most of all, I think I wanted my father to pay attention.

We would joke about this years later, when I was a senior in college and my father had remarried, when we'd both moved past the point when thinking about my teenage years brought tears to our eyes. Papi and I would play chess, sitting at the dining room table drinking Presidentes, me, taking way too long to make a move, and Papi waiting on me, like he'd been doing for years, sitting across the table telling stories. The time the school principal beat him with a yardstick so hard it broke, and he ran all the way home to tell Abuela. How in his early twenties, he'd had to take off one night, out of the blue, when one of the tiradores in El Caserío caught beef, how he fled Puerto Rico for New York and came back after a couple of years. How he enlisted in the army when I was a baby, but got a medical discharge after a few months. And how we were so much alike, me and my father: that time I jumped in Biscayne Bay after getting drunk and two men in a fishing boat had to pull me out. The day I got arrested for assaulting a police officer, knocking the glasses off his face. How I was *always* getting arrested, *always* running, and every time someone came knocking, every time the phone rang, he braced himself for bad news, Abuela always asking, "What did she do *now*?"

But that morning, before I was due in court, my father just said, "Good. Maybe *then* you'll learn." He was tired of having to lose sleep over me—he worked two jobs, seven days a week, and hadn't taken a vacation ever, since we moved to Miami from Puerto Rico.

That morning, Anthony had been running late for school, but he made sure to say goodbye to me before he walked out of our apartment.

"Hey, remember," he said, "if they lock you up, don't drop the soap!" He laughed his ass off as he strapped on his backpack and headed out the door.

As soon as he was gone, I went to the refrigerator for a plastic bottle of ketchup, and while Abuela did the dishes, I threw open the door to Anthony's closet, and squeezed a small pool of ketchup into the inside of his favorite sneakers. Left shoe, right shoe.

Across from 2-1, facing the courthouse's crowded entrance, I waited for the other girl. Every time a girl walked through the door or stopped to look up her name on the bulletin boards, Tanisha asked, "Is that her?"

One after another, teenagers and their parents filed into the room, took seats around us, waiting for their names to be called by the juvenile court bailiff. I didn't see her. Maybe she wouldn't even show.

Finally, one of the bailiffs came out of 2-1, called my name. He looked over the crowd, waiting for someone to respond.

I got up, looked around.

Another girl and her mother got up.

"Is that her?" Tanisha asked.

I wanted to say *yes*. But right then, I wasn't sure. It had been several weeks, and so much had happened since then, so many other fights, so much drinking, smoking. I didn't remember what she even looked like anymore. I would remember her face only from that day in the courthouse. Acne scars, wispy bangs. The way she rolled her eyes as she walked past me, the way she'd cuffed her T-shirt sleeves. I wouldn't remember hitting her weeks before, or how her face looked when I hit her, or if her eyes had been closed, or who else had been there, or if she'd hit me back, or if any of her friends had jumped in, or if she'd tangled her hands in my hair and pulled, or the dull ache in my scalp that would usually follow, or the rage, or the guilt I almost always felt after a fight. But I would stand before the judge, the prosecutor, the police officers, the girl, the girl's mother, and I would believe, without a doubt, that if they said I did it, then I did, and whatever sentence the judge handed down, I deserved.

GET YOURSELF A bunch of hoodlum friends. Start kickin' it with your local hood rats. And don't even flinch when one of the gang recruiters tells you that in order to prove that you have what it takes, you have to a) get jumped in, which means you get your ass kicked by five of their top enforcers, or b) let a mob of homeboys run a train on you.

Get used to shoplifting, vandalism, joyriding. Run away from home six, seven times. Drop out of school. Get arrested more times than you can count—spend more nights in juvie than you do at home. Do this just for the fuck of it. Enjoy this, because you're young, and invincible, and let's face it, you don't believe in consequences.

Spend your fourteenth birthday on the streets, smoking Newports and knocking back Cisco by the quart, not wanting much of anything. Don't think of your father. Or your abuela, who's been up all night wondering, again, where you are. If you're okay. If you're alive.

THAT WEEK, ME and Boogie took the bus to Hialeah to visit our boy Héctor, who'd been on house-arrest for three months. When we got there, he let us take his car, though neither of us had a license and barely knew how to drive. We went to la bodega de la esquina for some Newports and Philly blunts.

The dude who always worked the register was a friendly old guy everybody called Papi. *Hey, Papi*, we'd call out as we walked in, making a beeline for the coolers. *How you doing, Papi?* as we set Doritos and Pepsis on the counter.

Boogie made her way to the coolers. I asked for my cigarettes and five Phillies, and he set them down on the counter.

"You better bring ID next time," he said.

"They're not for me, Papi," I said, laughing. "They're for my mom."

He smiled. "Yeah, yeah."

Once we were out the door, Boogie pulled a small bottle of Cisco from each pocket of her baggy-ass jeans.

"Hang on to these," she said, handing them to me, and got in the driver's seat.

"Keep drinking that bum juice. You'll get a fucking hole in your stomach."

FOURTEEN, YOUR FRIENDS will say. They'll roll you a blunt, lace it with scutter, and tell you stories of all the shit they'd already done by the time they were fourteen.

Decide this is who you want to be. Decide that you can do anything, drink anything, smoke anything, and by your next birthday, you are addicted to the chaos, the violence, the excess. But mostly, you are just addicted.

AT HÉCTOR'S, AFTER a couple hours of drinking and smoking, Boogie and I decided to get tattoos.

"Put it on my ankle," I told Héctor.

And he did, his homemade tattoo machine buzzing. It was an odd thing, with a motor and two pencils duct-taped on either side of the makeshift needle tube, and I could swear it intensified the pain, because Héctor made it, and Héctor liked to see you squirm. Boogie knocked out on the couch, her hair tied in a moño, secured with a scrunchie. I tried to keep my leg absolutely still, which was next to impossible considering all the weed we'd just burned.

"Roll another one," I said, "so we can take a break."

He stopped, laughing and shaking his head. "Bendito nena, I thought you were all tough. It don't hurt *that* much." He handed me the quart of Olde E he'd been sipping from, and I chugged some, passed it back.

"Stay still," he said, grabbing my foot again, putting pressure on the skin just below my ankle. I braced myself. As the needles punctured my skin, I looked from Boogie, who had tattoos on both ankles, to Héctor, who was covered in them and shaved his head to show off the dragon on his skull. I could be stronger, I told myself. I sat still, just breathing. I checked out the pictures on the walls, on the coffee table, traced the patterns on the popcorn ceiling, closed my eyes. Anything to get my mind off the pain.

"How old were you when you got your first one?" I asked Héctor. He didn't say anything for a while, and I wondered if he was getting annoyed at me. Although Héctor acted like a teenager, he was well into his thirties. He was one of *those* guys—every barrio has one. That guy who gives all the local juvenile delinquents a place to burn their stash, an endless supply of Olde E and Newports and the occasional roll or bump of scutter.

Among the chaos of the mismatched furniture and plain old broken shit, every picture in Héctor's apartment was of his daughter, Vanessa. She'd died of meningitis when she was two, he'd told me one day. Never even got to see her. He'd been doing time in Metrowest her entire life, since before she was born. And her mother? She didn't even talk to him no more. He was dead to her. Héctor had two tears tattooed just beneath his right eye, one for each year of her life that he'd missed, and over his heart, her name in Olde English letters. At fourteen, I didn't know anything about losing a child, but I did know something about love. His story made me think of Alaina, my little sister, who was living with Mami while I was out on the street or on the beach, drinking and smoking without really giving a fuck about anything. Alaina, the one person I loved most in the world, who I only got to see sometimes, on the weekends, when she came to stay with us, who I'd left behind at Mami's after I couldn't stand to be there anymore. She had been there, always, and now she was having to deal with Mami all by herself. I had left her all alone.

Héctor stopped, took a deep breath. "Oh shit. How do you spell your name again?"

I must've flinched, must have made a face he found hysterical, because he laughed, put a hand to his forehead, laughed some more.

It looked like shit. And my ankle said *JACKI.*

LEARN TO FIGHT dirty, to bite the soft spots on the neck and inner thigh, to pull off earrings and hair weaves. Slather your face with Vaseline before a fight, so you don't get scratched, so the blows slide right off without leaving a mark. Keep five or six razorblades tucked in a loose bun on top of your head—in a girl-fight, they will always pull your hair. Learn that anything can be a weapon: pencils, bottles, rocks, belt buckles, a sock full of nickels, a Master combination lock. Eventually, you'll carry other weapons, brass knuckles and pocketknives, but never a gun, because what you really love is the fight. Besides, you're not crazy.

Learn to take a beat-down. On the streets, someone will always be bigger than you, stronger than you, badder than you. Someone will sucker punch you while you're sitting at the bus stop smoking and shooting the shit with your homegirls. Someone will crack a bottle of Olde English over your head while you're arguing with your man in front of Taco Bell. Walking home from a party, you'll get jumped by six girls who thought you looked at them wrong. And even though you did look at them wrong, and even though the night before you and your friends jumped some other girl at some other party, you'll still think they were dirty, and tomorrow you'll come back for them.

AFTER WE'D LEFT Héctor's, back at the Hialeah train station, Boogie and I smoked, shared the last bottle of Olde E, and talked about our next tattoos. A gold Monte Carlo pulled up in front of us, rolled down the driver's side rear window. I was already bracing myself—the car was packed full of people, and Hialeah girls always caught beef when we came around their neighborhood. They didn't say shit, just stared. But to me, and to loudmouth scuttered-up Boogie, it was clearly an invitation to fight.

I took one last drag, flicked my cigarette at the car, crossed my arms across my chest, and grilled them.

One of the girls stuck her head out the window. "Whatcha claim, girl?" she asked. She wanted to know where we were from before they jumped us.

I took off my hoops, slid them into my back pocket, and even though I knew what would happen, even though I'd been on the other end of a caserío beat-down enough times to know who walked away and who got carried away, I still said, "I claim these nuts, bitch."

I DON'T REMEMBER if I dropped my bottle of Olde E, if I put it down on the sidewalk, or when that same bottle came crashing down against my skull, glass blasting like buckshot. Or Boogie fighting girls off me when she realized I was down, taking a kick to the face from the driver, who she said looked like he was pumped full of fucking steroids. Don't remember when the Monte Carlo drove away, the driver yelling out the window that he was gonna bust a cap in both our asses, or when the ambulance arrived, and then the cops. But I do remember sitting on the curb, Boogie hollering in the background about glass in her eye, paramedics asking questions.

What's your name?

"What?" I said.

What's your name? He was holding my wrist, taking my pulse.

"Jaqui." I touched the back of my head, stared at my hand, my bloody fingers. Someone put pressure on the back of my head, said, *Stay still.*

Then more questions: *How old are you?* and *Do you know your phone number?* and *Do you know your address? Your parents' work number?*

What happened? somebody kept asking.

Do you know her phone number?

I tried to touch my head again, but someone pulled my hand away.

"We got jumped," I heard Boogie say, clearly, like she was in my head.

Look at me, another uniform said, touching the fresh tattoo on my ankle. *Look at me. Are you in a gang?*

I flinched, my ankle sore, hands on my head, more pain.

Look at me. Is that a gang tattoo?

FOURTEEN. YOU'LL DRINK and fight, get high and fight. Fifteen. You'll spend days smoking haze with your homeboy, J., raiding his old girl's stash, until she comes home, finds you sitting side by side on her living room floor, passing the Dutch and watching the Lost Boyz rapping about ghetto love on BET, the two of you naked except for your matching Jordans.

J. will say, *You wanna try some scutter*? And although you always say you never fuck with that shit, you do it anyway, and then decide to walk home, paranoid as hell.

MY FATHER NEVER told the story of what happened when he got to the hospital that day.

How he was at work when he got the call, so he asked one of the off-duty cops to give him a ride.

How the cop, a friend of his, recommended that he give me up to the state.

"Think of your other kids," he said.

"It's the best thing for her," he said.

"She's going to *kill* you," he said.

And although I promised myself that I would change, promised my father and Abuela, a week later I was back on the streets.

When I turned eighteen, I would cover the tattoo with roses. Almost a decade later, a friend who'd spent five years in lockup would tell me that in prison, a rose tattoo meant you'd spent a birthday behind bars.

AFTER I CAME home from the hospital, I spent a few days on the couch, watching TV with Abuela while Anthony was in school and Papi slept after his graveyard shift as a security guard. Abuela made bacalao guisa'o with caramelized onions, served it over guineítos with a side of aguacate, and we sat together on the couch, eating and watching reruns of our favorite Mexican novela, *El extraño retorno de Diana Salazar.* We yelled at the screen when we found out that Irene del Conde was really Lucrecia Treviño, an evil seventeenth-century witch who conspired to have Lucía Méndez burned at the stake for witchcraft so she could steal her true love, Mario Villareal.

Abuela shook her fist at the TV every time she saw Irene del Conde. "Maldita! And poor Mario has no idea!"

We laughed and laughed, and for a while it seemed Abuela had forgotten that I was the disappointing granddaughter, the one who was always causing trouble.

As the day turned to night, after the evening news, we watched *Dos mujeres, un camino,* and wondered how Erik Estrada had an acting job when he was such a terrible actor. We laughed at the TV every time he spoke, and secretly, I hated him, because he cheated on both his wife and on Bibi Gaytán, who I was madly in love with.

For almost a whole week, I stayed home with Abuela, pretending my head still hurt so she'd sit with me, so she'd whip us up some pancakes with extra butter, or some tembleque with extra canela. Just me and Abuela, neither of us talking about what had happened at the train station.

And then, one day, as we balanced bowls of dulce de lechosa on our laps, while Diana Salazar was having a dream of her past life as Doña Leonor de Santiago, Abuela stopped avoiding it.

She turned down the volume on the TV. "What's wrong, Jaqui?" she asked me.

I turned to her. "What do you mean?"

"This is not the life I want for you," she said.

This is not the life I want for you. That was my father's line. He would say those words to me again and again. At fifteen, when I get picked up by the cops after a fight at an Eckerd Pharmacy parking lot. At sixteen, when I pack my bags, leave his house, and drop out of high school. When I'm sitting in a courtroom after stabbing Anthony, facing attempted murder charges, waiting to hear if I'll be tried as an adult. When he takes me to my first Narcotics Anonymous meeting after three agonizing, delirious nights in detox, holding my hand, the two of us sitting up front, the night's speaker telling his story about a father and son, never taking his eyes off of me, and all I can think about is how easy it will be to get more scutter, more meth, how easy it will be to die, and afterward, the speaker will find me hiding in the shadows and say, *I was just like you, once upon a time*, and talk about how living is a choice we make. *Choose life*, he will say, and my father, trying to make up for all those years of absence, trying to be a better man than he'd been his whole life, will shake his hand, will wrap his arms around me, will say, *This is not the life I want for you*, and how my whole body will shake when he holds me, and he won't know it yet, but

I will spend my whole adult life trying to make him proud of me, trying to be everything I think he wants a daughter to be, trying to be the daughter I think he deserves, and I won't know it yet, but he will break my heart again and again, and part of me will think there is justice in that. Some girls grow up to be the kind of women who fall for men like their fathers. Some girls grow up to be just like them.

"What are you talking about?" I said to Abuela. "You're overreacting."

She looked at me a long time, her gray hair wrapped in four perfect moñitos, her lips pursed, with a sadness in her eyes I would not understand until years later, when I am a woman and she is gone.

SIXTEEN. FIND A girl you think deserves it, an ordinary girl you were friends with just last month, a girl who spent hundreds of hours on the phone with you, confessing her fears, her dreams.

Look at her, see her clearly, see yourself in her eyes before you do it. Punch her in the face again and again, until you're out of breath. Push her back against a parked car. Kick her in the stomach. When she falls forward, kick her in the face and break her nose. She will cling to your leg, holding it, bleeding all over your jeans, all over your sneakers, not understanding how you could do this to her. You, who once held her hair back as she threw up behind the handball courts after the two of you got drunk on Southern Comfort. You, who wrote poems in the margins of her notebooks, left them there for her to find. She will ask, *Why why why*. She'll still be wearing her backpack.

You'll be in the Burger King parking lot, and at least twenty other kids will be there, cheering you on. She will try to get away from you, but you won't let her go. You are like a rabid animal, the crowd fueling your rage. You are Macho Camacho in the ring, dancing all over José Luis Ramírez. You are Joe fucking Frazier at Madison Square Garden, and this is the fight of the century.

Forget how the two of you, you and that ordinary girl, laced each other's roller skates on Friday nights. How you held each other up, arm in arm, how you went around and around the skating rink rhyming along to Wu-Tang Clan, *Can it be that it was all so simple then*? Forget how you passed notes to each other in class, or how when she undressed in front of you for the first time your entire body throbbed. How more than once you thought to say I love you, but never ever dared.

Consider this training for the real world.

You'll be arrested, sent to juvie again. In court, you'll see your father for the first time in weeks. There will be tears in his eyes, but it won't be the first time you see him cry, or the last. He will embrace you, and you'll want to be his little girl again, and the look on his face will tell you all you need to know, that he wishes you were more like your little sister, who doesn't ever skip school and gets straight A's and never causes trouble. A proper, respectable girl—the girl Abuela raised. You'll want to tell him that you're sorry, that you're going to change. But you won't, because you've already said it so many times, and you don't know what's worse, if he doesn't believe you anymore, or if he still does.

Girls, Monsters

When we were twelve, we taught ourselves to fly.
—JOHN MURILLO, from "Renegades of Funk"

All of us girls, now women.
—T KIRA MADDEN, from "The Feels of Love"

That winter, the year Boogie turned fourteen, we got it in our heads that we could run away, leave Miami Beach and never come back. For months, I'd spent every night lost in a book, read whatever the librarian put in my hands, which usually meant books written by white men, about white people, for white people. The librarians at the Miami Beach Public Library never, ever, recommended books about black and brown people, about queer girls from the projects, about people like me. I didn't even know those books existed. So I read *The Virgin Suicides* over one weekend. I finished *Dracula* during three days we were without power because somebody didn't pay the FPL bill, used a flashlight to light its pages under my covers. I read Stephen King's *It* over several weeks and then walked around the neighborhood looking for the opening to the sewers under Miami Beach. Didn't find it. And then I read *The Catcher in the Rye* and lost my shit for Holden

Caulfield. I decided to do exactly what Holden did. I'd run away from everything. Home, school, everyone. Except Boogie. I'd take her with me.

I'd told Boogie about my plans one night while we smoked my mother's cigarettes in the park, how I'd been thinking of getting the hell out. We were sitting on a park bench, Boogie watching the boys play basketball, her auburn hair falling down her back in layers, her winged eyeliner making her brown eyes pop.

"Let's do it," she said. She was down. She'd seen my life, had spent hours huddled with me in my bottom bunk when I still lived with my mother, had held me while Mami, in the middle of a psychotic episode, ran around talking to herself, opening closets and cupboards and bedroom doors looking for a man she said had followed her home and was hiding in our apartment. Boogie had sat with me on my bedroom floor, her arms around my neck, after my mother came after me with a knife, had helped the men pull me out of the water when I jumped into Biscayne Bay and almost drowned.

Boogie had her own problems—her mom paid more attention to her man than to her, she was always fighting with her dad— but she was like me. She read books on the down low, dreamed of becoming a famous singer one day, getting the fuck out of Miami and traveling the world. We talked about what our lives would be— we'd get gigs playing jazz clubs around the country. She'd sing, because she could actually sing, and I'd play the piano or the bass and write all the songs. Eventually, when we got older, I'd write books about our time on the road. We dreamed up adventures, hitchhiking to New York City, although I wasn't looking for a specific place, since I didn't believe there was any place I belonged.

We wanted to meet exotic characters at subway stations, hang out at the Lavender Room, ice-skate in Central Park. We'd be just like Holden, except we'd take advantage of our time in the city and have sex. Lots of it. We'd find some New York rappers in baggy jeans and basketball jerseys and we'd have sex in the back of their limo while listening to Mobb Deep's "Shook Ones" or Wu-Tang's "C.R.E.A.M." We'd party at the Limelight, become club kids, wear Halloween costumes in February. Pink hair, silver glitter eye shadow, blue lipstick, leather dog collars. Noses, eyebrows, lips pierced. I'd be nothing like the ordinary girl who lived with her crazy mother across the street from Normandy Park, the girl who was full of secrets, who believed in monsters. I would finally be free.

THAT WINTER, WHEN the Christmas lights went up around Normandy Isle and South Beach, when all the Miami radio stations started playing "Feliz Navidad," Boogie and I took off. I didn't leave a note, didn't give any explanation, and neither did Boogie. There would be nothing left for our parents when they discovered that we were gone. We figured it'd be easier that way, that nobody would try to find us, or worse, stop us.

I tossed a change of clothes into my JanSport and we hit the street, walking along Normandy Drive, and I stuck my thumb out once we got to the corner of 71st and Collins.

"We can't just get into some random dude's car," Boogie said. "We need to be smart."

"Okay," I said, but when a green sedan pulled over, we climbed in without even a second glance at the driver.

His name was Carlos, and he was headed toward Bird Road. We had no idea where Bird Road was, but we took the ride anyway.

He was a middle-aged man with a thick mane of black hair that screamed "Just For Men." I rode shotgun while Carlos drove us down the 836, a lit cigarette pinched between his lips. He asked questions about our boyfriends and our parents, and what exactly two fourteen-year-olds were doing getting in cars with strangers.

"We ran away," I said, checking myself out in the visor mirror.

"Why's that?" he asked.

I shrugged. "Because home sucks. Because this whole fucking place sucks."

"You shouldn't talk that way," he said, "a pretty girl like you."

But I wasn't falling for his bullshit. From my mother, I'd learned that men always pretended to give a shit about you, saying exactly what you wanted to hear when there was something they wanted. And men always wanted *something*.

I reached into the center console for his Marlboros, plucked one out for myself, tossed the pack to Boogie. As he pulled off the road and we approached the sign for Santa's Enchanted Forest— Miami's Christmas theme park—I got an idea. Boogie and I had never been there, so it seemed like destiny: it was exactly where we were supposed to be.

I snuck a look at Boogie over my shoulder, gathering my curls into a ponytail. I smiled at Carlos like I'd never smiled at any man before, and asked him if he would take us to Santa's Enchanted Forest.

"I can drop you off out front," he said. But he hadn't caught my meaning. I hadn't meant for him to drop us off, since we barely had three dollars between the two of us and couldn't pay the entry fee, whatever it was. Then there were the rides, the food, the arcade.

"No," I said. "I mean *take us* take us."

We stopped at a red light, Carlos looking over the steering wheel without a word. I let go of my hair, my curls falling over my shoulders. Boogie sat in the back, eyebrows raised, waiting.

"Fine," he said. "Let's go."

I threw my hands up over my head, and Boogie hooted. Carlos smiled, adjusting himself in the driver's seat, tossing his cigarette out the window. And then the light changed.

Inside Santa's Enchanted Forest we caused all kinds of hell. We made Carlos pay the entry fees, treat us to ice cream, elephant ears, pizza. We cut in line, left him behind while we rode the Gravitron and the bumper cars. We got on every ride while he pretended he was some sort of throwback hustler, wearing his shades after the sun set, chain-smoking, bobbing his head to whatever music the DJ played. I never wondered why he took us, why he was paying for everything, never even considered the reason he'd spent all night waiting on two underage girls he picked up on the side of the road, because I knew—I knew, even if Boogie didn't, that there would come a moment when the night would end, when Carlos would show us what he really wanted, and what he really was.

AFTER HOURS IN Santa's Enchanted Forest, after we got tired of every other ride, Boogie and I rode the Ferris wheel, sucking on the Ring Pops Carlos had bought for us. We rode side by side, and as our car rose, we took in the whole park: the cast members dressed as Santa's elves and a carrot-nosed Frosty the Snowman, the fake cotton snow under the Christmas trees lining the main strip, kids finishing up their corn dogs and cotton candy as they boarded the carousel, everywhere the smell of cinnamon and fried dough, teenagers lining up for the Space Coaster and the MegaDrop. And then, when we got to the top, there it was: the tallest Christmas tree in South Florida.

Later, Carlos *would* change. He'd get mad at us for flirting with a group of boys from Treasure Island, and when Boogie kissed one of them outside Santa's Grotto. He'd corner me by the workshop assembly line, squeeze my breasts hard. I'd push him back, but it would do no good because he was stronger than me and his eyes were already glazed over with too much beer and too much desire. He'd reach down and grab me there, between my legs. And then he'd give me a look that only I could read, a look that said I owed him, this was the price for my wildness and my freedom, I was his. But then Boogie and the boys would show up and Carlos would let go, and I'd think, *Thank you thank you thank you oh my God*, grab Boogie and make a run for it, ditch Carlos and ditch the boys, too. We'd take the last bus back home, ride up front while the driver listened to the Jesus station, and years later I'd remember this moment and think about Holden, how he ran after Mr. Antolini tried to hit on him, how the whole book was about Holden running, but he didn't really go anywhere but home, because maybe in the end he had nowhere else to go.

But all that would come later. While we were still on that Ferris wheel, still in that moment on top of the world, Boogie and I had no idea. We just sucked on our Ring Pops and looked out at the theme park, at the people and the lights and the fake snow and the tacky-ass Christmas stuff, even though we were less than an hour away from Miami Beach, and in that instant, we let ourselves believe that we were on our way, or that we had somehow already made it. That we were already free.

. . .

THE SPRING CHINA turned fifteen, we were herded into a banquet hall for her quinces, all of us in our magenta ball gowns, elbow-length gloves, hair pinned up in elaborate twists, lips painted red. We walked down the aisle, our dance partners in their black tuxedoes, magenta bowties to match our skirts. As "Tiempo de Vals" blared from the speakers, we swayed to the music like we were in some old movie, counting *one two three four, one two three four* in our heads with the rhythm of the music, just like China's tía had taught us, the boys' hands at our waists, our palms sweaty in our tacky-ass gloves. We winked at each other from across the room, stuck our tongues out when we caught China's eye, giggling while her family watched from their extravagantly decorated tables. We twirled and twirled in our wide skirts, and when the song finished, we kept dancing, another song and another and another, all of us smiling and sweaty and breathless, overcome with too much Keith Sweat and Boyz II Men, too much "Freak Me" and "Rub You the Right Way." We stopped caring about how anybody saw us, what they might think.

After the boys had left the dance floor, after the pictures and the cutting of the cake, after all of us changed out of our magenta ball gowns and into little black dresses we'd picked out for ourselves, after we let our hair down and kicked off those ridiculous heels, we went back out on the dance floor, just the girls, hanging on to each other. We sang along to every song, our cheeks flushed, our curls sticking to our foreheads, the backs of our necks, our shoulders and backs glistening, and we stopped thinking about the real world, our real-world problems, who was on house arrest, whose brother had just gotten a ten-year sentence for racketeering, whose parents were living paycheck to paycheck. We felt the music vibrating through our bodies, fingers to toes, the beats hammering on our chests, filling us. We were beaming. We were breath and rhythm, laughing and laughing in each other's arms, and for a while, as the world was spinning, blue and red and yellow lights flashing all across the banquet hall, I looked around at us, at my girls, round faces covered in their mothers' makeup, how we would all be in high school in a few short months, and all I could see was how much I loved them, how much I loved *us*.

I didn't know it yet, none of us did, but it would be these hood girls, these ordinary girls, who would save me.

THE FALL AFTER China's quinces, the year we started high school, Shorty and I became friends. We'd known each other before, met when some friends and I were planning to fight some other Nautilus girls—a ridiculous one-minute roll on the sidewalk that ended with one of the girls having a seizure in front of Hunan Chinese Restaurant, the rest of us scrambling in ten different directions when the cop cars pulled up, lights flashing.

Shorty turned out to be one of my closest friends, even though we hadn't known each other long—she'd moved down from Chicago just a year before. We fell into an easy friendship, growing our hair long, dressing alike. She was small, with doe eyes and a dash of freckles across her nose, and she was always, always, smiling. That fall, that year, she was one of the few people I went to with my fears, my dreams, my anger.

In our first period music class, Advanced Chorus, we got split into separate sections, Shorty with the sopranos, and me with the altos. Every morning we'd walk in, sit together, talk shit about some of the other alto girls, the girlfriend of some dude Shorty had a crush on, the sister of a boy who'd snitched on me while I was skipping. Until Dr. Martin walked in and sent me on my way, back to the altos. From my spot on the second row, I watched Shorty, standing directly across from me in the semi-circle, smiling, her eyes wide. It killed me that I wasn't a soprano, that I couldn't reach those high-ass notes like Shorty. But also, that I couldn't sing next to her, that we never got to be side-by-side as we tried to sound like Alvin and the Chipmunks singing Billy Joel's "You May Be Right," or when we changed the lyrics to Boyz II Men's "End of the Road" to something nasty, or when we danced and clapped like a gospel choir while we sang "Oh Happy Day." I was secretly obsessed with *Sister Act 2: Back in the Habit*, and crushing hard on Lauryn Hill, so I didn't even mind singing about Jesus.

That winter, we watched *New York Undercover* on group phone calls, Boogie and China and Flaca and Shorty and me, all of us on the party line, screaming at the TV when Malik Yoba, Michael DeLorenzo, and Lauren Vélez took off down the street chasing some drug dealer. We cut pictures of Jodeci and Boyz II Men and 2Pac from magazines, taped them on the covers of our notebooks. We watched Janet and Pac fall in love in *Poetic Justice*, and we all wanted to be Janet, scribbling poems on the margins of our textbooks, strutting into school in baggy jeans and combat boots. We watched *The X-Files*, imagined ourselves solving paranormal mysteries, having alien babies, turning into monsters. And then we speculated about the size of Mulder's dick. We felt the warmth of that place between our legs and there was nothing monstrous or strange about it.

That winter, we measured out our life in songs, singing as we put on eyeliner in front of the mirror, as we passed each other in the halls at school, as we waited for the bus across from the park. We belted out Mariah's version of "I'll Be There" in China's mother's car on the way to a sleepover. We broke into fits of spontaneous booty shaking as we walked along West Avenue, when a car drove by blasting "Shake Whatcha Mama Gave Ya," as we rode the escalator in Aventura Mall. We choreographed dances to "Pop that Pussy" and "The Uncle Al Song" at China's house. We knew all the lyrics to every single DJ Uncle Al song—"Mix it Up," and "Hoes-N-Da-House," and "Bass Is Gonna Blow Your Mind." Uncle Al, who was known all over Miami for promoting nonviolence and peace in the hood, but was shot and killed outside his house in Allapattah. We dogged each other to "It's Your Birthday" while hanging from the monkey bars, *lightning in our limbs*, while drinking orange sodas at Miami Subs, while tagging the handball courts. Everywhere Boogie, China, Flaca, Shorty, Jaqui.

That spring, we paid tecatos at 7-Eleven to get us bottles of strawberry Cisco, took the bus to Bayside, got on the party boats, danced and danced and danced with older boys, handed them our phone numbers at the end of the night. We rode to the all-ages clubs, Pac Jam and Sugar Hill and Bootleggers, where they sold no alcohol but everybody smoked weed. We passed the blunt across the dance floor, all of us sweaty and smiling, and onstage, older girls dusted with baby powder shook and shook their asses, flashing us their tits, all the girls booing, all the boys screaming, cheering, fists in the air. We smiled at each other nervously, recognizing some of the girls we knew from school, two years ahead of us, three years ahead of us, our friends' cousin, a girl my brother dated once. And one day that winter, we would hear about one of those girls—see her face on the news—about how she and her best friend were found floating in Biscayne Bay, strangled, tied together. Their school pictures all over our TVs for days, for weeks, their story on the front page of the *Sun-Sentinel* with the headline "They Were Inseparable Friends—And They Were Slain Together." We would remember their dancing, speculate about the who, the how, the why. We would talk about how they were so young, had so much life left to live, as if we knew anything about life and living it. *We knew nothing but what eyes could see.*

That summer, on the last day of school, me and Shorty cut out after lunch, headed to the beach for National Skip Day, the two of us in Daisy Dukes and chancletas, our curly hair wild and frizzy and sun-streaked. At the South Pointe pier, high school kids in bathing suits and shades, seeing each other's bodies for the first time, blasting Bone Thugs-n-Harmony's "Thuggish Ruggish Bone" on their radios, catcalling girls across the way. Then, when a fight broke out, one dude holding the other underwater, arms swinging wildly, we ran toward the shore to see it. When he was finally able to get free, none of us saw it coming: the walk back to his car, the loaded gun pulled from his glove box. How we lost each other in the madness, Shorty running down the shoreline, and me, heading for the water. The bodies on the sand, all of us scrambling away from the gunfire. Later that night, we would watch ourselves on the news, all those teenagers loose on the beach, on the pier, no parents anywhere, the faraway spray of whitecaps breaking.

Just weeks later, me and Shorty were back on the beach, knocking back Olde E with some dudes we'd just met. The sun on our faces, bikinis under oversized T-shirts, we walked a couple blocks to their place. And once we were there, fifteen and sixteen and in a stranger's apartment, DJ Playero's "Underground" on the radio, it was so clear, so easy to see. How they separated us, knew exactly what to say. Shorty in the bathroom, me in the living room, the bottle half-empty on the floor. How I never thought to ask how old he was—old enough to buy alcohol, to have his own apartment. How he ripped my bathing suit, the banging on the bathroom door, his hand over my mouth, the music so loud. How I pushed back, kicking, reaching for the ashtray, the remote, anything, until finally, the bottle, and I was Shorty and Shorty was me and we were every girl, we had not been alone, *all of us* in that apartment, in that bathroom, *all of us* breathing, alive, *lightning in our limbs*, banging on that door for minutes, hours, a lifetime, and for a moment I thought it was possible that I could lose her, that I could be one of those girls.

It was the same the next summer, and the summer after that: we went right back to drinking, smoking, fighting, dancing dancing dancing, running away. We wanted to be seen, finally, to exist in the lives we'd mapped out for ourselves. We wanted more than noise—we wanted everything. We were ordinary girls, but we would've given anything to be monsters. We weren't creatures or aliens or women in disguise, but girls. We were girls.

PART THREE

Familia

Beach City

I.

One August afternoon, the year we started high school, I met Cheito. I was coming back from the beach with Boogie, walking barefoot on the scorching sidewalk because someone had stolen all my shit while I was in the water, including my chancletas. Boogie still had her sandals, her towel, her lipstick half melted in her backpack. But I had nothing except my shorts and bikini top—what I'd been wearing while swimming. I was trying to look cool while tiptoeing my ass all the way home when a blue Datsun stopped across the street.

"You need a ride?" the driver called out.

Boogie smiled. "It's your lucky day, girl."

I checked out the car, the Puerto Rican flag hanging from the car's mirror, counted two boys. I looked down at my burning feet. "Fuck it."

We crossed the street, and the boy riding shotgun moved to the back. Before Boogie could slide in and take his place, the driver pointed at me, looked me in the eyes. "Sit up front with me," he said.

Boogie sat in the back with his friend. I sat up front, check-ing him out. He had a dark tan, a low fade, hazel eyes that looked almost green in the sunlight. He kept smiling at me, confident—he was fine and he knew it. I was suspicious of his every move. I didn't smile back. "I'm going to Ninth and West Avenue," I said.

"No problem." He was quiet for a minute, then said, "My name's Cheito, by the way."

"Jaqui," I said, "and that's Boogie." I had already decided that I wouldn't make conversation with them, but giving them our names didn't seem like a big deal.

"Where you from?" he asked.

"Make a left on Fifth Street," I said.

He approached the light on Fifth. I sat back and ignored his question.

"Why you gotta be so rude, girl?" Boogie said. "She's Puerto Rican, and I'm Cuban."

"I was born in Caguas," Cheito said to me, "and my mom's family's from San Lorenzo. What about you? Were you born on the island?"

"En Humacao."

"Oh! So you like Tito Rojas? He's from Humacao." He turned up the volume on his radio, which was playing Tito Rojas's "Condéname a tu amor."

I smiled. "I love him. And Pedro Conga. But not a lot of people know about Pedro."

He looked sideways at me. "You dance salsa?"

"Claro que si. It's in the contract."

Boogie tapped my seat. "What do you mean? What contract?"

Cheito looked back at her. "You don't know about that. You're Cuban."

I smiled at him, then turned to her. "The Boricua Contract."

She rolled her eyes. "Dumbass."

Cheito and I both laughed, and he headed north on West Avenue toward my building, the windows down, the wind slapping at my face and hair.

When we pulled up to Southgate Towers a minute later, I opened the door, got out of the car quickly.

"Hold up!" Cheito said. "Can I call you?"

I shut the door, then leaned down and looked into the car. He seemed friendly enough. He'd given us a ride. He handed me a Taco Bell napkin, and I scribbled my phone number on it.

He shook his head. "Que mala," he said. "I can't believe you were just gonna walk away without giving me your number."

I handed it to him. "How do you know it's not fake?"

In the backseat, Boogie was still talking to his friend.

"I'm a call you and find out," Cheito said.

HE CALLED TWO days later and we talked for hours. We talked about Puerto Rico, about Puerto Rican food, Puerto Rican music. He told me about growing up in Hialeah and summers in Caguas and San Lorenzo. I told him about Humacao, Fajardo, Luquillo, about Miami Beach. We both raved about our abuelas, who'd raised us. We shared stories about our fathers, both mujeriegos, all the women they'd betrayed. We compared stories about our mothers, both of them hurt by the men they'd married. We played our favorite songs for each other. We listened to each other breathing on the line when we ran out of shit to talk about. At around 3:00 a.m., we started falling asleep on the line, but didn't get off until the sun rose, then agreed to talk again the next day.

The next day he picked me up and we went to the beach by the Fontainebleau Hilton. We swam in the ocean together, diving headfirst into the waves, racing each other underwater. He never let me win. When I got tired, he let me hang onto his shoulders.

In the water, he picked me up, lifted me until he was looking up at me, and I wrapped my legs around his waist. He was strong, I realized, much stronger than I'd thought. From the muscles in his arms, shoulders, and back, I could tell he lifted weights. He was two years older than me, and six feet tall, and didn't seem like a boy, but he also wasn't a man. He was funny as hell, and always asked what I wanted, and I liked every single thing about him. In the water, with my legs wrapped around his waist, I kissed him. Just a quick, soft kiss on the lips.

We'd kiss again when he dropped me off that night. I'd take my time reaching for the door handle, and then he'd lean over, ask, "Can I kiss you good night?"

I'd ride the elevator all the way up to our apartment on the eighth floor, the taste of his kiss on my lips, and I would know, don't ask me how, that some day I would marry that boy.

CHEITO ASKED TO meet my family right away, came over one afternoon and shook Abuela's hand, introduced himself, ate her food, charmed the fuck out of her when he spoke to her in Spanish. But not just any Spanish. He spoke with un acento Boricua, and Abuela, who spoke bien jíbara, who dragged her R's instead of rolling them, immediately loved him. Bringing home this boy, so

Puerto Rican, so respectful, who brought with him the sounds of home, of la isla, who went to school and had a job and his own car that he paid for himself, who would drive me around and take me to run errands like paying the light bill and picking up Adobo Goya and salsa de tomate when we were out? That was, in Abuela's eyes, my greatest accomplishment. She would tell me every time he came to see me, as soon as he left. "Don't fuck this up. He's the best thing that's ever happened to you."

He did the same with Papi. Shook his hand, introduced himself, spoke to him in Spanish, talked about salsa and cars and boxing and basketball, all the things my father loved. And then Alaina, Anthony, Mami, all my aunts, all my friends. He took an interest in every single person in my life, had conversations with them, made them laugh, gave them rides, did favors for them. He was good with people, animals, kids. Everybody loved him. Loved him so much they were afraid I'd lose him, push him away, run off with a gangbanger for a week, like I'd been known to do. When he didn't come around for a couple of days because he had to work, they'd worry, ask if everything was okay. Like they were just waiting for me to fuck it up. I loved them and resented them for it.

But the truth is, I was afraid, too. I'd never felt so loved before, never felt so happy. With him, I ate Puerto Rican food every chance I got, spent weekends on the beach, went to salsa and merengue concerts at Bayfront Park. He introduced me to his abuela, his father, his mom, his stepmom, his baby sister. His baby sister, who was a year old, adored me. We took her to the mall and pretended she was ours. I'd change her diaper, feed her, run a baby brush through her soft curls. When she started talking, she called me Tati. She'd have entire conversations with me in baby-talk that only *she* understood, and I'd nod and smile and ask her questions like I was expecting an adult response: When are you gonna go get a job and start paying rent? Why don't you make the bed, or do some dishes? Don't you think you need to help your parents around the house more?

But to the rest of his family I was just some loose caserío girl, a loudmouth with no table manners, a delinquent in baggy clothes who was going nowhere, a tomboy with too many piercings who refused to dress the way proper Puerto Rican women dress, refused to serve him the way a proper Puerto Rican woman is supposed to serve her man, definitely not who they thought he'd end up with.

Cheito told me again and again not to worry about them, that he loved me, loved all the ways I was loud and funny, loved my piercings and my baggy clothes, and that he wasn't interested in whatever they thought a proper girl was supposed to act like, and he definitely didn't need a woman to serve him or to take care of him because he could take care of himself. He just wanted to be with me, the real me. Just spend some time with them, he said, and they'll get to know you, and then they'll love you, too.

He took me to eat at his abuela's house at least once a week, and I loved going there, even if his family didn't like me. We'd walk in, and Cheito would give his abuela a hug, a kiss on the cheek, then hug and kiss his father, hug and kiss his stepmom. His baby sister would yell my name—*Tati!*—and run toward me, and I'd grab her, hoist her up onto my hip. I was amazed at how they all loved each other so much and were never afraid to show it, hugging and kissing each other the way I never saw in my own family. I had never, ever, seen Anthony kiss Papi. Men in my family did not hug and kiss other men. We hadn't sat at a table for a meal together in years. We barely talked to each other. I couldn't remember a single time my father told me he loved me, or the last time my mother had hugged me. I only sometimes hugged Alaina, usually when we were both crying about some fucked up shit Anthony had done to one of us. And Anthony? We'd never hugged. We'd never, ever, said I love you. We communicated by throwing shit across the room at each other. The only person who hugged me or kissed me or told me she loved me was Abuela.

When we sat down to eat at Cheito's abuela's house, I could feel the love in the room. I hadn't realized it was something I'd been missing until then, until we were all sitting at the round table with our plates full, everyone smiling, asking each other about their day, passing tostones across the table, saying *please* and *thank you* like an ordinary fucking family. This is what a family was supposed to be—people who actually loved each other. I felt robbed. I looked around the dining room, the way his stepmom scooped beans onto his dad's plate, the way his abuela fed his baby sister in her highchair, Cheito smiling at me from across the table. Damn it, I loved these people, even if they hated me. And I knew it then: this was everything I wanted.

But there was something else I knew, would always know. I was my father's daughter. When Cheito wasn't around, I was back to being the same old Jaqui: Fuck love. Fuck family. I'd skip fifth and sixth period, run off with friends to smoke at the park, or go hang out in Bayside, ride the party boats, get home drunk or high at three, four in the morning. Then somehow get up at 7:00 a.m. to make it to school. I was late every single day.

We had sex for the first time after being together a few months. We were on the beach, hanging out on the deck of a lifeguard stand after dark, talking and laughing and kissing. He was sitting on the deck, his back against the lifeguard stand's wall, and I climbed onto his lap, started unzipping his jeans. We'd talked about doing it for a while, but never any of the details. He was a virgin, and he said he wanted to wait for me to be ready, wanted me to decide when and where.

I straddled him until he came, and I was about to get up when one of the Beach Patrol cops rolled up in a four-wheeler, shining his flashlight in our direction.

We froze when we saw the light, our arms around each other.

"Not the time or the place," the cop said. He kept his flashlight trained on us.

"We're leaving," Cheito told him. "We're leaving right now."

The Beach Patrol pulled away when he saw us getting up. Cheito zipped up his pants, buckled them, and I slid my shorts back on.

"Are you okay?" he asked me.

"I'm fine," I said. And I was. I picked up my sneakers, my socks. Then we both started laughing.

"I'm sorry," he said.

THE NEXT TIME, he got us a room at a motel in Hialeah, on Okeechobee Road, a place with a queen-sized bed and a Jacuzzi and free cable and porn on every single TV channel. He bought a bottle of Mr. Bubble from the guy at the front desk—I guess he was trying to make it up to me—but we never even used it.

When we got into the room, I turned on the TV, watched every one of those old pornos for a few seconds, hairy ass men with beer bellies, balding and sporting mustaches thick as brooms, jerking off on women's tits. I cringed.

"Is this what guys like?" I asked. "Because it's definitely not what girls like." But I had no idea what girls liked, not really.

He turned off the TV, kissed me, turned on the radio, kissed me again. He put on 99 Jamz, which was playing an R&B mix. He lay me down on the bed, kissing me on the lips, biting my neck, kissing then biting my thighs. I took off my bra, tossed it aside. He pulled off my underwear and put his head between my legs, and then slid on top of me, kissing me on the lips, on my neck. He wrapped the sheet around us both, then held me until I fell asleep.

When I woke up, maybe an hour later, he was still holding me, the music still playing. I turned over, stretching my arms, then sat up. He sat up, too, pulled me toward him and buried his face in my hair.

"Hey," he said, kissing the top of my head.

We fell into each other, kissing, and he got on top of me, spread my legs, and worked himself inside me slowly. He never stopped kissing me.

We went on like this for hours, until I couldn't take any more, then fell asleep in each other's arms.

It was all new, but I loved every second of it. I wanted to be with him, always. To wake up next to him every morning. For the first time in my life, I thought, it was clear that somebody loved me. And I loved him, too.

EVEN THOUGH I was fifteen, I thought I was grown, like I was in complete control of my life, and even when I wasn't, that I definitely should be. I was sick of people treating me like a child, trying to control me. So I started saving up money. I got a job waiting tables, and then, when I turned sixteen, I dropped out of school and started working at a pharmacy. A few weeks after that, I moved out of my father's house into a hotel. A month later, Cheito and I got a tiny apartment across the street from the beach.

We were teenagers, both of us working full time just to make rent, taking the bus to and from work. We didn't have much—our clothes, an old TV that Cheito had had in his childhood bedroom, a folding table from Target, a bed and small dresser his father had given us. We were struggling, but we made it work. There were so many jobs: the pharmacy, valet parking, another pharmacy, a clothing store at the mall, another restaurant. Then one day, Cheito decided he wanted to stop living paycheck to paycheck. He wanted a career, a future full of things he could never have if he stayed in Miami Beach, working just to pay for our small place on the beach.

He called the local Marine Corps recruiter. He came from a family of military veterans, had uncles and cousins in the Army and the Marines, and had been talking to them about this for months.

I pleaded with him to stay. He could go to college, I insisted. I would get a second job.

But he didn't want me to get a second job. He wanted to make enough money to do more than just survive, he said. He wanted us to be able to travel, see the world. I wanted him to have all those things, too, but not without me.

We could get married, he said, as soon as he got out of boot camp and finished school. Then he could take me with him wherever he went.

What if there's a war? I asked. What then? It felt like I was losing my entire world. He'd been the only person who believed in me, the only person who thought I was good. He was my family.

On the day he was supposed to fly off to Parris Island for basic training, standing outside the Miami Military Entrance Processing Station, his mom, his abuela, and I, all crying, begging him to stay, his father gave him a hug, told him to go.

"You have no future here," his father said. "If you stay here just for a girl, you'll regret it for the rest of your life."

A few weeks after he left, his father picked up the bed, the dresser, and the TV. Exactly three months after that, I was evicted from our apartment.

II.

We talked about Miami Beach like it belonged only to us, convinced that the tourists and spring breakers who came down to swim in our ocean and dance in our nightclubs were fucking up our city. We were seventeen-, eighteen-, nineteen-year-old hoodlums, our hair in cornrows and too-tight ponytails, too much hairspray and dark brown lip liner, noses and belly buttons pierced, door-knocker earrings, jailhouse ankle tattoos. We didn't have time for boys from Hollywood or North Miami, busters who drove their hoopties with the windows down because they didn't have A/C, who called out to us trying to get phone numbers as we crossed Washington Avenue or Lincoln Road, our chancletas slapping the sidewalk.

What did they know about surfing during hurricane winds, fucking on lifeguard stands, breathing under water? What did they know about millions of stray cats pissing in the sand dunes, entire flocks of rogue seagulls dropping shit torpedoes, about refugees and kilos of cocaine and bodies washing up on our shores?

We were the ones who knew what it meant to belong here, to be made whole during full moon drum circles, dancing, drinking, smoking it up with our homeboys. We knew what it meant to bloody our knuckles here, to break teeth here, to live and breathe these streets day in, day out, the glow of the neon hotel signs on the waterfront, the salt and sweat of this beach city.

ONE NIGHT WE parked Brown's old Mustang behind the roller skating rink on Collins and hoofed it to the beach. We took our bottles of Olde English and Mad Dog 20/20, the six of us passing a blunt and listening to 2Pac's "Hit 'Em Up" blaring from somebody's radio, and every time they sang, *Grab your Glocks when you see 2Pac*, the boys grabbed their dicks and we all laughed our asses off. Brown started dancing and stripping off his clothes while we cheered him on, me and A.J. hopping around, keeling over, slapping our knees. Flaca, China, and Cisco climbed to the top of the lifeguard stand, singing, "Go, Brown! Go, Brown!" When everything but his boxer briefs had come off, Brown gave up, and we all booed him, threw our balled-up socks and sneakers at him.

Cisco changed the song, and Flaca and China came down from the lifeguard stand and the three of us ran toward the shore, dipping our feet in the water. I kicked at the rolling waves, splashing them, and China screamed. I kept splashing them, dipping my hands in the water and aiming it at their heads, but China took off, running up the beach.

"You're gonna fuck up my hair!" Flaca yelled. She splashed me back, kicking and kicking her long legs at the small waves, holding her quart in one hand. She was laughing, her brown hair in a bun high up on her head, the baby hairs on her forehead and temples plastered to her skin with so much hairspray that not even the saltwater would mess it up. She took a few steps back and gave me the middle finger, and for a moment, she looked just like she had when we were fifth graders.

China and Flaca and I had been in the fourth grade at Fisher when we met, and we'd always been close friends. Flaca's dad and Papi knew each other, had been friends for years. He was also close friends with my uncle Junior. As kids, we'd spent every October 31 at the Lincoln Road Halloween street party, dressed as hippies, punk rockers, witches. We'd spent the last year going on missions, riding the bus to the mall, borrowing China's mother's car and riding to Grand Prix Race-O-Rama, where we spent hours playing Mortal Kombat, riding go carts, shooting Lil' Hoops, and posing for ridiculous pictures in the photo booth. When we all got together, we'd go back to being those same kids.

Flaca and I laughed and laughed, until suddenly, out of the darkness, Brown appeared, wearing nothing but his underwear, and started walking into the ocean.

"Sorry, but I have to pee," he said.

We exchanged looks, then Flaca and I both yelled, "Ew!" and ran back up toward the lifeguard stand to find China.

We found China, dancing around with Cisco and A.J., a bottle of Mad Dog in one hand. When the music stopped, she took one sip, then another, and another, and somebody yelled, "Chug it!" and then she was chugging, and all of us joined in, clapping our hands, calling out "Chug it!" and screaming when she finished the bottle, held it upside down for all of us to see.

Out behind the lifeguard stand, me and A.J., sand between our toes, feeling for each other in the dark. We ran around laughing and laughing, and I took his hand and danced circles around him in slow motion.

I don't remember when A.J. first told me he loved me, or even *if* he told me, but I knew. I felt it every time he came around, every time our thighs touched while sitting together on China's couch, or when the six of us had to squeeze into Brown's Mustang and I had to sit sideways on his lap, trying not to put all my weight on him, my lip brushing against his ear, his arms around my waist. Or when we stayed up all night talking even though he had to get up early for school the next morning—something I didn't have to worry about since I was a high school dropout. Or on nights when the liquor and the weed made my head spin, the heat and the high coming down on me all at once, and only A.J. around to keep me from falling.

Down by the shore, Brown was so fucked up he dropped to his knees, then lay down sideways on the sand. Later, we would all carry him back to his car. Flaca would drive us to her place a few blocks away. We would all stagger up the stairs to her little studio, put Brown to sleep in the bathtub, and smoke Newports on the balcony. He would wake up with the munchies an hour later. "You got any cheese?" he'd call out from the bathroom. A.J. would grab an entire pack of Kraft Singles from Flaca's fridge, and the two of us would toss them into the tub, slice by slice, while Brown tried to catch them in his mouth.

But before all that, the six of us dancing and running around on the beach, China chugging on that Mad Dog, Flaca and Cisco kissing on the steps of the lifeguard stand, and A.J. looking at me under the moonlight, a cloud of smoke all around us, I wrapped my arms around him and said, "Don't let me go."

We were laughing, hitting the blunt.

We were the faraway waves breaking, the music and the ocean and the heat rising rising rising, like a fever.

We were bodies made of smoke and water.

THE TRUTH WAS that I wasn't into A.J.—we were just friends. I'd spent the last few months waiting for Cheito, bitter, getting blackout drunk, snorting coke, fighting, and sneaking into clubs on Washington Avenue. I'd gotten my GED and started taking classes at Miami Dade Community College, but was failing every one of them because I almost never went to class, and when I did, I was drunk or high or just not interested. I'd been sleeping on my father's couch for months.

After Cheito finished his MOS school, he'd come home on leave. We stayed in a hotel for two weeks. That first night, he asked me to marry him.

I'd just turned seventeen, and was madly in love and so happy to have him back, even if only for two weeks, and we were half naked, kissing in bed, when he pulled out a small white box. A ring.

The day before he had to fly off to Marine Combat Training, we went to Miami Beach's Old City Hall and got married.

FOR THE NEXT year, married life was Cheito in Camp Lejeune, training, and then school, and then shipped off to Okinawa; and me, sleeping on Papi's couch, not going to class, only getting up to go to work or go get fucked up, and then coming home and passing out on the couch again.

Most nights I hung out with Flaca and China. Occasionally A.J., Brown, and Cisco would join us, and we'd all go to Society Hill, this hole-in-the-wall dive bar on Washington that had no cover and served us drinks and never asked for ID. The place was all painted black and dark green and had some of the regulars' names tagged on the walls in spray paint, South Beach legends, people we'd grown up with that everybody knew. Society Hill was so small you could barely dance in there, but someone would always fire up a blunt and pass it, and we'd all end up dancing anyway, our bodies close, dodging elbows to the face and pushing back dudes who tried to grind on us from behind. Afterward, we'd end up on the beach, smoking until the world slowed down, dancing like we had something to celebrate. While we were together, we forgot we were kids with adult problems. Some of us were already married, some of us already had kids, some of us had dropped out of high school and had no choice but to work, some of us had parents facing deportation, some of us had lost our mothers, some of us were living on our own, trying to make rent. While other girls were saving up for prom dresses and graduation pictures, I was saving up to make a deposit on a small apartment on West Avenue, which was taking longer than expected since I was spending half my paycheck on drugs and alcohol. Flaca was working so she could afford to pay her half of the rent. China was working to take care of herself, and her brothers and sister. Everybody had some shit going on. But those nights on the beach, we pretended we were kids again, taking pictures with Flaca's camera, writing our names on the lifeguard stands, always leaving something behind, wanting the night, the beach, to remember us, as if somehow we knew these moments were precious, fleeting. As if somehow we knew we were running out of time.

And we were. High school was ending for them, and it had already ended for me. For them, there would be grad weekend, trips to Disney World. There would be a big deal on prom night, when I'd spend hours doing Flaca's and China's hair and makeup, helping them get ready. I wouldn't go, because something about seeing all those people again after being unhappily married and flunking out of college made me feel like a failure. But afterward, we'd go to the beach, Flaca and China kicking off their heels and running on the sand, their long skirts flapping in the wind, the rest of us chasing them, and I'd think, *This is just like the movies*, and catch myself feeling hopeful.

BUT THAT WOULDN'T last long. There would be another night, all of us sliding into another friend's car, all of us driving north to Grand Prix Race-o-Rama, me riding shotgun, and everyone else packed into the backseat of his Chevy Impala.

He was older, in his twenties, and he sold scutter and meth to make rent. He called me every Friday, asked if I wanted to go out, and I'd feel guilty, but also, I resented Cheito for leaving me, so I did. I always brought China and Flaca, got him to take us out to eat, take us dancing, buy us drinks. He did everything I asked, bought us Taco Bell, brought me bottles of Palo Viejo, brought me pre-rolled blunts laced with scutter or stank. He called me Jaquira, saying it the right way, rolling his R's, and something about that made him seem familiar, made him seem safe. His name was Nate, and the only thing I liked about him was how he said my name. And that he brought me drugs.

That night he would bring me two blunts—one for my friends, and one special for me, laced with so much stank the whole car smelled like Elmer's glue for hours after I smoked it. We would get to Grand Prix, play arcade games for a couple hours, and then I'd snort so much of his powdered meth I would be gone, completely gone. There would be pictures of that night, Flaca and China and I making faces in the photo booth, looking like girls. High school girls. And then the night would start to fade, my heart pounding in my chest, the feeling that I would die, that I wanted to die. Flaca and China and Nate would take me outside, and I'd rip my hoops out, fling them across the parking lot because my ears were on fire. They'd put me in the backseat, and when the car started rolling out of the parking lot, I would try to jump out until somebody grabbed my collar, my arms, my legs. And then, my whole body on fire, in the back of the car, Flaca on one side, China on the other, the two of them would hold me, try to rock me to sleep, keep me from reaching for the door handle while Nate drove me home. Flaca would yell at him, *What the fuck did you give her?!* And Nate would lie, say, *Yo, that's on you, girl. I didn't give her shit.*

And later, after Cheito and I are separated and I'm living with Nate, after Nate beats my ass in the street and I try to leave, after he drags me from the hallway back into his apartment and into his bedroom, after I reach for the phone and he rips it off the wall, wraps the telephone cord around my neck, promises that if I leave him again he'll kill me, after I wait for him to fall asleep or take a shower, after I run next door and knock on the neighbors' windows and make phone call after phone call after phone call, it would be Flaca who'd show up in her boyfriend's mother's car in the middle of the night. She'd take my backpack and toss it into the backseat and check out my face, my neck, say, *That fucking asshole.* She'd get back in the car, and as we pulled away, she'd say it again. *That fucking asshole.*

I wouldn't tell her that I'd done this all before. That the last time I'd called my father, and he'd pulled up to the back of the building, his friend riding shotgun, both of them determined to kick Nate's ass, until I said, *Let's just go, before someone calls the cops*, and got in the van, all their bravado fading. I wouldn't say that the next morning he'd called, sorry, so sorry, and that I'd let him pick me up from work, went back to his apartment. Or that it had only been a week.

We wouldn't talk about it at all afterward. But the next time I heard from him, weeks later, he was calling collect from Dade County Jail. I accepted the call only because I wanted to ask how long he'd be locked up.

"Ten months," he said.

"Good," I said, then hung up.

And that was the last I ever heard from him.

A FEW MONTHS after I turned eighteen, the six of us were all sitting around China's living room passing around a Philly, China, Flaca, A.J., Brown, Cisco, and me, listening to music and occasionally jumping off the couch to shake it to D.J. Laz's "Esa Morena." It was still early in the night, and we were all waiting for Society Hill to open so we could walk the eight blocks to Washington.

Cheito had been in Okinawa for almost a year. I couldn't see a future for us. I couldn't really see any future at all. I was still exactly where I'd been a year before, sleeping on my father's couch, a high school dropout with a GED and some failed community college classes. All I'd done over the past year was drink and smoke and snort coke. I'd done more drugs than homework, barely even made it to classes, spent every night at Society Hill, and then the beach. It was all the same. The same people standing outside the club, the same people passing blunts across the dance floor or trying to grind on you or trying to get your phone number, forgetting that just last week you'd said you weren't interested, or that the week before that they'd walked up trying to look cute and spilled a drink on your tits. Nothing had changed. Alaina was in high school, and she was living with Papi, too, but I barely ever saw her. After school, she worked at a surf shop on Lincoln Road, selling T-shirts and bikinis and surfboards. Anthony was waiting tables at some tourist trap restaurant on South Beach. Papi was dating a couple of different women, who all hated me. Abuela was cooking and cleaning, chain-smoking on the balcony, and watching novelas. Mami was living in Normandy Isles by herself, getting evicted every couple of months, and crashing with Mercy when she needed a place to stay. And here I was, doing absolutely nothing, with a husband somewhere at the other end of the world. I was failing at life.

I'd been thinking about it for a while, but it was right then when it occurred to me—all of us heading in the same direction, working odd jobs or failing out of school or just going through the motions. China and Flaca both working full time, barely making enough to make rent and buy sneakers and pay their phone bills. And not one of us knew where we were headed.

That night, I followed China and Flaca out the back door, where we lit some cigarettes and sat on China's steps, joking and laughing, and when I finished mine, I snubbed it out on the bottom step, then tossed it. It would be the last one I smoked. I was done.

"Hey," I said, "I think I figured out what I'm gonna do with my life." Cheito had done it, and he got to get the fuck out, see the world. Why couldn't I? "I think I'm going into the military."

They both looked at me, blinked. "Say *what*?"

Battle Stations

We arrived at the Great Lakes Naval Recruit Training Command in the summer of 1998, the summer of *Armageddon* and *The Miseducation of Lauryn Hill* and Michael Jordan's game-winning fadeaway jumper during his final five seconds as a Chicago Bull. We arrived on buses, fresh off our flights from Miami, from California, from New York, tired and sweaty and restless in our seats. We were eighteen, nineteen, early twenties, our hair cropped short, our family photos tucked into our backpacks, our friends' addresses scribbled on notebook paper, folded into the pockets of our jeans.

When we stepped off the bus, the petty officer on duty smiled at every single one of us, and then, once everyone was standing outside, he yelled, at the top of his lungs, "Attention!"

We stood at attention, like our recruiters taught us, some of us excited, some of us terrified. The petty officer smiled again, walking up and down, checking us out, then he took a step back to see the entire group, some of us women, most of us ordinary girls.

"What a sad, sad bunch of recruits," he said. "Welcome to Great Lakes, or as some of you will come to know it, Great Mistakes."

We filed inside the processing center, got our assignments, picked up our uniforms, our boots, sheets for our bunks. We were there for a future, most of us, recruited with promises of college funds and medical benefits and seeing the world. Some of us were military brats. Some of us just wanted to prove something, make our parents proud. By the time I got to Great Lakes, I'd come to think of the military as the only way I could save myself.

In the navy, I became a completely different girl. I took orders. I followed the rules. I worked hard—harder than I'd worked my whole life. I earned the recruit division commanders' trust and respect. They made me a section leader. I aced my safety classes, personnel inspections, physical fitness tests. I aced the firefighter training, the gas chamber, weapons training. I felt like I was a fucking superstar. I would ace Battle Stations, the final test of all our navy skills, and before I graduated, I'd get a meritorious promotion.

In the navy, for the first time in my life, I believed I could be good at something, that I could have a life full of promise and opportunity. It was the first time in my life that people expected me to succeed, that they looked at me and saw someone who was smart, and capable, with a future. And it scared the hell out of me. It had been easier to let people assume I would end up dead, or in jail, or strung out and living on the streets. It had been easier to want nothing, to believe in nothing.

DURING THE DAY, the navy's Recruit Training Command looked alive, like the world was moving faster. The ships full of recruits, the galley full of sailors in their dungarees or smurf suits calling out their numbers to the turnstile, the drill halls with entire divisions marching inside, practicing their flag drills. Outside, sailors and recruits marched in step, calling out cadences, jogging from one place to the next, from the USS Carr to the drill halls to the galley to the Navy Exchange, their RECRUIT ball caps blocking out the sun.

We were fitted for uniforms, the steel-toed boots we were supposed to call boondockers, canteens firmly attached to guard belts, flight jackets, rain coats.

After a few weeks, on a sweltering summer day in Great Lakes, I got down to formation with all my gear, fell in line next to Seaman Recruit Santiago, a tattooed dark-skinned Chicano from California. Santiago, who I called G-mo when we were alone, was in our brother division, and my partner in almost every phase of training. We were both section leaders and always marched side by side, ran together, sat next to each other at chow and in class. We'd been inseparable since the second week of boot camp, sending each other letters through the US mail, passing each other notes in class, talking while standing in formation, while doing push ups in PT or marching to the drill halls.

G-mo looked around for signs of a recruit division commander, then quickly took my hand, squeezed it.

"How you doing, Jaqui?"

He let go of my hand and looked straight ahead, trying to avoid being spotted by an RDC.

"I'm cool," I said.

Brooks, our brother division's RPOC, who usually called cadence and relayed orders from RDCs, was standing on the sidelines, watching us. He walked over, pretending he spotted something on the ground.

"You fools need to chill out with that PDA," he said.

Behind us, Jones was adjusting his safety belt and laughing at us. "Ain't y'all so sweet. Wait until you get recycled for fraternizing."

I didn't know why Jones was hating. Just a couple weeks ago he had a boot camp girlfriend he couldn't stay away from, until she had to go back to the first week of training with another division. She'd gotten recycled after she got caught sneaking into the male sleeping quarters during her 2:00 a.m. watch. Recycling—sending someone back to start bootcamp over with another division—was what they did to recruits who needed discipline, who fraternized or broke the rules. Basically, it was for recruits who got caught.

Out of the corner of my eye, I spotted Petty Officer Thompson, one of the RDCs, making a beeline straight for us. I braced myself. She was not the one to fuck with.

Petty Officer Thompson strutted up to Jones. "What's your seventh general order, recruit?" She was the only woman RDC out of the six who ran our two divisions, and the toughest. She had to be. Being a woman in the military, especially a black woman, meant you had to work with men who thought they were better than you, faster than you, stronger than you. It meant you had to constantly prove yourself, every minute of every day, when even the rules said you weren't good enough. Back then, women were not allowed to be SEALs, were not allowed to serve on submarines, were not allowed to be rescue divers. But when PO Thompson trained with us, she outperformed all the men. And that was just the physical part. Being a black woman in the military also meant you had to be twice as smart, twice as capable. You had to know your job and everyone else's, and watch people who were less qualified get all the promotions. All the other RDCs had higher ranks than Petty Officer Thompson, but she was the one who knew everything, the one the men turned to when they needed questions answered, when they needed someone who knew all the SOP. She was the one getting us up at 4:00 a.m., the one who could recall military history off the top of her head, the one who was always on time. It was clear to all of us: she ran this shit. And when we were alone with her in the female quarters, she reminded us, told us every time she got the chance, *You need to show them that this is our world, that we run this. Don't you ever let them think otherwise.*

Jones, who was caught off guard, stood at attention with a dumbstruck look on his face. And I didn't realize I'd been looking sideways at him until Thompson turned to me and smiled. Damn. I turned my face forward, stood at attention, and kept my eyes open, even though I knew what was coming.

She took a deep breath, then yelled across the formation at the division, "Seaman Recruit Díaz lost her military bearing!" She took a step toward me, put her face right next to mine, so close I could hear her breathing, hard. "Let's see if she can help you out, Jones," she said. "What's your seventh general order, Díaz?"

"To talk to no one except in the line of duty, Petty Officer!" I yelled.

She smiled, turned to Jones, and said, "Jones, drop." She turned back to me. "Díaz, help him out."

I stepped out of formation, then dropped to push-up position, started pumping them out as fast as I could, counting out loud as

I went. "One, Petty Officer, two, Petty Officer, three, Petty Officer, four, Petty Officer . . ."

Beside me, Jones had already reached twenty. He stopped counting, holding his last push up, then turned to Petty Officer Thompson, and said, "Petty Officer, I respectfully request permission to recover."

"You recover when I say you recover," she said. "Now, push!"

Jones kept pumping them out. I struggled to keep up, but I kept going.

When Petty Officer Thompson walked off to inspect the rest of the division, Jones looked over at me. "Hey, you alright, Díaz?" He smiled.

I turned my head toward him, smiled back, then stuck out my tongue.

We both started laughing out loud, and unable to hold myself up in push-up position, I hit the ground. I could hear G-mo laughing, but I got back up and kept pushing before Petty Officer Thompson came back around.

"Díaz, recover," Thompson ordered. "Jones, recover."

We both got up, brushed ourselves off, and fell back in line.

NIGHTS INSIDE THE USS Carr, I lay in my rack listening to the silence, the other recruits sleeping and breathing and farting, some of them talking in their sleep. I had insomnia, and sometimes it would be hours and I'd still be up. I'd be on the top bunk, looking up into the darkness, trying to remember what a Pepsi tasted like, the noise on the streets back home. The smell of Abuela's kitchen—sofrito, lechón roasting in the oven. Alaina's unwashed curls, greasy, tangled. How Papi knelt in the living room to pray every night before leaving for work. This was all I had, so even though I didn't believe in prayer, I prayed for those things to hold me together for the rest of my time in boot camp.

Those nights I couldn't sleep, I wrote letter after letter. I wrote every single person in my family. I wrote Cheito. I wrote Cheito's family. I wrote every single one of my friends. I wrote G-mo. I wrote in my journals, wrote like my life depended on it. But Cheito's family never wrote. My own family barely wrote me. Once in a while I'd get a letter from Flaca or China. Once I got a letter from Alaina, and then six postcards in a row. Cheito wrote me every week, telling me how proud he was, how strong I was, how he missed me. I felt guilty every time I opened one of his letters. When Cheito left for boot camp, I had only written him three times the whole twelve weeks he was there. I resented him—he'd broken my heart. And then there was also G-mo.

The letters from Flaca and China and Alaina made me feel like shit. I missed them, I missed home, and while I was gone, the whole world kept on going like I was never even there:

Papi got evicted, and they had to move to some other neighborhood.

Alaina smoked her first joint.

A gang war was sweeping Miami and Miami Beach.

A couple of our friends got convicted of attempted murder and racketeering. One would serve seven years in prison. The other got a twenty-year sentence.

Our old middle school was demolished, an institution built in its place.

Society Hill burned down.

. . .

IN BOOT CAMP, far from home, far from friends and family, I met Eliza. She was in my division, and we sometimes had fire watch together in the middle of the night. She was tall and strong, with broad shoulders and a buzz cut, and I sometimes watched her from afar. I knew she was gay. I could just tell.

One morning in the galley, while we were sitting down to breakfast after physical training, Eliza across from me, our eyes met. We looked at each other for a long time, not saying anything because we weren't allowed to speak, watching each other longer than was acceptable, longer than was comfortable, and I just knew. It was like we found each other in a crowd, like all we could see was each other. After a while, I looked away, hoping that G-mo, sitting next to me, hadn't noticed. I could still feel her eyes on me then, and afterward, as we all got up to bus our trays, as we all headed back outside to get in formation, as we double-timed it back to the USS Carr to get in the showers, and then while we were in the showers. I knew every single curve of her body, every tattoo. And she knew mine.

It went on like that for a while, Eliza and I looking at each other, not saying anything. Sometimes, while we were sitting in class, I'd catch her watching me from across the room, and she'd look away. Other times, I'd be sitting in the back, watching her, waiting for her to look back at me, and most of the time she wouldn't, but sometimes, it was like she could feel me watching her, too.

ON THE MORNING before Battle Stations, we were given all the equipment we needed to survive an attack on the USS Carr. Fire safety equipment, gas masks, Kevlar helmets, extra canteens so we could stay hydrated for the five-mile run. We'd learned how to put out all kinds of fires, how to get a ship underway, what to do if one of our shipmates fell overboard, how to shoot a pistol, an M16, how to swim and tread water, how to make a floating device using our waterproof dungarees. During Battle Stations, we had to prove that we could use all those skills. We'd been living on the third deck of a simulated aircraft carrier for the last eight weeks, and everything we'd learned since we got there had been to prepare us for this night. In three hours, we'd be attacked by an enemy navy.

At midnight, we were awakened by the sound of mock explosions, fire alarms, and Atkins, our RPOC, hollering orders in her Tennessee twang.

"Get up!" Atkins yelled. "Battle stations! Battle stations!"

Our division commander, Petty Officer Thompson, was on the 1MC, her voice blaring throughout the whole ship: "General quarters, general quarters, all hands man your battle stations. Battle stations, all hands man your battle stations."

I jumped off the top bunk, landing on my feet, headed straight for my wall-locker.

"You have three minutes to secure all gear adrift," the RPOC was saying.

We were supposed to run past the quarterdeck and report to formation wearing every piece of equipment we had: gas masks cleaned, canteens filled and clipped to our safety belts, our ten-pound Kevlar helmets, chin-straps fastened securely across our chins, dungarees tucked into our boondockers, gym shorts under our dungarees, swimsuits under our gym shorts. Those of us who were section leaders got extra shit to carry: I had another seabag filled with first aid supplies, extra canteens, spare gas masks, sanitary pads, tampons, panty liners.

When I got down to formation with all my gear, I fell in line next to G-mo. We were early. Less than half of us were in formation.

"Good luck, Jaqui," he said.

I smiled. "Good luck."

Suddenly, Petty Officer Thompson came out of the ship, rushing, breaking us into squads of five or six. In our group, we had Jones, Brooks, G-mo, Williams—who was our ship's female recruit master at arms—and me. Brooks and G-mo were strong and in shape, always got high scores in anything fitness-related. Jones was little and fast as hell. But I was worried about Williams, who was older than the rest of us, and especially about myself. At least Williams could shoot. But Battle Stations was all about making it as a team, and if one person didn't make it, it wouldn't look good for the rest of us. I was afraid I'd be holding the rest of them back. I liked all the people on my squad. They'd become my friends over the last two months, like family. Everyone loved Brooks because he was fair, and because he didn't hesitate when you needed help, and because he was always repping Brooklyn, knew all the words to every single Notorious B.I.G. song. Williams, the only white girl in our group, was crazy loud, but funny as hell. Since she worked as one of the ship's masters at arms, she got to come and go without permission, and she sometimes snuck G-mo notes from me, brought me back notes from him. And Jones and I were always joking around. He played basketball, and sometimes we called him Muggsy, because he loved Muggsy Bogues, but also because he was small but could still shoot.

Petty Officer Thompson started calling over groups, ordering them off. When she reached us, she said, "Brooks, get your shipmates and fall out!"

And we broke into a run.

WE RAN TOWARD the drill halls, the old airplane hangars. Inside, we separated into squads as we entered the obstacle course: a maze of compartments, bulkheads, hatches, ladders, artillery, hoses, ropes. Our first event was a rescue mission. One of our shipmates was hurt, and we had to carry them on a stretcher, run the whole obstacle course without dropping them. If we dropped them, or left them, or if they ran out of oxygen or drowned, we'd all die and fail the event.

We picked Jones for the stretcher, since he was the smallest, and we carried him into the first obstacle, a compartment that had lost all power. We found our way in the dark, without tripping or knocking the stretcher into a bulkhead, and did it fast, to avoid running out of oxygen.

Then we carried him through a collapsed bulkhead over a deck, everything covered with debris—sand, gravel, large rocks, dirt, broken equipment. With just a foot and a half of space, we had to drag ourselves across the gravel through the hole in the bulkhead to make it to the next compartment, all without putting down the stretcher. Brooks was the first to go through to the other side, dragging himself across the gravel. He stuck out his arm to hold one end of the stretcher while Williams went through, and then I came through, leaving Joe to hold one end and push the stretcher through the hole just before dragging himself to the other side. After that we ran through what looked like a beach, all gravel, the

sky above lighting up with blinking, blinding lights, and everywhere what sounded like bullets whooshing past us, explosions
somewhere in the distance.

We finally made it to the area where they were keeping the
injured, set the combat stretcher down, and as soon as we did, a
couple of sailors ushered us past the area: "Go, go, go!"

THE NEXT COMPARTMENT was a large storage room, and as soon
as we carried the stretcher across, we were approached by a damage controlman.

"There's been a fire!" he said, and then the sprinklers went off,
water raining on us. We followed him to the front of the room,
where fifty large active missiles were stacked on top of each other.
He told us that we needed to move all the missiles out and into
the next chamber before the room got flooded, being careful not
to drop them, not to bang them against each other and blow ourselves up. And then he left the compartment, climbed into a small
hatch to the next chamber, to watch.

We each picked up a missile and climbed into the hatch and
laid it on the floor in the next compartment. But that was taking
too long, so we made a line and started passing missiles to each
other, until Brooks, at the end, set each one down in the room. The
sprinklers were spraying water, the water rising fast, then faster,
until one of the sprinklers burst.

"Fuck!" I said. "We gotta move faster!"

"If the water comes up to our waist, we have to go," G-mo said.

We seemed to be moving so slow—we'd never be able to move
all those missiles.

G-mo started lifting faster, moving faster. "Let's go!"

I tried to move as fast as G-mo, pass the missile to Williams, but it was too heavy to move that fast. And Williams was struggling, too. It was starting to feel like G-mo and Brooks were carrying us.

Suddenly, another sprinkler burst. The water was rising faster, and we were all soaked, and all our gear was soaked, and everything was getting heavier. I was so tired, sleep-deprived, moving through the water slowly, my seabag so soaked and heavy. I felt like I might collapse.

Suddenly, all the sprinklers burst, and everyone started splashing across the compartment, grabbing whatever they could and running toward the hatch. If the water reached the hatch, it would flood the other chamber. We needed to move.

G-mo and Brooks carried the last of the rounds, sloppily, hurriedly. We climbed through the hatch, passed through to the other side, securing the door behind us.

SINCE OUR SHIP was attacked, flooded, and on fire, it was sinking. We'd spend the next twelve hours moving from one scenario to the other: We had to pull all the ropes and secure them to get the ship underway. We had to carry the wounded to safety. We had to walk through a maze in a part of the ship that had been almost entirely destroyed by fire, feel our way toward the flames in the dark without touching the hot bulkheads, walk through the smoke, hold on to the firehouse as we pointed it at the flames in the dark. We had to abandon ship, jump over the edge into the ocean, and swim to the nearest rescue boat while avoiding shark attacks.

During boot camp, we'd been trained to abandon ship by climbing a fifteen-foot tower and jumping feet first into the deep end of an Olympic-sized pool. In Battle Stations, the tower was twice as high and there were Navy SEALs in the water, pretending to be sharks. If one of them caught you, you were dead.

I was standing at the top of the thirty-five foot tower, after my whole squad had jumped. They were all in the water, swimming among the sharks toward the rescue boat. And I was frozen.

I was supposed to jump. If I didn't, I'd get recycled and my team could get fucked. They might not pass Battle Stations.

I moved closer to the edge, measured the distance between the tower and the rescue boat. I looked straight ahead at the clock on the wall across the pool, but I couldn't make out the time. It was the middle of the night. By tomorrow afternoon, Battle Stations would be over, and most of our two divisions would be handed their official NAVY covers. Those who didn't pass would have to keep wearing their RECRUIT ballcaps and wouldn't be able to graduate. Everyone would know.

I had to jump. I had to go over the edge, land feet-first in the water and swim. But I couldn't get off that tower.

In the pool, one of the Navy SEALs surfaced, started treading water, pulled his snorkel out of his mouth. When he saw me, he called up to me, "Get off that tower, recruit!"

Behind me, another Navy SEAL was climbing the ladder, coming after me.

Everyone in the water was looking up at the tower, at me. In the rescue boat, Brooks and G-mo were already sitting back, watching, Jones and Williams climbing onto the boat.

"You better get off this tower, recruit!" the Navy SEAL behind me said.

There I was, in front of my whole squad, Brooks and Jones and Williams and G-mo, and all the other squads that had already finished the event, drying off by the side of the pool. Everyone watching.

"You better get off this tower before I throw you off!" the Navy SEAL said, and I flinched.

All those times I'd considered jumping off the balcony in Southgate Towers, the eighth floor, the fifteenth floor. That time I jumped off the roof of a two-story building. I'd been so high. But now, on this tower, I was sober, painfully sober, and everyone was looking toward me expecting some kind of bravery. But didn't they know? I wasn't brave. I was a girl who was scared of the dark. A girl so scared of being hurt she would always leave first. I'd never been brave.

And then I heard G-mo's voice. "Come on, Jaqui," he yelled. "Come on!" In front of our entire division, in front all the RDCs, everybody looking from G-mo, to me, realizing that he'd called me by a nickname, not my last name, not even my first name. Nobody in the navy knew me as Jaqui. Only G-mo. He didn't know it yet, and maybe I didn't either, but before the month was up, I would fuck him over. We'd both be out of boot camp, in Tech Core, and he'd be the same G-mo, this earnest, smart, hard-working, funny guy from California who liked lowriders and played spades and wanted kids some day. Exactly who he'd always said he was. He'd come visit me in my barracks and I'd be a completely different person, and he'd look me in the eyes and not recognize me, say, *What happened to you, Jaqui? This isn't you.* He wouldn't know it, but by then I'd already be gone.

I looked down again, then straight ahead. I folded my arms across my chest, feet together, deep breath. I closed my eyes and stepped off the tower, felt the hollow in the pit of my stomach. I had dreamed of this moment so many times, my body falling falling falling through the air, the concrete below, the ocean below, nothing below. Is this what the French woman felt? What if gravity is a lie we've been told? What if I never land? What if I fall forever?

I heard myself scream all the way down. And then I hit water.

I KEPT A journal during all of boot camp, all those weeks, months. I didn't want to forget that there had been a time when I thought I'd end up exactly like my mother, that maybe the navy had saved my life. I didn't want to forget my shipmates after we all graduated, friends that had been like family, after we shipped off to school or our first deployments, after months at sea. Or how on Battle Stations night, all of us sleep-deprived and hungry and nervous, we were jerked from our dreamless sleep by the sound of whooping fire alarms, the recruit division commanders hollering on the 1MC. How we strapped on our battle gear, Kevlar helmets, gas masks, canteens, ran across the base to the USS Marlinspike, a guided-missile destroyer, and for an entire night we put out fires, emptied flooding compartments of their heavy artillery, dragged ourselves across gravel and underneath barbed wire in the dark, carrying our wounded shipmate on a combat stretcher, playing at war. How on that final run, weighed down by all our gear, carrying each other, crying, the pride I felt when I crossed that finish line. How until that moment, I didn't know I could be that strong, didn't really believe I could be saved.

. . .

AFTER BATTLE STATIONS, late one night, Eliza and I were assigned to do the laundry for our entire division during watch. It was the first time we had a real conversation, after weeks of just watching each other, and sitting across from each other, and almost smiling at each other when we passed each other in the USS Carr, or in the classroom, or the galley.

That night, we loaded the washers, added the soap, and then sat on the laundry room floor, listening to Dru Hill on her Discman, sharing her headphones, the two of us singing "We're Not Making Love No More." After Battle Stations, everything was less tense, and the RDCs barely came up to check on us while everybody was sleeping. So we could just hang out. We folded laundry, told each other stories. She told me about her daughter, who was at home with her ex-husband.

"Do you miss her?" I asked.

"It's hard," she said. "But I'm doing all this for her. She understands."

I was surprised she had a daughter, an ex-husband, an entire life that included a family. She was butch, muscular, with a husky voice, and she was comfortable in her own body. She was older than me, and it seemed she knew exactly who she was. How freely she just took my hand and sang to me and asked whatever she wanted to know. How easily she could break my heart. Even in her NAVY T-shirt and ridiculous gym shorts she was sexy. I couldn't picture her with a man. As hard as I tried, I could only picture her with *me*.

I didn't tell her about Cheito.

We sat there for a while, listening to music and singing, and when she kissed me, I kissed her back. I wanted to put my hands all over her, but didn't know how. I licked the soft tendons of her neck, her shoulder blades, the small of her back, all sweat and salt. There was no art to what we did—when she fucked me, it was fast, the two of us watching the laundry room doors, exasperated, like we were grasping at something, the clock on the wall ticking like it was set to detonate.

As soon as it was over, I was already thinking in the past tense. As much as I'd dreamed of this moment, and even though for the first time in my life I finally felt like myself, like the woman I was supposed to be, and even though I knew I could've loved her, the truth is I never intended to love her in the real world. That's who I was. A girl who ran.

MONTHS AFTER BOOT camp, after I'd moved on to electronics school, walking down the corridors in the Tech Core school build-ing, I heard a couple sailors whispering and laughing and calling out, *Hey, don't ask, don't tell!*

I kept walking, not really paying attention, until I heard it again, *Don't ask, don't tell!*

I turned around, and saw the two of them laughing, covering their mouths, and realized that I was the only other person in the hallway. They were talking to *me*, laughing at *me*.

Every day after that, walking past the groups of mostly guys huddled in the hallways, I had to hear and not hear and keep walk-ing as they said it again and again and again, *Don't ask, don't tell. Hey, don't ask, don't tell.* Until "Don't Ask, Don't Tell" became my nickname.

A few days later, as we lined up in formation outside the bar-racks, one of my boot camp shipmates came up to me. Jones. He stood right next to me, smiling.

"What's up?" I said.

He didn't reply, just smiled. Like he knew something I didn't know.

Behind him, another sailor lined up. "Hey, Díaz, I heard you like to eat pussy," he said, loud enough so that our whole group heard. Everybody laughed.

Jones was still smiling, and I realized, in on the joke.

I didn't say anything. I turned and faced forward, kept my military bearing, face expressionless, heart pounding in my chest.

He kept talking. "Everybody knows. Everybody's talking about it. Somebody, I can't say who, even made up a song about you."

For weeks afterward, on the street, in the barracks' corridors, as I mopped the floors on the quarterdeck while on duty, guys would rap as they walked behind me, would break into spontaneous rhyming the second I stepped into a room. Later, after I'd gotten kicked out of Tech Core, after a long period of unauthorized absences, after I'd gone AWOL and become a military deserter, after turning myself in, standing in my old barracks in front of a petty officer who would look at me with disgust and call me "coward" and "traitor," words that would stick to me, that would define how I saw myself for years, after everyone had heard I was back, after another petty officer cornered me in the hallway, ordered me to stand at attention, screamed in my face, tiny splatters of his spit landing on my cheek, and after a seaman recruit, two ranks below me, came up to me in the chow line, asked, *What are you doing breathing my air, Díaz? What the hell are you doing in my navy?* it would still be Jones I thought of. I'd see the five of us, our squad carrying him in the combat stretcher, our squad carrying each other during that last run, after twelve hours, that final mile,

Brooks pulling Williams' wet seabag off her shoulders, strapping it on himself. G-mo behind me, not letting me slow down. Jones next to me, when I knew he could run faster, much faster, saying, *You better keep pounding that pavement, Díaz, you better keep pushing.*

I had loved boot camp, the navy. It was in the navy where I'd been able to imagine living past eighteen, where I'd finally felt like I mattered. But I would eventually run.

Secrets

and I am going to keep telling this
if it kills me
—AUDRE LORDE, "For the Record"

It's more than a year after you get out of the navy, after you've
returned to Miami Beach. You're walking south on Biscayne
Boulevard, where it's mostly drug dealers, sex workers strolling
the streets at dawn, grimy motels. The Stardust, the Vagabond,
the Shalimar. Iconic Miami. The sun is almost up and you've been
walking for what seems like hours. Just walking, hoping no one
will notice your bare feet. You have one sandal. You hold it with
both hands, press it tight against your body, cradle it like a baby.
You bought the pair while shopping on Lincoln Road with your
best friend. They were expensive, but you were getting ready for
her twenty-first birthday party, and you figured you'd get to wear
them for your own twenty-first birthday party, in a few months.
You only wore them once. And now you only have one.

You walk faster, and every time a car passes, you turn your
face, flip your curls to cover it. You hope no one you know will
recognize you if they drive by on their way to work or school.
When a man on a bike passes, you pull up the torn strap of your

dress, try to readjust it, put it back in place as if it could somehow reattach itself. As if you could make yourself presentable. Your feet are bloody, and every step is a spike, piercing, and just when you think you can't walk anymore, you see a payphone. You cross the street to get to it. Pick it up. But you have no money. All you have is the sandal. You dial 0, call your little sister collect. Please pick up. There's a pause. You're holding your breath.

Then a voice. Hello? Your sister. And you can breathe again.

IN FOURTH GRADE, Ida M. Fisher Elementary, our whole class sitting in the bleachers during PE, my friend Beba came up to me. "You have to hear this," she said, her voice shaky, breathless.

Yvonne, who we weren't really close to, was with her. Yvonne, with red hair that fell down her back and shoulders, a mass of freckles on her cheeks and nose.

"Come on," Beba said to us, and we moved over to one corner of the bleachers, where no one would hear our conversation. The rest of our class, playing "Around the World," waited for their turn at the basketball. Beba and I listened as Yvonne described how her stepfather came into her room at night, how he took off her clothes and felt her naked body under the covers. How sometimes he took off his own clothes, made her touch him.

"Why don't you tell someone?" I asked. It was my first instinct. To tell.

"I told my mom," Yvonne said. "But she didn't believe me."

"What do you mean she didn't believe you?" Beba asked. She was angry, furious. It didn't make any sense. "Let's tell Ms. Carey. She'll know what to do."

But Yvonne didn't want us to tell. She shook her head. She searched our faces for something, I didn't know what. She begged us, with tears in her eyes, to keep her secret. "Please," she said.

And we did.

YEARS LATER, AT twenty-two, long after I'd forgotten about Yvonne, on a beach road trip from Miami to Maine with some friends, we'd stop at a diner in Myrtle Beach, South Carolina for breakfast. We'd talk about our trip, where we were heading next, the Outer Banks, Virginia Beach, the Wildwoods. We'd ask the waiter about the coastal towns in the area, where to get the best ice cream, the best pizza. Where to go dancing. We were from Miami Beach, we said.

We were leaving, and one of my friends headed to the register to pay the bill, the rest of us headed outside, when I saw her. She was wearing a waitress uniform. Black pants, white shirt, black apron. She was placing drinks on a table. As soon as I saw her, the memory came back to me: the three of us sitting on those bleachers at Fisher, that gym where we played basketball and square-danced awkwardly with greasy-faced boys. Yvonne, Beba, and I. Just girls.

My friends left the diner, but I stood there watching her, looking for a name tag, something to tell me that it was really her. That somehow she'd turned out fine. There was no name tag, nothing to confirm that she'd made it. But I knew it was her.

I don't think she saw me. Or if she did, I like to think that she didn't recognize me. I wanted to go up to her, say something. I thought about the three of us in the fourth grade that day, her face as she told us about her stepfather, as she asked us to keep her secret. Do this for me, she'd said. Do this one thing.

I'd kept her secret. All those years, I kept it. You could argue that I was a child, that I didn't know any better, that it was what she wanted. But I didn't do it for her. The truth is I did it for me. I kept it because I didn't want to get involved, because the thought of putting the words together to recreate what Yvonne said had seemed like too much to bear. It had been easier not to tell.

I didn't say hello that morning in the restaurant. I didn't say anything. I left, without a word.

Her name, as you probably already guessed, was not Yvonne.

YOUR SISTER DRIVES you to Mount Sinai Hospital. You don't remember the drive there, but when you look up, you are there. She parks the car in the ambulance lane and the two of you get out. You walk into the emergency room, where a nurse hands you a clipboard. You don't write your name on it. Instead, you look around the sitting area at all the people, waiting. Some of the faces look back at you. You look at your bare feet, bloody, then back at the nurse. You have to wait. Like everybody else.

You leave the clipboard on the counter, walk out of the emergency room, ignoring your sister's pleas as you head back to the car. In the backseat, you wait for her to start the engine.

You have to let me help you, she says. She's only sixteen, but she's so grown up. She looks like you, but different, so much more like herself. She has dyed blue streaks into her long curls. She dresses to match her mood, faded punk-rock band T-shirts, handmade leather bracelets, Chuck Taylors in every color. You are twenty, but feel like a child, and you'd never wear Chucks. Instead, you splurge on expensive midi dresses and uncomfortable strappy heels that cut into your toes, or basketball jerseys with Jordans that run you almost a week's paycheck.

I don't know how, you want to tell her. There is so much you want to say, so much you don't.

I MET BEBA when I was nine, in fourth grade. I'd just been transferred into her class, and my new teacher, Ms. Carey, yelled across the room for me to sit next to Beba. I did as she said, put down my backpack, looking around for familiar faces. It was three weeks into the school year and I'd just been yanked from my small ESOL class, my fourth-grade friends, and dropped off in this enormous classroom with at least thirty strangers who all spoke perfect English and this screaming lady who was supposed to be my teacher.

"We're going to art in five minutes," Beba said. She was drawing on a manila folder, and she didn't take her eyes off of it, not even when she spoke to me.

"What's your name?" I asked.

"Beba," she said. Her pencil raced across the folder's surface. Horses, so many horses, then a rabbit, a squirrel, a few birds, some grass, a tree. With a single stroke of her pencil, faster than I could take a breath, she signed her name on the bottom, then dated it.

"What's *your* name?" she asked.

"Jaquira," I said.

She looked up, puzzled. "How do you spell that?"

I spelled it for her, and she wrote it on the folder's upper right corner, handed it to me.

. . .

YOU DON'T REMEMBER the drive to your apartment either. But you don't take the elevator. You run up the stairs until you get to the sixth floor, stop in front of your door when you realize you don't have your keys. You wait for your sister to open the door for you. When she opens it, you realize you are still holding the sandal. You walk into your studio apartment, open the closet. You want to put the sandal on the floor, imagine that the other one will be there, what it would mean if that were true.

You consider throwing it away, but they are brand new. You refuse to think of them as a single thing. They are a pair.

You go into your bathroom, open the hamper, stuff it inside, under all the clothes. At the very bottom. Later, when you are sorting clothes, you will find it and think of how useless the one sandal is. Brand new, but useless.

There's a knock on your door. You think people wouldn't knock if they knew what their knocking did to you. Your sister opens. Come in, she says.

There's a cop in your apartment. She wants to know what happened.

I didn't call you here, you say.

I called her, your sister says.

BEBA AND I sat together in art class while Ms. McKinney explained our assignment. She had placed pictures of Ocean Drive all around the room, several of them at our table. We were supposed to create imitations of one of the Art Deco hotels, first using pencils on poster board, then using colored pencils, pastels, crayons, or water colors to fill them in. I sat with a blue pencil in my hand, watched Beba as she drew an exact replica of the picture Ms. McKinney had set at our table. It took her all of ten minutes to sketch and paint the picture, write her name on it and walk it over to Ms. McKinney.

When she returned to our table, Beba noticed my poster board was blank. I was sitting there awkwardly, everyone ignoring me, the new girl.

Beba smiled. "Just draw it!" she said.

But I couldn't *just draw* anything.

"Draw a big square," she said.

I hesitated, but I drew a square.

"Now draw small squares for windows," she said, pointing to where windows should go, "here, here, here, and here."

I drew small squares.

We continued this way, Beba guiding me through the entire picture until I had an actual building with windows and doors, with palm trees on the side, with a sidewalk, and cars parked out front. It looked like something someone else had drawn. Afterward, she showed me how to draw horses.

THEY WANT YOU to go with them. It's not like Mount Sinai, they say. You won't have to wait. I will be with you the entire time, someone says, but you don't know if it's your sister, or the cop. Either way, it doesn't matter. You're not looking at them. You're not paying attention. You are looking at yourself now. You are bloody. No, you are *bleeding*. There is blood running down between your legs. You want to wipe it, wash it off, but you're afraid to learn where the blood is coming from. You know, but you don't. You think of that first time, with all its violence, all that blood, and how you never told a single person. You agree to go with them, only because you don't want to see it. You want them to do it. You want them to be the ones to wash it off.

WHEN WE WERE both ten, Beba and I were shooting hoops in Flamingo Park with Frank and Jorge, some kids from the neighborhood. After Beba and I fought over the ball and pushed each other around, I walked off the court and headed toward the girls' bathroom. I was bending over the water fountain when I felt someone grab me from behind. *What the hell?* I thought. I turned around, thinking it was Beba, and I swung my arm at her. We were always fighting and making up, so I didn't swing too hard, since I was just annoyed. But when I turned around, it wasn't Beba.

It was a man. He was pulling me toward the boys' bathroom. I was almost inside when I realized what was happening. He was attacking me, trying to take me away, and I didn't understand why. I pushed him as hard as I could, trying to fight him off. I put one hand out in front of me, pushed against his face, and I felt his mouth against the palm of my hand, his lips, his teeth.

I pulled my hand back when I felt those teeth, that sticky mouth, the wetness there, pushed against his chest. And then, I could smell him. He smelled like garbage. But it wasn't just him— the smell was all over me. *He* was all over me. He was trying to pull me into the boys' bathroom again, and for a while time seemed to slow down and I kept thinking, *Not the boys' bathroom*, again and again, *Not the boys' bathroom*, until I thought to scream, until I had no air left in my lungs and I didn't know if anyone could hear me. I tried to run, but he had me. I didn't know where he was holding me, my arms or my torso, only that I couldn't pull away. I kicked, and kicked, and kicked, but I didn't hit anything, and then I started swinging my arms, trying to hit him in the face, the shoulders, anywhere, and when he finally let me go, I realized that Beba was hitting him, too, and Frank and Jorge, the four of us, as I tried to catch my breath, the four of us punching and kicking and slapping, and I flung my whole body at him, hands, feet, knees, until I was almost flying, and then he was running running running, and we ran, too, picking up rocks in our path, until I pegged him square in the back, and he raised his shoulders in pain but kept running, and we chased him, throwing our rocks, out for revenge, out for blood, but lost track of him in the small residential blocks between Flamingo Park and Alton Road.

Beba wanted to tell.

She thought we should go to the cops, her mother, her aunts. But I was afraid Papi and Abuela wouldn't let me go out by myself anymore if they found out. I preferred the secret. Besides, I told Beba, nothing happened.

The next day at school, Beba passed me a sheet of paper with some of her drawings on it. A comic strip. The four of us playing basketball. Me, with springy curls and a thought bubble over my head that said, "Peace, love, and hair grease," walking away from the courts. The man grabbing me. Beba, Frank, and Jorge running toward us. Then all of us stomping him, a dust cloud rising between us. And after all the pictures, she wrote, "We kicked his ass!"

Today, I remember how hard I fought to stay out of the boys' bathroom, how maybe it was that part, how forbidden the place had seemed, that scared me the most, and I wondered if I would've fought as hard if it had been the girls' bathroom.

YOUR MEMORIES OF the clinic aren't complete. You remember a crime scene technician rubbing cotton swabs along the inside of your fingernails, wiping off the blood along the three nails you broke off, taking pictures of your hand. Sometime during all this, your dress and your bra are stuffed in a paper bag, labeled, taken away. Your sister helps you into a sweatshirt, which you put over the hospital gown. You still can't take a shower.

They keep asking about your panties. Somewhere in that alley, that's all you can say. You remember to memorize this phrase, *Somewhere in that alley*, because every question is asked three, four, ten times. When they keep asking, you stop talking. You decide to look straight at the wall. Maybe if they think you're crazy, they'll stop asking questions.

Your sister gets upset. She already told you that. Didn't you hear?

You lift up the back of your sweatshirt so the woman with the camera can take pictures of the bruises and cuts on your back. You don't remember her asking you to do that. She asks to take pictures of your face. You refuse. She tries to explain. If they catch the guy, they need to have pictures of the bruises and cuts to show the extent of the damage. But you don't want any evidence, no pictures to prove that you are damaged. That's not what she meant, she reassures you. She's so, so sorry.

After you are showered, dressed, when you think the looks and the questions are over, they sit you at a table. You're going to speak to a detective.

When the detective arrives, she sits across from you. Tell me what happened, she says.

I already told the other police officer, you say.

I know, but I need you to tell it to *me*. She doesn't ask what you want. Doesn't ask what you need. You refuse to tell the story one more time.

She needs to know the truth, she says, she needs the whole story. Were you drinking? Were you using drugs? She begins to explain how your words could put an innocent person behind bars, how you could ruin someone's life. This is not a game, she says. This is serious. And then, finally, you understand.

You hide your face in your hands. You just want to go home, you tell her, but she keeps talking, which makes you think maybe you didn't really say it.

You get up, leave her sitting there. You have nothing else to say.

THE SUMMER BEFORE I started middle school, Alaina and I stayed with Mami for a few weeks. I kept bouncing between Mami's and Papi's apartments, running from one place to the other, or just plain running away. On July 4, Alaina and I sat outside watching fireworks after a long afternoon of running around the neighborhood with the other kids. We were sitting on the curb drinking Capri Suns. I was trying to make mine last—we usually couldn't afford to spring for luxuries like Capri Sun or Coca-Cola, and we had to settle for the generic orange drink or grape drink you could buy at the corner bodega for a dollar a gallon.

When one of Alaina's second-grade classmates, who lived in our neighborhood, walked over, she introduced us. "Hi, Barbarito! This is my big sister," she said, smiling. He probably already knew who I was, since Alaina was a miniature me.

"Hey," he said, and sat with us on the curb.

We watched the fireworks for a while, and when it got darker, after we'd flung our juice pouches into the street and most of the neighborhood kids had been called home by their parents, Alaina went inside. I stayed behind a few more minutes, until Barbarito said he had to go. We both got up, and I headed toward our building, and he started walking up the block toward his. Suddenly, he turned around and ran to me and grabbed both of my breasts as if it was a normal thing. I'd just turned twelve, but I was already wearing a B-cup. I pushed him away, but he came back at me, wrapped his arms around me from behind, and stuck his hand down my shorts. I tried to elbow him, tried to peel him off me, but he was behind me, and was much shorter and faster. I realized that for a moment this little kid, who was probably only eight or nine years old, was in complete control. I couldn't get him off of me. It was only when *he* decided that it would be over. Then, suddenly, he just let me go.

I stood there in shock, watched him walk away, asking myself, *What just happened?*

Then, as if to show me that he was still in control, he stopped, smiled at me. "Byyyye!" he said.

I crossed my arms, hugging myself, feeling like my body had betrayed me, my breasts inviting violence. Even though I'd been attacked by the homeless man in the park nearly two years before, when I was younger, smaller, it was this little kid, one of my little sister's classmates, someone I could probably beat within a minute of his life, who'd made me feel powerless.

I never told Alaina. I never told anybody. But the next day, Alaina and I went back to Papi's place.

You make your sister drive you back to your apartment. She tries to convince you to go forward with it. She tries, in her best tone, to explain that if you don't, you will regret it for the rest of your life. In front of your door, she asks if you want company. She can sleep over. You tell her you want to be alone.

She stays anyway, sits in bed with you while you pretend to sleep. You get up at three in the morning, pick up the phone, dial your ex-husband in Jacksonville, North Carolina. By this time next week, your apartment will be packed up, stored, and you will be in another state.

The year I'm in boot camp, lying awake in my rack night after night, writing letters home, standing at the top of the tower looking at the water below, Beba is fighting with her boyfriend. I haven't spoken to her in about four years, and as I'm marching next to G-mo and practicing flag drills and spit-shining my boondockers, I don't think of Beba once. And she probably doesn't think of me.

That year, as I'm passing Battle Stations, Beba is breaking up with her boyfriend. After that last argument, in the middle of the night, she leaves her boyfriend's house, headed to a friend's place. As she's walking down Biscayne Boulevard, a cab driver is getting robbed, knife at his throat. He can't move, watches the ceiling while the guy in the back takes his wallet, his watch. The attacker cuts him, and the cab driver clutches his chest, his arm, his eyes shut tight, his whole body rigid, and steps on the gas pedal.

As Beba crosses the street, she is struck, the taxi dragging her three, four, five blocks.

The taxi crashes into a house on a side street, comes to a stop. The police are called, the taxi driver rushed to the hospital, the car taken away. The attacker is long gone. The scene is cleared.

At the hospital, the cab driver tells them the story. He was robbed, thinks he hit someone, but isn't sure.

There was no victim at the scene, the officer tells him. No one. You got lucky.

Thank you, the cab driver says, nodding, relieved. Thank you.

A few blocks from the accident, in a small house in the neighborhood, Marcus Jess can't sleep. His dog won't stop barking. He steps out on the front porch, but the night is dark. He can't see anything. He gets back inside, shuts the door behind him. Dog still won't stop barking.

A few hours later, when the dog finally stops barking, Marcus Jess has to get up for work. He takes the dog for a walk. As they cross, they reach the fence where the dog usually does his business, Marcus Jess sees a body. A teenage girl. Again, the cops are called. The scene is cleared.

Marcus Jess doesn't make it to work that day. His dog was barking all night, he tells the cops. All night.

There's nothing you could've done, one police officer says.

Thank you, Marcus Jess says. Thank you.

That year, as a drug war is sweeping the city of Miami, the worst South Florida has seen in decades, with multiple drive-by shootings, as police raid homes and confiscate pistols, knives, two hand grenades, as the *Miami Herald* is reporting armed robberies and three different deadly gang-related shootings on the same day, as a fifteen-year-old boy is shot down in front of his house, Miami

Police Lieutenant Bill Schwartz is quoted in several South Florida newspapers: "Our homicide rate is down."

YOU WILL COME back to Miami eventually, after six months in North Carolina.

You will know that moving to Jacksonville was a mistake.

It will not be the only thing you'll regret.

It will be a long time before you buy another pair of strappy sandals.

But you will.

Mother, Mercy

The summer of the Casey Anthony trial, seven years after I've left Miami for college, while news stations across the country are reporting on the Florida woman accused of murdering her two-year-old daughter, my grandma Mercy dies. I'm living in central Florida and haven't seen Mercy or my mother in the seven years since I left. Only once in all that time has Mercy called to see how I was doing. That was three weeks ago. She was sixty-nine years old.

They find five empty bottles of sleeping pills on the floor next to Mercy's bed. They find a gift she left for my little cousin Lia: a necklace with an angel pendant. They find a note.

It's my cousin Junito who calls with the news.

I ask if my mother knows yet.

"No one's heard from her all day," Junito says.

My mother hardly ever has a working phone. She still lives in a tiny efficiency in Miami Beach—a city she hasn't left since we moved from Puerto Rico in 1987—a few blocks from Mercy. Anthony is still a waiter in the same tourist trap restaurant he started working in when he was eighteen, so he's in Miami Beach every day, and sometimes takes care of her, as much as you can take care of someone like my mother.

For many years, Mami and Mercy, both addicts, kept each other company. Mercy took pills mostly: Xanax, Ativan, Oxy. My mother prefers crack, cocaine, meth. Both have been prescribed powerful antipsychotic medications for schizophrenia. Before Mercy died, they saw each other every day. They were each other's refuge, enabling each other, bailing each other out, sometimes living on the streets together. Loving and hating each other the way addicts do.

I ask Junito what the suicide note says, not sure if I'm ready to hear the answer.

He exhales loudly. "You don't want to know."

I ask about our aunts in Virginia and Puerto Rico—do they know?

"You're the first person I called," he says, and then he starts sobbing. He says he always imagined that when Mercy died he wouldn't care, wouldn't cry, wouldn't feel a thing.

"I'm sorry," I say, as if she weren't my grandmother, too. As if this were something that happened to him, not us, not *me*. Later, I will call my aunts in Virginia, and they will wail. I will listen to their ragged breathing and imagine what the news will do to my mother. "I'm sorry," I will say. "I'm so, so sorry."

I RAN AWAY from Miami seven years before Mercy's death. Cheito and I had gotten back together and bought a townhouse after I left the military. I'd taken night classes at Miami Dade Community College, and then applied for a transfer to the University of Central Florida. I wanted to get out of Miami, wanted to get away from my mother, from Mercy.

When I got the acceptance, I decided to go. I didn't have a conversation with Cheito about it—we weren't happy, and I'd decided months before that I would leave him. It seemed easier to just go, so I packed whatever clothes and shoes I could fit into my car and drove north, left him with the mortgage, the car payments, the dogs. I stayed with family for a couple of weeks until I found a job and an apartment.

On the day of my college orientation at UCF, after declaring English as my major, I was given an appointment to meet with the English department for an advising session with a group of about eight other transfer students. We were handed forms to fill out, a list of courses and their prerequisites, requirements, electives.

We all sat at a small table with our paperwork. While all the other students filled out their forms, I looked at the concentrations: Literature, Technical Communication, Creative Writing. I looked over at the guy sitting next to me. He'd checked Literature. The woman next to him. Literature. The woman to my right. Literature. A guy across from me. Technical Communication. Not one person had checked Creative Writing. Maybe they knew something I didn't, I thought. Did writers even make money?

As we waited on the advisor, I tapped the paper in front of me. I considered my life. I'd come all this way. I'd left my husband, my house, my job. My *dogs*. I'd left my whole life. I looked around the table one more time. What the fuck was "Technical Communication" anyway?

I put an X next to Creative Writing. And then circled it, twice, just to make sure there was no confusion. My whole life, I'd always known. But the x, the two circles, they made it feel real. Now other people would know, too. And I would do whatever I had to do, but I would be a writer.

As I walked to my car that afternoon, for the first time in my life, I actually felt like a woman, not a girl. Months after my college orientation, when it was clear that I wouldn't go back, Cheito packed up our place in Miami and followed me to Orlando.

As I GET off the phone with Junito, I think maybe I should be crying, but I'm not. I want to ask Cheito if it's normal that I'm not crying. He knows me better than anyone. Our two boxers, Taína and Chapo, hop onto the love seat with me. Taína puts her head on my lap, and Chapo licks my face. They do this when I'm sad, so I know I must be sad.

On TV, the Casey Anthony murder trial is on without any sound. I turn the volume up. Casey Anthony's mother is on the stand, and I think, *That poor woman. Oh God, that poor woman.*

My grandmother is dead, and I'm feeling sorry for a murder suspect's mother.

Three weeks ago, Mercy called me unexpectedly. She was living with Tanisha, her youngest. Mami was at the house, too, but it was Mercy who'd dialed my number. She wanted to see how I was, she said. She asked how many years Cheito and I had been together.

"Too many," I said, and we both laughed.

We talked about the Casey Anthony trial.

"What kind of woman loses a baby and never calls the police?" she asked.

"A guilty one."

We talked about the Baby Lollipops murder case. I was in the middle of writing about the toddler, about his mother—had been

for months. I'd spent hours poring over newspaper articles and
court documents the night before. Reading witness testimony I
hadn't seen before had left me unable to sleep. I'd been battling
insomnia my whole life, but lately, it had gotten worse.

I asked if she remembered the baby boy whose body had been
dumped beneath some bushes in Miami Beach when I was a girl.

"I remember," she said. "It was his mother and her lesbian lover
who killed him."

I waited for Mercy to say more, braced myself for some hateful homophobic rant. More than ten years earlier, after Alaina had
come out, my mother had called me to ask if it was true. The whole
time I'd heard Mercy yelling in the background about how my sister
was dead to her, how she didn't want any fucking patas in her family.

"Put her on the phone," I'd told my mother, coming to Alaina's
defense, but Mercy wouldn't take the receiver. I'd finally said, "Tell
that bitch she can go fuck herself!"

But instead of unleashing hateful slurs about Ana María
Cardona, Mercy took a deep breath and said, "That was, like,
twenty years ago," her voice heavy, exhausted. I assumed it was all
the pills she took: antipsychotics, antidepressants, anxiety pills.

Sitting on the couch now, I wonder: Was she high during that
conversation? Was it the pills that made her call me, or was it
something else?

I call Alaina and give her the news. She is silent for a long
pause, and then she says, "Wow."

I give her all the details Junito gave me, and ask if she's coming
for the funeral, even though I know she can't. Alaina left Miami
Beach for good as soon as she turned eighteen—left for college and
never looked back. She lives in Spain, where she's an artist and

social justice activist, and doesn't make a lot of money. Whenever she gets a little extra cash, she uses it to rescue stray dogs. But even if she could afford it, she probably wouldn't come anyway. I don't blame her. I don't know if I'll make it either.

This is not how it feels to lose a grandmother. When Abuela, my real grandmother, died two years ago, I felt a deep, insurmountable grief, like I was completely lost. It was because of her that Mercy didn't destroy my sense of self-worth. Abuela, who had raised us to love ourselves, our blackness, who when Alaina came out, looked her in the eye and said, "I love you just the way you are. I just want you to be happy." But this? I don't know what this is. What does it mean to lose someone who hates everything you are, hates the people you love?

On the TV, Casey Anthony's mother describes how her granddaughter had been missing for a month before she called the police herself, how she hadn't known Caley was missing until that very moment. The newscasters play sections of the grandmother's 911 calls over and over again. They speculate about what kind of mother goes shopping and partying and drinking, what kind of mother gets tattooed when her daughter has just died tragically. They call her "Tot Mom." Tot Mom. It's fucking absurd.

Abruptly, I jump up off the love seat, frightening Taína and Chapo, and run to our bathroom, where Cheito is in the shower. They run after me, wagging their nubs as I sit on top of the toilet and stare at the waffle-weave shower curtain. It all seems so pointless now: this overpriced shower curtain from Pottery Barn, our oversized four-bedroom house, the flat-screen TVs, the expensive furniture, the two-car garage, the two cars, the motorcycle. We'd bought this house five years ago, a debt we couldn't afford even with our two salaries. Here I am living in this house with more rooms than I even know what to do with, and my mother is living on the streets half the time and doesn't even have a phone.

"My grandmother is dead," I say to Cheito through the curtain.

He doesn't say anything, and I realize it's probably because he thinks I'm talking about Abuela. Every time in the past two years I've said those words to him—*My grandmother is dead*—it's been the beginning of a new wave of grief, followed by days in bed, unable to eat or sleep, unable to have a conversation. How long has it been since I've referred to Mercy as *my grandmother*? How long has it been since I even mentioned her?

"I mean Mercy," I say. "She took a bunch of pills."

MERCY HAD BECOME a mother at fifteen, a grandmother at thirty-two. In her youth, she was known for brawling in the street with other women, with grown men. She never, ever backed down from a fight, no matter who threatened her. Once, Alaina and I watched her attack a neighbor outside a drugstore, knocked her down and started kicking her, because the woman had called Mercy crazy. Later, we found out that the woman was dating Papi.

Mercy was fierce and unforgiving, had a list of every person who'd ever wronged her, loved to tell stories of how she'd gotten people back. The woman who'd cut in front of her in line at the supermarket? Mercy had purposely bumped into her and told her to fuck off. The guy on a bike who'd looked at her wrong? She'd slashed his tires later. The boy who'd beaten up one of her daughters? The next morning she'd gone to his sister's job and slapped her, told her it was a message for her brother, and that the next time she would cut up his face with a razorblade.

The first time Papi left Mami, Mercy was livid. The only reason a man leaves the mother of his children is another woman, she said. Together she and my mother concocted a plan to get him back: I was supposed to listen to all of Papi's phone calls and find out the woman's name. Then they'd scare her into staying away from him, drag her out of her house and kick her ass in the street. Mercy would use her straight razor and carve my mother's initials into the woman's face.

But instead of spying on my father, I told him about their plan. When she found out, Mercy called me a chota, said I was dead to her for helping my father cheat on my own mother, and if she couldn't find out who the woman was, my father would do. She would give him gills, like a fish.

My uncle Junior, Titi Xiomara's husband, was also on Mercy's list. Junior and Xiomara had fallen in love when they were teenagers, then had two boys, Junito and Angel. They loved their boys—and each other—fiercely. Alaina and I had grown up with Junito and Angel. They were like our brothers. When we lived with Mami, Xiomara often came to check on us, brought us food. Sometimes Xiomara and Junior rescued us, took us to their house when Mami was having one of her breakdowns. Junior had rescued Mercy, too. Once, he beat up a guy who'd felt her up at a party, tried to assault her. But still, when Junior pissed her off, Mercy would threaten him like anybody else.

Like my father, Junior was black, so Mercy had been against their marriage from the beginning, and even in front of Junito and Angel, she would remind them: how Xiomara came from a white family, how Mercy's father was a blue-eyed blond, how Junior's family were a bunch of negros. Mercy claimed that Junior's mother was a witch who used brujos against her daughter, that she had left a voodoo hex outside Xiomara's door one afternoon: a green bell pepper used as a pincushion, with a long, X-shaped needle inside. *X for Xiomara.*

Once, after a telephone argument with Junior, Mercy finally decided to follow through on her threats. Xiomara and the kids had spent an afternoon at Mercy's house. Junior went to pick them up, strapped the kids into their car seats as Xiomara got in the passenger seat. Then, right there in her neighborhood, in the middle of the moonlit sidewalk, people walking their dogs and riding their bikes and returning home from the grocery store, as Junior closed Xiomara's passenger door, Mercy pulled out a box cutter and sliced his face.

He ended up in the hospital, had to get about twelve stitches that left him with a v-shaped scar above his eyebrow.

Years later, when I was thirteen, after getting into a nasty fight with an ex-boyfriend, I threatened to carve my initials into his face.

GROWING UP, I thought my aunts in Virginia and Puerto Rico were lucky. Their mothers, the women who'd actually raised them, were loving and self-sacrificing. Abuela was the same way for me, even if I hadn't always gotten to live with her. Abuela died the week of Mother's Day. Ever since, I've thought of myself as motherless.

Every Mother's Day, I spend hours at the drug store looking at cards. I buy one and leave it sitting out for weeks, then store it in a shoebox in my closet. This year's card is still on the kitchen counter, next to the glass bowl where we keep our car keys. Staring at it, I wonder what will happen to my mother now that Mercy's gone. Who will keep her company? Who will make her morning coffee? Who will be there late at night when she comes home wasted?

All these years, I've thought of myself as a runaway, having left Miami Beach to be as far away from my mother and Mercy, and their drama, as possible. Before I left Miami, my mother had been living on the streets. She'd gotten arrested a few times, and I'd wanted to send her to a rehab facility in Virginia, where my aunts could check in on her once in a while. It was a place that specialized in treating women addicts who also suffered from mental illnesses, a place that could help her get her life together. But when Mercy found out I intended to get a court order to send my mother away, she told Mami I was going to lock her up in a mental hospital. Every day for a week my mother called, threatening me. I had been a mistake, she said, a failed abortion. Who the fuck did I think I was? Shortly after that, I left.

Since then, I'd gone to college, then graduate school. I had been a teacher, worked as a financial aid counselor, edited a magazine. Alaina and I had taken care of Abuela. We both had worked our asses off to have the kind of lives we wanted. But most importantly, we had separated ourselves from Mercy, and from Mami.

But now, as soon as I hear the news, Mercy's death becomes like a release, and it arrives like a flood, the desire to see my mother.

I tell Cheito I need to see her, to make sure she's okay. We pack our bags, hustle the two dogs into the car, and make the 220-mile drive south to Miami Beach. I listen to the radio and stare out the window while Cheito drives.

IN CLEWISTON, WE stop at a burger joint to use the bathroom. I wash my face in the sink and study myself in the mirror, my eyes rimmed with red, my lips chapped, face pale.

A year ago, during a trip to Washington, DC, I stopped by my titi Iris's house. I hadn't seen her since I was a fifteen-year-old juvenile delinquent, my hair in cornrows, wearing dark brown lip liner and over-plucked eyebrows, a nose ring and gold door-knockers and sixteen other piercings. When I'd come to her house this time, with no piercings and very little makeup, she took my face in her hands.

"My God, Jaqui," she said. "You look just like your mother."

I didn't believe her, but when I got home a few days later, I searched through old photo albums and found a picture of my mother at twenty-one, her blond hair cut in a short bob, and for the first time in my life I realized that I had her round face, her cheeks, her smile.

Now, staring at myself in the bathroom mirror, I don't see any resemblance.

Back on the road, my cellphone won't stop ringing. Junito calls. Angel calls. Papi calls. Alaina. Titi Xiomara.

Xiomara is in Mercy's apartment, says the paramedics came and went, and now the cops are there. People keep walking in and out of the bedroom while the body is just lying there, she says. It's been hours. She still can't find my mother.

I turn off my phone. From the driver's seat Cheito takes my hand. I'm glad he's not the type of man who says shit like, "She's in a better place," or, "You have to remember the good times." But in the car, I find myself doing exactly that—trying to remember something good about Mercy.

There is this: she told me stories. When I was a kid, she told me about her first love—my grandfather—a man she met in New York. She was just a teenager, and he was much older and married, but she loved him anyway. She told me about all the men she'd loved, about her baby brother who'd died, about her supernatural experiences: She'd once lived in a haunted house and seen the ghost of a woman who'd died by drowning. She'd been bitten by a poisonous alacrán and survived through the power of prayer. She'd witnessed an entire caldero of rice just throw itself across the room. Things like that happened to Mercy all the time. Chairs would move on their own. Empty glasses would fill with water. Cars would flip over seventeen times, and she'd make it out alive, without even a scratch. Dead birds would be resurrected in her hands when she prayed over them. And once in a while, she'd run into someone she'd known in another life.

It was when she told these stories that I knew I loved her. But I was never sure if she loved me—or any of her grandchildren, or her daughters, for that matter. She never hugged us or kissed us. She withheld food as a punishment. She regularly kicked our asses. She threw us out on the street, called the cops on us, even threatened to kill a few of us. And she had nasty nicknames for us, even her own grandchildren: Pimple Face, The Anorexic, The Slut, The Fat One, The Bastard, The Alcoholic, La Ganguera, La Delincuente.

And then there is this: suicide was our family legacy. Her own father, she told us, had been so heartbroken when her mother died, he'd tried to kill himself, but survived. But she would make sure she got it right.

All my life my grandmother threatened to kill herself. She threatened to jump in front of a bus and leave behind a flattened corpse, to climb to the fifteenth floor of our apartment building and fling herself from the balcony, to take a straight razor to her wrists, to swallow three hundred sleeping pills. And when we found her dead body, she said, we would regret all that we'd done to her. Oh, how sorry we would all be.

IT'S MEMORIAL DAY weekend, and traffic is at a standstill on the MacArthur Causeway. We ride with the windows down, sweaty and silent, watching a bright-red sky turn dark. We've barely moved in almost an hour.

The dogs stick their heads out the window, and I stare out at the Venetian Islands—royal palms and mansions with wraparound balconies and Spanish-style homes with elaborate tile roofs. When I was a kid, I used to check out these houses from the bus on my way to downtown Miami. I'd imagine myself in one of them, only I'd be a different girl, with a different family, and I'd swim in the pool and then go play the grand piano in the living room or watch movies in our personal home theater. The fantasy never got old, no matter how many times I rode the same bus and looked out the same window.

Miami Beach is overcrowded with tourists, partygoers, club-hoppers. Parking is impossible. By the time we pull up to the building, Mercy's body has been taken to the medical examiner's office. We double-park with the flashers on and get out to walk Taína and Chapo. Cheito volunteers to stay with the car and the dogs while I go upstairs and visit with my family, but the last thing I want is to go inside Tanisha's apartment, the place Mercy called home, and stand in the room where they found her body.

We wait on the sidewalk as family members arrive, teary-eyed and exhausted: my cousins Junito and Angel, three of my titis, their husbands, their kids. Cheito and I hug them one by one, Taína and Chapo wagging their nubby tails and playing with the kids. Everybody talks about how friendly and well-behaved the dogs are. They ask questions about the ride down, the traffic, my job, Cheito's job. No one says a word about Mercy.

I meet Tanisha's kids, Lia and Jayden, who are eight and three years old, for the first time. They eye me warily, then go back to playing with the dogs. Lia, the older one, stops abruptly and stands with her arms crossed and head down. Then it hits me: just an hour ago Lia and Jayden were in the same room with our grand-mother's body. I wonder if they loved her. But what am I thinking? *Of course* they loved her.

My titi Iris takes my hand, pulls me off to the side. She looks into my eyes. "Your mother," she says, shaking her head. "Oh my God, Jaqui, tu mamá."

Then everybody goes quiet.

Up the street, a scraggly old woman shuffles toward us in worn Converse Chuck Taylors. She wears a dingy black sweater and tattered jeans with holes in them, her hair in a buzz cut. Coming closer, she smiles a toothless smile at me and Cheito. I steel myself—she's going to ask for spare change, a cigarette, some-thing. Cheito starts digging in his pockets and pulls out a handful of coins. I reach for his hand, sending nickels and quarters flying to the concrete, rolling down the sidewalk. I'm still holding on to him when the woman wraps her arms around me, and I feel her bones, sharp and fragile against me. She kisses my cheek, this small, shattered creature who smells like dirty laundry and cat piss and cigarettes, this stranger. Then she pulls back, and this is how it happens, all at once—the cars blocking the intersection, the tour-ists headed this way and that, my family gathered on the sidewalk, the dogs barking and wagging their tails, my husband holding my hand. I look into her green eyes and something like a wave breaks inside my chest, and I know, or maybe I always knew: I am seeing my mother for the first time in seven years.

WHEN I WAS a kid, my mother often showed up unannounced wherever I was, sometimes with Mercy in tow. They'd walk all over Miami Beach looking for me. They'd show up at my friends' houses demanding to see me and drag me outside because I hadn't asked permission to be there. They'd show up at the movies, open the door to the packed theater, and call my name in the darkness. They'd show up at the skating rink, the public pool, the basketball courts of three different parks. Sometimes, if I was staying at my father's house, my mother would get there early in the morning and insist on walking me to school. I'd be terrified that the other kids might see us together and find out she was my mother. Eventually they did. They called her "homeless lady" and "crazy lady" and, as I got older, "crackhead" and "scutterhead" and "junkie."

MY MOTHER IS nearly unrecognizable. I remember a while back she called to tell me that she'd had most of her teeth removed and needed money to fix the few she had left. Anthony called the next day. "She didn't have them 'removed,'" he said, "they fell out."

She has meth mouth. I've known this for years, but the knowledge did not prepare me for the sight of it. Cheito squeezes my hand, but it makes me feel worse, maybe because he has a mother who's not an addict, two grandmothers who adore him, even a doting stepmom who considers him like her own son.

Mami hugs me again, says, "She didn't look dead. She looked like she was just sleeping."

I wrap my arms around her, but not too tight. I'm afraid I might crush her, that her collarbone will fracture, that her ribs will crack, that I will break her with my need to put her back together again.

As she pulls away, asks my aunt for a cigarette, I take a couple of steps back. Unable to steady myself, I sit on the curb, lean forward with my face in my hands. I'm relieved that my mother is alive, but I can't believe that I've let this happen. I shouldn't have left it up to my brother and Mercy to take care of her.

I wipe the sweat from my upper lip with the back of my hand. Junito sits next to me. He looks so much older than the last time I saw him, just a few months ago. I ask, just loud enough for him to hear, if he read the note. He says they all did, even my little cousin Lia.

"Lia? Oh, my God. Why would Tanisha let her read that?"

He says it was Lia who found the note. It was Lia who found the body.

Lia and her brother Jayden are still playing with the dogs. Junito calls her over, and she sits on the curb with us. She's small, with dark skin, dark hair, dark eyes. I wonder how Mercy felt about that.

Lia tells us how she likes to read, how she reads to her little brother at night, how she wants to be a marine biologist.

"Wow," I say. "What do marine biologists do?"

"They study sharks." She tells me all about the great white shark and the hammerhead and the tiger shark. She tells me how she'll be graduating from the fourth grade this week, and how Mimi won't be there.

"Who's Mimi?" I ask.

"My grandmother," she says. "She died today."

I listen as my ten-year-old cousin tells me about the woman she called Mimi, who lived with her and her little brother and her mom, a woman who went to church every day, who made her breakfast in the mornings and walked her to school afterward. Mimi taught her passages from the Bible, brushed her hair, sang songs to her about Jesus, told her she loved her.

This is the way I want to remember my grandmother, tender and gentle and loving, a woman who cherished her grandchildren and took care of them, who made them feel safe. But these are not my memories. This Mimi is not the woman I know.

Lia shows me the angel pendant she wears on a silver chain around her neck. She says Mimi left it for her when she died.

Junito takes her hand. He has tears in his eyes, and suddenly he looks like the boy he used to be.

"She was my grandmother, too," I say.

Lia looks at me curiously, crinkling her brow. "Really?"

I explain that Jeannette, her aunt, is my mom, so that makes us cousins.

"But you're old," she says.

Junito and I both laugh, and then I tell her I know Mimi loved her.

"I miss her," Lia says, caressing the angel pendant with her fingertips.

"I miss her, too," I say.

"I know," she says, as if no other possibility could ever occur to her.

THREE WEEKS BEFORE she died, my grandmother called me. She told me she was living with Tanisha and the kids, that she was in a wheelchair now because she'd slipped in the bathroom and broken both her legs. She'd sued her landlord over the fall, a leaky pipe the landlord had neglected to fix. I was skeptical about the details, but I figured the less I knew, the better. She told me a nurse came to care for her once in a while. She talked about her favorite grand-daughter, Lia, how big she was, and how smart, and how Lia's little brother, Jayden, was three years old and had a foul mouth, just like his mother. We both laughed at this.

She told me about some of her friends who had died recently, said she was getting old, that most of the people she loved were dying off. Cancer, overdoses, heart attacks.

"I'm the last one left," she said. "The last one."

I reminded her that she still had her family. She said she missed my sister and me, that she wanted to see us. It had been so long.

We talked for almost two hours, like we hadn't done in years, probably in my whole life.

A WEEK LATER, as we're preparing for the funeral, my aunts Xiomara and Iris bicker and yell over every arrangement, insults escalating like guerilla warfare. Each calls the other selfish, crazy, a gossip, mala, maldita hija de puta.

Xiomara walks around the apartment looking through Mercy's things, trying to find answers, her amber hair pinned up in a doobie, her eyes red and puffy. Once in a while, she breaks down, in tears, wailing, asking, "¿Porque? Dios mío. ¿Porque?"

Iris tries to be levelheaded, calm. She makes phone calls. She calls my other aunts in Virginia to let them know what's happening, every single step of the arrangements. She calls her job, her husband, my cousin Amir. She calls my titi Jenesis, her twin sister, asks about the kids, my cousins Nasir and Halimah. She's okay as long as she's busy. I never see her cry.

My mother chain-smokes outside on the steps, talking to herself.

Lia and Jayden sit in their room, refusing to eat the sandwiches I brought them from Sergio's Latin Cafe. Who can blame them? Their grandmother has just died.

Tanisha and her man hurl insults at each other, coming to blows, then fling shoes and hairbrushes and perfume bottles across the bedroom where my grandmother's body was found, each blaming the other for Mercy's suicide.

Iris singlehandedly breaks up the fight, picks up Tanisha's man in a headlock, and deposits him outside the back door while we all watch.

"Not today, honey," she says. "Not in this house." She slams the door behind him.

I exchange looks with my cousins Junito and Angel. Welcome to our family.

I wish Alaina was here. Two years ago, when Abuela was dying of cancer, Alaina made the trip back to Miami to be with Abuela during her last days. Papi, his wife Meira, and I had slept at the hospital for weeks, taking turns between sleeping on a chair next to Abuela's bed, or in the waiting room. Anthony and I had spent those last few weeks fighting; but when Alaina arrived, I felt like everything would be okay. Later, in the funeral home, after Anthony had left, after most people had fallen asleep in their chairs, Papi and Tío David talking late into the night, Alaina and I lay down together, sharing one couch, our feet pointing in opposite directions. It was like we were kids again, except we were orphans now. Losing Abuela was like losing everything I thought I knew about myself, losing everything that had once tethered me to the world, to Puerto Rico, to my family.

Growing up, Junito and Angel, Alaina and I, we had an unspoken pact: as fucked up as our family was, we would not fight each other. We were the normal ones, the four of us against the world.

When Junito and Angel start arguing, I storm out, grabbing my keys, my purse, heading to my car.

Cheito and the dogs have been back home for two days, so I make the four-hour drive alone from Miami Beach to Winter Haven, barreling north on US Highway 27 with the radio blasting. I'm somewhere outside South Bay when Iris calls to ask where I went.

"If you think I'm going to stay for that," I say, "you're crazy." I remind her that this is why I left Miami in the first place, that our family can't be civil, even for a funeral.

Angel calls just to tell me he loves me. Junito calls to tell me not to feel guilty—he's not going either. When Xiomara calls, she just cries on the line. After a while, I turn off my phone.

Every time I leave Miami, I tell myself I'm never coming back, only to end up right back where I started. I leave and come back again and again. Miami, like my family, is a place you learn to love and hate simultaneously. You can find yourself leaving it your whole life but never manage to leave, spend the rest of your life going back to it and never really get there.

When I reach Lake Okeechobee, less than halfway home, I pull into John Stretch Memorial Park, drive around aimlessly for a while, then park. All around me there is water—the park's smaller lake, the waterway that runs parallel to US-27, and then Lake Okeechobee. In the sky, a flock of turkey vultures, bodies tilting at slight angles, wings upturned like V's. I sit on the shore of the smaller lake, watching the vultures for a long time, the pendulum swing of their bodies in the air, and wonder if they've spotted their prey, if they're waiting for something to die out here. Later, I will read that a group of vultures in flight is called a kettle, and a flock of feeding vultures, a wake.

All my life my grandmother threatened to kill herself. I visited her at the hospital when I was a kid, after she swallowed two bottles of pills and then asked Tanisha to call 911. I watched my uncle Junior wrestle a steak knife from her hands when she swore she would stab herself in the heart. Until she finally made good on her threats, my grandmother had been killing herself for over twenty-five years. And in some ways, she had taken me with her: the first time I attempted suicide I was eleven. The second time, thirteen. And there would be a third, a fourth.

On the shore, vultures circling overhead, I realize that maybe I always knew I wouldn't go to the funeral. Maybe this is where I need to be: somewhere that is not Miami, somewhere that is not Winter Haven, somewhere that is not home.

Sometimes I can't believe she did it. Sometimes I think I always knew she would, that I've been like a bird, waiting, circling, waiting.

AFTER I GET back from Miami Beach, I will watch almost every hour of the Casey Anthony murder trial. When the jury comes back with a not-guilty verdict, I will have the overwhelming urge to call Mercy, to tell her.

I will keep thinking about that last phone call, return to it again and again. I will wonder if she'd already thought of doing it, if she was reaching out to me. I will lie awake at night thinking about what it means to want to die so badly, and remember all the times I'd held my mother's pills in my own hands. I will wonder if she felt alone, if she was scared or tired or bitter. Was it an act of revenge, or was it despair? Did she think about me, about my mother, about any of us? How hard it must have been for her to see my mother deteriorate over the years, to enable her, to try to rescue her but fail again and again. I wonder if my grandmother, in her wheelchair, both legs broken, could no longer live with that.

I'd like to imagine that on her last day, Mercy got up, dressed, read her Bible. That she was walking again, both her casts removed the week before. That she went outside on the balcony, felt the sun on her face, the ocean breeze blowing back her hair. That she fed the neighborhood's feral cats, as Miami Beach residents have been known to do, left an open can of tuna in the alley behind her building. That after dropping off Lia in front of her classroom at Ida M. Fisher Elementary, she stopped by a friend's house, talked about last night's novela, maybe the Casey Anthony trial on TV. I imagine that later that afternoon, she went to my mother's apartment for one last visit. She would've given her a few cigarettes, pressed a couple crumpled dollar bills into the palm of her hand, for Cuban toast and café con leche from Puerto Sagua. She would've checked the refrigerator to make sure my mother had eggs, milk, cheese. She would've made sure my mother had her Metro pass, that she took her pills that morning.

I tell myself that at the moment of her death, she thought of my mother, that she was transformed into that girl she'd been all those years ago: Mercy at fifteen, a mother for the first time, her baby girl in her arms. I imagine my mother, tiny and innocent and smiling, looking up at her with those green eyes. And Mercy, when she looks at her baby, she suddenly feels like she's looking into the center of the universe, the whole world in her arms, the whole world terrifying.

PART FOUR
//\\//\\//\\//\\//\\//\\//\\//

Regresando

Returning

The first time Cheito and I split, after I've been out of the navy for a few weeks and he is living with another woman, I go back to Miami and land a job ringing up cough syrup and cigarettes for six bucks an hour. I take the Metrobus to and from work every day, sometimes running into people I knew in high school. I avoid them, stare out the window, pretend I'm lost in neon lights and Art Deco hotels, reluctant to give them the sordid details of my latest disappointments. Failed marriage, dropped out of college, left the military, living with parents. Yes, again.

One Friday, I get off work early, cash my paycheck at the bodega around the corner, take the L headed to the Beach. I sit in the back, keeping an eye on both exits as we approach the 79th Street Bridge. All this cash is making me paranoid.

A man sits across from me, bald, with a goatee, insists that he knows me from el barrio. He sips from a quart of malt liquor wrapped in a paper bag. I clutch my purse. When I tell him, *No, I never lived in Spanish Harlem*, he says, *You sure?*

Positive.

I get up, move to the front of the bus, sit right behind the driver. Across the street, the regulars are lining up for the early show at The Fat Black Pussy Cat. Two seats away, another stranger. He takes his eyes off his copy of *Vibe*, looks me up and down. You got beautiful feet, he says, for a fat girl. He goes back to his magazine. This dude is sober.

Then *she* gets on, dirty-faced and scrawny, matted hair in a messy black ponytail, her lighter roots growing out. She doesn't pay her fare. She stumbles all the way to the back, asking if anyone can spare change so she can make it home to her kids. She was mugged, she says, they took everything. Most people ignore her. They've heard this line a hundred times, probably on this same bus. Probably from this same woman. A few hand over their change just to get rid of her.

When she makes her way back to me, just as I'm about to deliver my line, *Sorry, I don't have any cash*, I realize I know her. We went to school together. I ate lunch at her house a few times and we watched *Dirty Dancing* over cold slices of Domino's pizza, and we both swore one day, when one of us married Patrick Swayze, the other would be a bridesmaid. Then we fought over a sixth-grade boyfriend, and because I was a closeted queer girl in a homophobic place, I started a rumor that she was a lesbian, and because she knew exactly what would hurt me, she said my mom was a crackhead bitch.

I *know* her.

Except she's not like I remember. She looks twice her age, skinny, battered, her nails ragged, the whites of her eyes a mix of bloodshot and yellow, her face covered in lesions. She's lost some of her teeth— probably meth mouth. And she doesn't seem to know me.

Years later I will hear that she was attacked by a john, or a pimp, that he took a knife to her throat, slit from left to right, and left her to bleed out. But she will live, and after she gets out of the hospital, she will go right back to the streets, get arrested at least four more times, the scar on her throat visible in every single one of those mugshots.

But that is years away. Right now, on this bus, she holds out her hand, says, *Excuse me, miss, can you spare a quarter?* Says it not like it's a question, but like an apology. And what is a quarter, a dollar, a twenty? Wouldn't I give the $192 in my purse just to be back in her living room, eating cardboard pizza, dreaming of a future in which we were both movie stars and happy? And isn't it possible that in another life, under different circumstances, *there but for the grace of God*, this could've been me?

I rifle through my pockets as she waits. The other passengers sit still, their faces all turned toward us. The bus stops at a red light. And then I remember: all my cash, my entire paycheck, down to the last dollar, is in an envelope they handed me at the bodega and I can't pull it out right here, on this bus, where anyone can see it, probably rob me before I even make it home from the bus stop.

I take a deep breath. Exhale.

"I'm sorry. I don't have any cash."

In my head, I say her name.

Orlando, 2004

IN COLLEGE, ALONG with pages and pages of notes about La Masacre de Ponce, the Jayuya Uprising, el Grito de Lares, and the Cerro Maravilla murders, I carry a portrait of a young Lolita

Lebrón, who'd always been a controversial figure, even for Puerto Ricans, because of her role in the March 1954 shooting inside the house of representatives.

Lolita's interest in politics and activism deepened after the Ponce massacre, after she moved to New York in order to find work. There, she saw the way Boricua workers were marginalized and mistreated. She got sick of the racism, the insults, day in, day out. She joined the Puerto Rican Nationalist Party. Eventually, she would rise through the ranks to become a leader of the movement, following in the footsteps of Blanca Canales, who'd helped found the women's branch of the Nationalist Party, the Daughters of Freedom, and led the Jayuya Uprising. After the Nationalist Revolts of 1950, after Blanca Canales was already serving life in a federal prison, after the Utuado Massacre, after the Gag Law had been suppressing the rights of Puerto Ricans for years, Lolita Lebrón started corresponding with Pedro Albizu Campos. He wrote her from his prison cell in La Princesa. Together, seventeen years after La Masacre de Ponce, they organized the attack on Capitol Hill.

In the photograph, Lolita is stoic, determined. A small woman restrained by armed police officers, she wears high heels, a long dress, jewelry, a hat. It was taken before she was sentenced, when she was thirty-five. Fifty years after the attack, in 2004, the *Washington Post* runs a story about Lolita Lebrón and uses that photo. They call it "When Terror Wore Lipstick."

I'm conflicted about Lolita. I tell myself I can't make sense of the shooting, of the violence. But I still carry the picture. I want to believe that she's not the sum of the worst things she did during her lifetime. I want to be the kind of person who believes in

redemption, the kind of person who, in a few years, will write letters to Ana María Cardona while she's on death row for her son's
murder and torture.

But also, I never want to forget how the world sees us. How
Lolita Lebrón, a controversial figure, a hero to some, a terrorist
to others, a woman who led a revolt on Capitol Hill, was written about in the *Washington Post,* a publication that in 2004 has
thirty-one Pulitzer Prizes. How even all these years later, the headline doesn't mention her life, or her death, or her pistol, or the
shooting, or the planning, or the wounded victims, or Puerto Rico,
or the flag, or colonialism, or freedom, or liberation, or racism, or
torture, or motherhood, or the loss of her children, or the years
she spent in prison, or the voices she heard or the visions she saw
while incarcerated, or what she yelled when she pulled out her gun
in the visitor's gallery of the US Capitol, *¡Viva Puerto Rico Libre!,*
or what she said when she was arrested, or what she said in any of
her dozens of interviews, or what she said when she was protesting
the occupation of Puerto Rican land and the oppression of Puerto
Rican people, or anything related to who she was or what she did.
Instead, the headline mentions her fucking red lipstick.

Orlando, 2006

ON THE MORNING of my college graduation, a Saturday in July,
my family arrives from Miami. My tío David flies in from Puerto
Rico, then drives up with Anthony, Papi, and Meira, my stepmom.
Alaina brings Abuela.

Cheito and I pull in to the parking lot outside the university arena, find them all waiting there, Alaina pushing Abuela's

wheelchair, Papi smiling and holding a camera, Anthony and Tío having a deep conversation about where we'll be having lunch later.

I bend to hug Abuela first, and she kisses me soft on the cheek. "Mírala," she says to everyone. "Did you ever think this day would come?"

My brother chuckles. "Nope."

Cheito hugs Abuela. "I always knew."

Papi wraps his arms around me, then pulls away, looking at me. "I'm proud of you," he says in English, his eyes watery. Meira, my stepmom, takes a picture of us. They've only been together five years, but she feels like family.

Alaina hugs me, smiling, her eyes watery, too. Alaina, who is also in college, will graduate next year, then she'll be off to see the world. "I'm so proud of you," she says.

Once we're inside the arena, as I'm lining up with all the other graduates, I will look for my family in the crowd. I will find them: Abuela sitting next to Alaina in a spot reserved for wheelchairs, and a few rows up, Papi, Meira, Anthony, Tío, and Cheito. As I sit there, in my cap and gown, all the other graduates in their caps and gowns, the arena loud with talking and laughter, flashes going off, people still finding their seats, I can't stop smiling. I am overwhelmed with happiness, with love, with hope, with the certainty that I will be a writer someday. But also, more than anything else, I wish my mother was here.

Miami, 2008

IT'S HALLOWEEN AND my stepmom, Meira, and her daughter are throwing a party. It's my stepsister's house, three bedrooms, a pool, everybody out on the pool deck, evil fairies and werewolves, so many vampires, Elvira, Mistress of the Dark, at least three different witches. I count four women in black sexy cat costumes from the party supply store, a sexy Cat in the Hat, a sexy leopard, a sexy pink kitty cat who is clearly wearing something from Frederick's of Hollywood.

China and Flaca come with their kids—Flaca with her four-year-old son, another one on the way, and China with her two girls, six and eight. Out of all my friends, I'm the only one who doesn't have kids.

When Flaca sees me, she takes a step back, laughing and laughing. "Girl, you look crazy as hell." She grabs my hand, checks out my blue Ring Pop, then plucks one of the lollipops sticking out of the back pocket of my baggy jeans.

When China sees me, she covers her mouth, her eyes wide, then circles me, checking over every single detail of my costume. "Where did you get those bamboo doorknockers?" she asks.

I hand her a lollipop. "Aventura Mall."

China and her two girls are also wearing cat costumes, furry leopard-print ears, tails, furry cuffs around their wrists, black noses, whiskers painted on with black eyeliner. Flaca is a black cat, a kitten in her belly. Her son is Batman, running around the pool deck with the other kids, flapping his Batman cape.

People I don't even know come around, check me out, trying to figure out my costume, everybody asking, *What are you supposed to be?*

My stepbrother, Quentin, spots us from across the way, shouts my name, "Jaquiiiiii!" It's how he always greets me. He comes over, gives me a bear hug, and I introduce him to Flaca and China. He is Michael Jackson. He looks me up and down. "You supposed to be a rapper?"

Flaca and China laugh. I laugh, too. He doesn't get it. He didn't know me as a teenager. But Flaca and China get it. They knew the moment they saw me.

I'm wearing baggy jeans, a baggy white T-shirt, high-top Jordans, a gold chain around my neck, my hair in cornrows. I put in my seventeen piercings, fake gold doorknockers, tiny gold hoops. I'm wearing penciled-on dark brown lip liner, brown lipstick, thick black winged eyeliner, lord knows how many coats of mascara. I painted on a fake black eye, put fake blood under my nose, on my knuckles. I stuffed my pockets with Charms Blow Pops and Ring Pops.

"I'm me," I say. "Teenage me."

And then China and Flaca and I start telling stories, remembering when we were just girls. The time me and Kilo egged some guys that came back later with a gun. That time we all painted our faces white like in *Dead Presidents*, put on camo pants and went to Society Hill, danced until the place closed down, how we didn't know that months later, it would all go up in flames. The year I bought my first car, a Mazda Millenia I got from a used car dealer, how we packed the car with people, me and Flaca and Cisco and Omar and China and Flaca's little sister, how we all rode out to Orlando, and smoked two blunts before stumbling into Terror on Church Street, all of us so faded we screamed and laughed so hard we cried.

Flaca and China go play with the kids, and I spend the rest of the party flirting with Quentin, and later that night, alone in my father's bathroom, I'll remember when Halloween was all about monsters, how one Halloween night eighteen years ago Ana María Cardona and Olivia González dumped Lázaro's body outside the house on North Bay Road, how every Halloween since I've thought of him, all those lollipops in my pockets, how he'd be a man now. And when I'm standing in front of my father's medicine cabinet, when I'm washing all the makeup off, when I'm drying my face with a towel my stepmom has left for me on the sink, when I'm looking at myself in the mirror, my lips and my tongue blue from all that candy, how impossible it seems that we were ever those people, that I was ever that girl. How we will never be those people, those girls, again.

Miami Beach, 2014

IN THE SUMMER, after being away for almost a decade—seven cities in under ten years—I move back home with Cheito. I wanted to be closer to Mami, close enough to walk to her place, to take her to the beach on Saturday mornings, to be a part of her life again, to have her in mine.

I find an apartment in North Beach, two blocks from the ocean, a ten-minute walk to Normandy Isle. In the morning, I ride the bus to Downtown Miami for work. In the afternoon, I ride the bus back, get off by the North Beach Bandshell, which used to be the roller skating rink back in the day, before the modeling agencies and fancy restaurants, back when movie producers and music video crews steered clear of our neighborhood, unless they were looking to buy dope.

I've been back in Miami Beach just a few weeks when I get a phone call from Titi Xiomara.

"Your mother is dying," she says, her voice breaking. "We have to do something."

After all these years of living with schizophrenia, addiction, and drug-induced Parkinsonism, my mother has also been diagnosed with emphysema, hoarding disorder, and several other illnesses. Most days, she can barely breathe. In a couple of years, they will remove a mass from her breast, and months after that, another one from her lung.

I returned to Miami Beach for my mother, but on the day Titi Xiomara calls, I've yet to see her.

I keep going to her apartment building, knocking and knocking until the neighbors open their doors to stare me down, ask who I'm looking for.

"I didn't know she had a daughter," they sometimes say, but I can never tell if what they actually mean is "She never talks about you" or "How can you let your mother live like this?"

It's true. My mother is dying. Painfully. Of addiction and mental illness, of loneliness, despair. My mother has been dying for over twenty-five years.

Miami Beach, 2015

ANA MARÍA CARDONA had spent twenty-two years on death row when I received her first letter. When she arrived at Florida's Lowell Correctional Institution in 1992, she was thirty, a young mother.

In her letters, she tells me she was sexually assaulted when she was a kid, that she attempted suicide several times as a teen, that by sixteen she was using drugs, drinking, having sex on the streets. She came to the US in 1980 during the Mariel boatlift, she says, alone and pregnant, and got into sex work out of desperation. She lived on the streets for some time, had two children and then met Fidel Figueroa, Lázaro's father, a Miami drug trafficker. Soon, she started using cocaine. Before she knew it, she was addicted.

Ten years after her first conviction, after several appeals and investigations, there was a discovery: in 2002, an appeals court found that the state of Florida withheld evidence from the defense it should've disclosed. During her interviews with police, Olivia González confessed that she'd lied to investigators, that she hit Lázaro on the head with a baseball bat. She reluctantly admitted that the blow was so hard there was a possibility it might've caused Lázaro's death. And there was crucial evidence to support that González had killed him: the medical examiner himself had originally reported blunt force trauma had been the cause of death.

One afternoon in May, I get another letter:

My whole family died in Cuba, she writes. *All I have left is God and my children. It's hard. You find yourself on the streets with little children, like I did, and not a single person extends a hand.*

She denies torturing Lázaro, insists that she was on drugs while he was being abused. She believes he'd be alive if it wasn't for Olivia González, admits that she let Olivia beat him while she was strung out on crack cocaine, that she failed to protect him. She did what she could do to put a roof over their heads, including, she claims, enduring a relationship with Olivia.

I've read most of this before, in her letters, in trial transcripts. I've read account after account, minor details changing here and there. Sometimes, there are huge discrepancies: Some reports say

Cardona has three children. Some say four. She tells me she has three surviving children. I don't ask about them, their names, their ages. I don't want to know—all those years ago, they were also victims. But she won't stop talking about them. They are her life, she says. They're all adults now, and she hopes to have a relationship with them if she gets out of prison.

As I keep reading, she finally says one thing I haven't heard before: when her second trial started, she was offered a plea deal. If she'd pled guilty to a lesser charge, she would've been sentenced to twenty years. With time served, she would be out by now.

But I refused, she writes. *I won't sign a paper that says something I didn't do. I am prepared to die . . .* She wants her kids to know that she did not kill Lázaro, she says. She wants them to know the truth.

ANTHONY MOVES MAMI into an apartment just a few blocks from my building, a short walk to the beach. For a while, I stop by Mami's place almost every day. I clean her bathroom, bring her dinner from her favorite Chinese restaurant on Collins Avenue, drop a few dollar bills on her kitchen counter. Sometimes I cook for her at home, walk over and drop off Tupperware containers of rice and beans, pork chops, beef stew, fried chicken and tostones. Sometimes I drop off sheets for her bed, towels, a dress, a pair of sneakers, toothpaste, soap.

On Mother's Day, I buy Mami a card, an arrangement of carnations from Walgreens, nothing fancy. I make a home-cooked meal and sit with her out on the patio. We drink café con leche while she chain-smokes, tosses pieces of bread at pigeons, works in her small garden. When the sun goes down, she opens a can of tuna and leaves it outside for a stray cat she calls Mishoo, a skinny tuxedo with only one ear.

I live so close to the ocean, so close to my mother, a short walk from the park where so many of my memories live.

I haven't been sleeping well. Sometimes I slip on my chancletas and go for walks along the shore. Sometimes I run on the boardwalk. Sometimes I ride my bike all the way to Haulover and back. I think maybe this will help me sleep, but then I lie in bed, awake.

And everywhere I go, as I'm riding my bike on the boardwalk, laying out on the beach, pushing my shopping cart inside the neighborhood bodega, waiting on the bus on my way to work, I think I see her, my grandmother, Mercy. She's been dead at least four years, but it's her. I'm sure of it. The same green eyes as my mother, the same swing in her hips. My grandmother, like a ghost, haunting.

And I wonder if Mami sees her, too.

SOMETIMES I WAKE in the middle of the night, pulled from a dream by Ana's words, her letters. *I did not kill my baby*, she says.

I get dressed, grab my car keys, take a drive to the house on North Bay Road. I know this is crazy as I'm driving south on Alton Road at 2:00 a.m., as I slow down, turn onto 54th Street, as I come to a complete stop in front of the circular driveway. But there's something about that house.

I did not kill my baby, she says in her letters, although I never asked if she did. At least not in those words. I don't want to be the kind of person who asks that kind of question, the kind of person who combs through newspaper articles and watches footage of news coverage that aired more than twenty years ago, the kind of person who spends days poring over trial transcripts and leaving messages for defense attorneys and prosecutors.

It's after 2:00 a.m. and I'm sitting in my car, in front of the house on North Bay Road. In less than a year, her conviction will be overturned. In less than a year, she'll be released from death row.

Tomorrow, I will send another letter.

I'VE BEEN BACK in Miami Beach for about a year, after a summer in Puerto Rico, where I'd been to several demonstrations—underpaid teachers protesting the privatization of public schools, students protesting the island's colonial status under the United States government, activists calling for the release of Oscar López Rivera, the longest-incarcerated Puerto Rican political prisoner, who is serving a seventy-year sentence for "seditious conspiracy."

Since I've been back, both my parents have been chronically ill, one after the other. Both have been in and out of hospitals for months. Even though I've been writing, I find myself unable to write anything meaningful.

It comes on without warning, a crippling, major depression. The suicidal kind. It keeps getting worse, and suddenly I am self-destructing. I walk out of my job one day and never go back. I have another reckless affair. I destroy my marriage, again, and destroy Cheito, a man who adores me.

One night, after not sleeping for days, I find myself sitting on the kitchen floor with a knife, not remembering how I got there, but trying to build up enough courage to slit my wrists. For days, I've been thinking of Mercy. For days, the five bottles of pills, the suicide note. For days, I think it makes perfect sense, that it is the beginning of the end, that it has always been ending.

Cheito finds me in the kitchen that night, takes the knife from me, takes me to bed. He lies down with me, holds me until I fall asleep. He doesn't know it yet, and neither do I, but soon, I will pack my clothes, my books, all my things, and leave him for the last time.

The next day, China and Boogie call from Boogie's car. They're outside my building.

"Get dressed," Boogie says. "We're going to dinner."

I throw on a tank top, jeans, chancletas. We sit in Flanigan's, talking shit for hours, eating ribs and fries and key lime pie.

"How's the writing going?" Boogie asks.

I don't tell them about the sadness, the not sleeping, the nights I throw on a T-shirt and shorts and walk out, heading to the beach at midnight, at 1:00 a.m., while Cheito sleeps. How I stand in the darkness, listening to the waves crashing. How once, when I was sixteen, a customer at the pharmacy where I worked—his cheeks red, his eyes bloodshot, smelling like a week-long bender—told me he could see my future. *You are a child of Yemayá,* he said, *madre del agua.* How he said it was the ocean that made me, and to the ocean I would return. *You will die by drowning, when Yemayá calls you home.*

We talk about movies and TV, about Daddy Yankee and Rihanna and Drake. We laugh when the waiter brings three spoons for my key lime pie and I tell him to take two spoons away because I ain't sharing shit. We laugh when somebody plays Ginuwine's "So Anxious" on the jukebox and it's been more than ten years since I heard it but I know all the words, and suddenly we all feel how old we are.

"Fuck that," I say. "I stopped aging at twenty-seven."

Nothing is better, not yet, and I know it, but at least I have my girls. It's like they heard me calling from miles and miles away. And that night, and the night after that, I will sleep, finally.

Puerto Rico, 2015

DURING THE SUMMER, I return to El Caserío Padre Rivera. I drive past the candy store and turn, past the gate, ready to check out la cancha where Papi taught me to shoot hoops. I check out our old apartment, my first elementary school, drive around Eggy's old building to see if I can park close to la plaza. I wonder if he still lives here, but I know how unlikely that is. I remember how back in the day, kids rode around on their bikes carrying guns, how I heard on the news this morning that there was a shootout here just last week, and two people were killed.

I've been inside El Caserío less than five minutes when a boy on a bike approaches the car, motions for me to roll down my window.

"What are you doing here?" he asks in Spanish. He can't be more than sixteen.

"Just visiting," I say. "I was born here." I tell him how I went to school in the elementary school on the next block, how I lived across the street, how I used to ride my bike out here. I point to my old building.

He keeps his hands on the handlebars, checks out the inside of my car for a while, then gives me directions to the nearest exit, even though I haven't asked for them.

"I know my way around," I say. "I used to live here."

"You do not belong here," he says, then pedals away, disappearing around the corner.

Puerto Rico, 1950

TWO YEARS AFTER Law 53 was passed in Puerto Rico, a gag law meant to suppress independence activists, which made it a crime to display or own a Puerto Rican flag, to sing "La Borinqueña," to organize or speak against the US government, citizens and Boricua Nationalists were being arrested all over the island. Their crimes: displaying la bandera, advocating for independence, speaking out against the United States government or the US-appointed governor. Each person served up to ten years in La Princesa, without a trial, without due process.

The cops had been trying to catch Pedro Albizu Campos, who'd been out of prison for about three years. He'd been gaining a following, speaking publically about independence, organizing. So they targeted his friends, other members of the Nationalist Party, anyone they suspected could be aiding him. On October 27, the Peñuelas Police murdered four people during a traffic stop.

That day, Albizu Campos was arrested in his home in San Juan, sent back to La Princesa, where he'd live out the rest of his days. Years later, we would hear about how he had been tortured with radiation. We would read the doctors' statements confirming that the wounds on his legs were radiation burns. We'd see photos of his swollen, charred legs, the man unable to stand. And we would know that he was killed by a colonial government, in his own country, for wanting independence.

Three days after his arrest, the Nationalists revolted.

In Jayuya, Blanca Canales, who had been amassing weapons and ammunition, armed a group of Nationalists, led them to the police station, the post office, and through the town. There, in the center of Jayuya, they raised the banned Puerto Rican flag, declaring Puerto Rico a free republic. For three days, Puerto Rico—or Jayuya, at least—was free.

In Utuado, another Nationalist group exchanged fire with police. Most were killed; the rest retreated, hiding in the home of one of the leaders. To deal with them, the Governor, Luis Muñoz Marín, called the US National Guard. And so, in November 1950, American bomber pilots bombed the pueblos of Jayuya and Utuado.

Later, after the pueblos had been decimated by American bombs, after the people of Utuado and Jayuya had died, after the National Guard walking the streets with their machine guns and their bayonets had occupied the land that had been stolen again and again, after they ordered the surviving Nationalists to surrender, after they walked them down Calle Doctor Cueto to the Plaza de Utuado, where they were ordered to remove their shoes, their belts, everything they owned taken, everyone heard the shots. The National Guardsmen had rounded up the survivors. They had walked them behind the local police station. They had lined them up. Their backs to the wall, their eyes open. The youngest only seventeen, pleading for water, begging for his life, bayoneted time and time again until he died. Julio Colón Feliciano, Antonio Ramos, Agustín Quiñones Mercado, Heriberto Castro, and Antonio González. All of them executed by American soldiers without a trial.

Puerto Rico, 2016

I'M WRITING A feature for *The Guardian* about Oscar López Rivera. After speaking with his lawyer on the phone, I meet a group of activists in el Viejo San Juan. We talk for a few minutes, then walk. Along the cobblestone streets, I come across a chalkboard mural on a building on Calle de Tetuan where someone has written, "Mandela is still ashamed of you. Free Oscar." All over the city, people are wearing FREE OSCAR T-shirts, college students hitting the streets with makeshift signs, calling for his release.

That afternoon, walking in el Viejo San Juan, I go into the old prison, La Princesa, where Juan Antonio Corretjer and Pedro Albizu Campos were locked up. In 1993, La Princesa was renamed, and now it's the Compañía de Turismo de Puerto Rico, an air-conditioned building housing an art gallery, a grand piano, and the Puerto Rico Tourism Company's offices, where you can get trolley maps of Old San Juan.

La Princesa is full. Families walking around, tourists taking selfies, studying their maps, checking out the sculptures and paintings, handing me their cell phones so I can take their photos where so many people died, where, during the years of the Gag Law, people were imprisoned for waving Puerto Rican flags, for holding assemblies, for wanting independence. La Princesa, a house of torture where people starved, where Pedro Albizu Campos spent decades living among the rats, enduring radiation burns, his legs swollen and charred. La Princesa, a place where our ghosts live, our history right there for us to see, but none of us actually *seeing*.

I know something about the in-between, of being seen but not really *seen*. I have lived there my whole life. I mean quite literally that I'm a child of colonialism, born into poverty on an island that was seized and exploited, first by Spanish colonizers, then by Americans. My family, although they're also US citizens, are colonial subjects, and most of what we know about our black family is limited because of slavery. We can trace as far back as Haiti, but before then, nothing. Like most black people in the US, the Caribbean, and Latin America, our histories, our cultures, our *people*, were stolen.

In the courtyard, two of the cells are in their original condition—stone walls, rusted bars, the stench of dried piss, pigeon shit. Even in the summer heat, the tourists are lining up for photos.

A woman approaches, asks if I will take a photo of her and her two kids. I take her phone, stand in front of one of the cells. I take their picture.

"Gracias, mamita," she says.

And then, without thinking, I hand her my phone so she can take one of me.

How strong our collective desire to erase our history, our pain. How easily we let ourselves forget.

After leaving San Juan, I spend a couple days driving up and down winding mountain roads, hugging the curves, singing along to Héctor Lavoe's "Un amor de la calle." I call Papi from the road to fill him in, tell him about my drive up the mountain, deep into the island, no cell reception, no GPS, all the way up to Cerro Maravilla, where two young pro-independence activists, college students, were murdered by the police in 1978. How next to the communication tower's antenna at the top of Cerro Maravilla, I found a small memorial under a Puerto Rican flag raised in their names, two crosses, one for Carlos Soto Arriví, one for Arnaldo Darío Rosado, their portraits, the words *Prohibido Olvidar.*

"Call me again tomorrow," Papi says before we say goodbye.

I take a drive to Comerío to see my tío David. Across the street from the Catholic church in la plaza de Comerío, across from la Parroquia Santo Cristo de la Salud, where my tío is one of the priests, I find a mural: Oscar López Rivera's face, the mountains, the flag. Oscar is not forgotten.

Tío and I have lunch at a new restaurant in the Hotel Media Luna, overlooking the cliffs, where we talk about how much Comerío is growing. He's aged, his close-cropped Afro has some gray in it now, his eyeglasses have gotten thicker. But he is smiling so wide. He is happy.

"How's your father?" he asks, and for the next hour we talk, we laugh. We order beers and talk about Papi, who is divorced now and living with Anthony. We talk about Anthony, who has a baby now. We talk about Alaina, who is abroad, seeing the world, rescuing animals. We talk about my writing.

"Tu abuela," he says, "she did something right." I understand that he means he is proud of me, and realize that even though he's a priest, and a man, I'm a lot like my tío. He's an independentista, like my father was all those years ago, who still reads the poetry of Corretjer and de Burgos, who looks at the mural for Oscar López Rivera across the street from the parroquia and feels proud to live in a pueblo that still holds on tightly to Puerto Rican culture. We don't know it yet, but in a year, Hurricane María will hit Puerto Rico, leave our people in the dark, without power, without water, without help. It will pass right through Comerío, strike so hard that the Hotel Media Luna will be damaged, the area all around the hotel will be flooded, and the water levels in Río de la Plata will rise more than eleven feet above flood stage, causing flash floods, destroying most of the houses, leveling much of the pueblo. I will not be able to get ahold of Tío for more than a month. But we don't know any of this yet, so for now, we are fine.

When I drop him off in la parroquia, I hug him hard, promise to come back later this week.

I drive through the Comerío mountains, pull over on the side of Route 167, overlooking one of Río de la Plata's hydroelectric dams. I get out of the car, step out onto the rocky ledge over the dam and the river. After María hits, the dam will break and the river will flood all of Comerío, drowning entire houses, and for weeks, people in the community will be digging mud out of their living rooms, out of their bedrooms. But not this summer. This summer there is a drought, and the southwest of the island is completely dry, parched. Yesterday, driving to Ponce, I saw a small fire along the side of the road, the dead grass charred black. But here, the water falls over the dam, green mountains all around us, houses hidden among the trees, the rocky river below. The air is hot and humid, and I hear nothing but the sound of the waterfall, a long, soft shushing *shhhhhhhh*. Clouds of mist rise, tiny droplets covering my bare arms and face, the pull of the water, reaching for me.

Tomorrow, I will get back in the car and drive to Ciales. A handful of men will be playing dominoes on somebody's front porch as I turn into the main street. A pack of satos will roam the neighborhood. A woman will push her baby stroller across the street. And then, standing in the same plaza where I first saw Juan Antonio Corretjer, my notebook in my messenger bag, Lolita Lebrón's photo tucked between its pages, I will try to memorize the blue of that sky, and I will be that little girl again, my father's daughter.

Miami, 2017

SHORTY PICKS ME up in Miami. Her two kids, Arianna, who is twelve, and Sean, thirteen, ride in the back of the SUV while I ride shotgun. We head south toward their house, stop at a Peruvian restaurant on the way. I sit next to Shorty and the kids laugh across the table from us, sipping on their juices and poking fun at each other, smiling. It's frightening how much they look like her, how much they both smile, how happy they are, how funny. They have her eyes, her smile, her goofy laugh, her dimples.

"I can't believe you made two humans," I say, "and they look so much like you."

It's something I say again and again, to each of my friends, because it's true. I can't believe we're this old, that we actually made it, that they all have children, and some of those kids are grown. Some of them are in college, have their own cars, relationships.

Arianna is into music and art, and we talk about her drawings, reading music, singing, a new friend she made in school. Sean is a writer. He writes satire about presidential candidates, long stories about heroes and magic, essays about his family. When we get to their house later, he will print out one of his stories, give it to me, and I will read it, give him some notes, and before I leave their house, he will hug me, and Arianna will hug me, and my heart will ache for a family of my own.

PLEASE WRITE, SHE says in a letter dated July 20. *I've been thinking about you a lot. I need your help.*

I don't write back.

Please write, she says in a letter dated July 27. *My new trial starts November 27. I am fighting for my life.*

I don't write back.

Please write, she says in a letter dated July 30. *I need your help. I did not kill my son.*

I don't write back.

At the end of November, when Ana María Cardona's third trial begins, I fly to Miami from Ohio, where I'm living temporarily for a writing fellowship.

In the courthouse, day after day, I sit with other journalists covering the story for *Rolling Stone*, the *Miami Herald*, ABC News, NBC. We all take notes furiously, look away when our eyes meet. They all wear suits, blazers, dry-cleaned pantsuits. I wear a gray hoodie, jeans, sneakers. They all have full time jobs reporting for *Newsweek* and CBS. I've been trying to make it with freelancing gigs and fellowships and teaching.

Ana is sitting with her defense lawyer, Steve Yermish, who I talked to on the phone a few months back. In the jury box, the jurors take notes, listening attentively as the prosecution presents evidence. Not one of the jurors is looking at Ana.

After a few hours, one of the jurors starts nodding off. I watch him for a while. His head bobs unexpectedly, and he catches me watching him, shuffles his feet. From now on, he will watch *me*, look for me in the courtroom to see if I've caught him nodding off again. And I have, several times. Every time our eyes meet, we will both know this.

Once, when the lawyers ask for a sidebar, Ana Cardona looks over to the other side of the courthouse, where I've been sitting the whole time. It's the first time I've seen her look my way. She looks gaunt, tired. When our eyes meet, I wonder if she knows who I am. She watches me a little too long, no expression on her face. When Mr. Yermish returns to his seat next to her, she looks away.

The prosecutor, Reid Rubin, pulls out a photo, sets it on a projector to display for the jury, for the entire courtroom to see. It's Lázaro's body on the autopsy table. I've seen this before. One side of his face bruised, blackened, his eye swollen shut, his skinny, malnourished body broken. I gasp, look away, look down at my sneakers, at my notes. Behind me, several people gasp, a woman says, "Ay Dios mío."

Reid Rubin raises his voice. "She killed him slowly," he says. "Over time."

I glance across the courtroom at Ana.

Her eyes widen. "Oh my God," she says in English, dramatically, shaking her head.

Mr. Yermish places a hand on her hand, whispers something I can't make out, and she quiets.

The prosecutor pulls out another photo, projects it. A different angle. He begins to describe all of the injuries, each one, in detail.

I start to feel sick, anxious. My eyes start to water. Behind me, a woman says, "Ay Dios mío," every time the prosecutor describes another injury.

I consider leaving, check behind me for the other journalists, writers, reporters.

No one gets up.

I stay.

In front of the court, facing the jury, Reid Rubin says, "After Lázaro died, they went to Disney World. As the police were driving her to Miami from Orlando, she was making out with Olivia in the back of the police car."

And then I see: as Mr. Rubin describes injury after injury, the details of every broken bone, pointing at the enlarged photo, to every broken tooth and cigarette burn and skull fracture, Ana is nodding off, her eyes closed. Behind me, a woman says, "Is she falling asleep? Wow. Unbelievable."

Mr. Rubin looks at the jury, points at the enlarged photo of Lázaro on the autopsy table, says, "According to the medical examiner, the baby had looked that way for months."

Mr. Rubin looks at the jury, says, "Ladies and gentlemen, you heard her. On the stand, she said the last time she saw her son was in August. And then when I asked her what they did for the baby's birthday, she said that she sang him "Happy Birthday," that she hugged him."

Mr. Rubin looks at the jury, says, "By the way, his birthday was October 18. Less than two weeks before he died."

Mr. Rubin looks at the jury, says, "She confessed three times on the stand. She got caught in three separate lies."

In a few months, after the third trial is over, a friend will ask, *Why are you so drawn to people who do terrible things? How come all the people you write about are in prison?*

In the jury box, all the jurors are wide awake, taking notes. Across the courtroom, Ana is nodding off.

Gambier, 2017

I'M NEARING THE end of my writing fellowship, getting ready to move back to Miami, again, when I find out about Chanty. It's China who calls to tell me.

"Oh my God, Jaqui. Have you looked at Facebook today?"

I was busy all day, teaching, writing, grading student work. "What happened?"

"Chanty died," she says. She keeps talking, explaining what she read on Chanty's page, people saying goodbye, how she had been struggling with drug addiction for so long.

I don't say anything. I haven't seen Chanty in almost twenty years, haven't talked to her since I was sixteen and working at the pharmacy.

I take the phone over to the dining table and log in to Facebook on my laptop, check out Chanty's page. "It's true," I say finally.

"I know, Jaqui. I just told you."

I sit with China on the phone for a long time, quiet while she talks. "I can't believe it," she starts to say, and then I stop listening.

I scroll through all the messages posted on her page, all from people I don't know. There's not a single message, not one, from a person I know. I look for messages from her sisters, her mother. And then I realize that that's what I'm looking for—her mother. I want to know if her mom is okay.

"I can't believe it either," I tell China.

Later, in the shower, I'll think about reaching out to her mom. But I won't, because I won't know what to say, how to say it. What could I possibly say? That Chanty was one of the very first friends I had when we came to Miami. That she sat in front of me in fourth grade. That she was smart, and funny, and loud. That I had a gap between my two front teeth and she sometimes called me Gapita. That we sang together in sixth grade, in chorus, walking the hallways at Ida M. Fisher Elementary, Wilson Phillips and Whitney Houston and Mariah Carey. That she was right to keep me away, that I know she was trying to protect Chanty. That Chanty was my friend. That I cared for her. That I'm sorry she's gone.

Puerto Rico, 2017

AFTER HURRICANE MARÍA decimates Puerto Rico, I can't find my uncle. I call everyone I know on the island. I reach out to volunteer organizations. I post pictures of him all over social media. I get in touch with a group of volunteer firefighters traveling all over the island doing rescues and wellness checks using satellite phones, a makeshift website for victims to check in, to ask for help, using a rescue map. I call. I call. I call. There are rescue teams on the ground, I'm told, but some roads are destroyed, some roads are flooded, some bridges have collapsed. There's no way to make it to Comerío right now.

In San Juan, the navy's hospital ship hasn't arrived. In Humacao, my titi Jenesis, who is diabetic, needs to see a doctor, but can't get to the hospital. In Caguas, a cousin loses his house. In Naguabo, no one has seen or heard from FEMA, no one has water or power.

On TV, Trump throws paper towels at hurricane survivors, shoots the rolls like he's shooting hoops. He smiles for a selfie, then looks into the camera. "There's a lot of love in this room," he says. "A lot of love in this room."

Later, during a press conference, he will claim that only sixteen people died in Puerto Rico. That we should be "very proud" that we didn't have "a real catastrophe like Katrina." A year later, Harvard researchers will find that more than four thousand Puerto Rican people died.

But right now, my uncle is missing and people have no water and no power and no help, and Trump is throwing paper towels at them and congratulating himself and telling us we should be proud.

I keep calling. I send money for gas, for food, for water. I send boxes of supplies. I call. I call. I don't sleep. Every day, my uncle is missing. Every day he could be hurt, or dead, or dying of thirst. Vox reports that there is a suicide crisis on the island after the hurricane. Almost ten thousand people call the health department's suicide hotline in three months. Every day my uncle is missing. Every day, I don't sleep. Every day, I feel nothing, except rage. And then finally, one day the phone rings, and it's him.

Miami Beach, 2017

I ARRIVE IN Miami the week of Thanksgiving. I've been gone for a year and a half, and during that time, my mother's health has deteriorated. She's been in the hospital at least four times this year.

We spend Thursday in the hospital, Mami hooked up to oxygen. She has pneumonia for the second time this year, has trouble breathing, speaking, and doesn't want any more treatment. She will eat only Jell-O and broth and nothing else. I will drink black coffee for four hours straight and then lock myself in the bathroom with heart palpitations. I will not sleep for three days. I will leave her in a week. When I'm gone, Anthony will make arrangements for an assisted living facility that will not quite care for her, but where she'll be able to live with her oxygen tank, where they'll prepare meals for her, where they'll make sure she's not alone at night, that she doesn't smoke with her oxygen tank, that she doesn't go out into the streets alone.

I will make plans to come back to Miami Beach, again, and at night, I will close my eyes and see us exactly as we were two years ago:

As I walk along the boardwalk on the north shore, the roller skating rink–turned–bandshell just a block away, women jogging in pairs, kids riding their skateboards, weaving in and out and almost running over pedestrians, I make a right toward the sand, toward my favorite lifeguard stand, blue and orange and yellow. I kick off my chancletas, head to the water, then walk north along the shore, toward Surfside, the waves washing away my footprints. And then, I run into my mother walking along the same route, in the opposite direction, heading south, smoking a Camel, her sneakers in her hand, bare feet kicking up clouds of sand. When I see her, the sun on her face, the wind in her hair, the seagulls' choking calls in the distance, I know that we will always feel the same pull, the ocean calling.

Even when she is gone, we will always find each other here.

Miami, 2018

China and I arrive half an hour late. It's my fault. I took three hours getting ready, doing my hair, my makeup. I changed my dress three times. On the way to pick up China, I got lost, even though I'd been to her house over a dozen times.

When we finally arrive, it's the groom who gets the door for us. He introduces himself, hugs me. China already knows him—she was there when they met—but it's the first time I lay eyes on him.

"Thank you for coming," he says, smiling. "It's so nice to finally meet you. I've heard so much about you."

"Felicidades," China says.

"Felicidades," I say, too, not sure what else I'm supposed to say to this man who is marrying one of my best friends, someone she met just a month ago. They fell in love right away, she told me on the phone. She couldn't believe it either.

He leads us upstairs, where everyone is waiting on us, and there she is, in a white dress she picked out herself. Boogie. She hugs China first. And then she wraps her arms around me, and I try not to cry when she says, "I love you."

China will be la madrina, and I will stand back, take pictures with my iPhone, watch him place the ring on her finger. She will smile the whole time, and there will be tears in her eyes, and even though we haven't talked much in the last year, selfishly, I will feel like I'm losing her, like I've already lost her.

Puerto Rico, 2018

EXACTLY ONE YEAR after Hurricane María, I fly to Puerto Rico. My friend James comes along to keep me company. He rides shotgun as I drive the Jeep, listens as I rage at the traffic, at the news, at people's performative allyship while the island is in crisis, at the cryptocurrency fuckers and their money, at the vendepatria governor, at Trump, who keeps denying the thousands of Puerto Ricans who died, everyone pretending things are going back to normal when black Puerto Ricans have always been in crisis. One year later, and I'm still in a constant state of rage.

We eat in San Juan, drive to Humacao, to El Caserío, and I park the Jeep in front of my old elementary school for a few minutes. It starts to rain. James asks what exactly I'm looking for. The truth is, I don't know.

We drive to El Malecón de Naguabo, where I spent so many weekends, so many summers listening to salsa and eating alcapurrias and ensalada de pulpo across from the ocean. We buy a couple beers, walk across el malecón, looking out at the waves, the cliff-side houses across the water. Half of the kioskos are closed down, damaged after María. A nearby oceanfront house is crumbling. This is where my abuela was born, I tell James. This is where my family was from. In those days, my abuela's barrio had the largest black community in Naguabo.

We drive to Fajardo, to Santiago Iglesias Pantín, where my father's liquor store was, Abuela's house on top. As I approach the square, la plaza across the street, I know the way. I see it right away.

The last time I saw my abuela's house, a year before, it looked empty, abandoned. But now, it's destroyed. Abuela's house, which used to be yellow and white, is painted guava and blue, pieces of the cement and cinderblock crumbling, holes where the windows used to be. On the side of the house, someone has spraypainted *XL Los Black Magic* and *BM* in white. Downstairs, where Papi's liquor store was, all the windows and doors are gone. There are broken boards on some windows, as if someone tried to board it up. There are rusted metal bars on the front entrance, broken, falling apart. Inside, there are bottles and cans, the remnants of squatters, a dirty blanket, so much trash.

I have dreamed about this place so many times, the balcony where Abuela kept her plants, the chickens she raised out back, Abuela's kitchen, Abuelo's portrait on the wall, Caviche Liquors, my father hauling in wood for the floors, nailing down boards, buffing, staining, finishing. How he built this from the ground up.

How do we keep living in the world when everything we built is gone? How do we even go on?

In the car, on the way back, I'll keep it together. James will read Octavia Butler for a while, and then he'll read me a Dionne Brand interview, and we'll talk and laugh, but later, after he's asleep, I will go into the bathroom and cry. I'll grip the sink with both hands and steady myself, and I will feel this thing in my chest, something I have no words for, something so thick, so heavy, I can barely breathe.

Capitol Hill, 1954

AFTER HER INCARCERATION, Lolita spoke of visions. In prison, she said, she'd heard the voice of God Himself. Visited by angels, Jesucristo, la Virgen María in her prison cell. God had given her a divine mission.

I imagine that long after being convicted and sentenced to fifty-six years in federal prison, the day of the shooting had become to her like something willed by God: The train ride from New York to Washington, DC, Lolita sitting by the window watching the countryside, surrendering herself to the idea of dying in the name of freedom. How she met Rafael Cancel Miranda, Irvin Flores, and Andres Figueroa Cordero, the three men who would follow her into the house of representatives, up to what they called "the Ladies' Gallery." How after a meal at Union Station, running late, the four of them got lost. How they wandered the streets, strangers in this foreign place, this city so far from home, until finally they asked for directions. How when it started raining, on the steps of the United States Capitol, Rafael pointed to the time on his watch, asked Lolita to wait. How she ignored the time, the rain, the three nervous men, everything testing her resolve. How she saw the hesitation, the fear in each of their faces, and thought, *I am alone.* How she had decided, back on that train, that she would sacrifice her life for her island. And then she said it, "Yo estoy sola," leaving the three men behind to follow or turn back. She had come here to die.

Lolita standing in front of that government building, one woman among all those men. How she'd been living in a country that didn't feel hers. How she remembered the European settlers that raped and enslaved and killed the Taíno who didn't deliver tributes of gold and spun cotton, hands hacked off, bodies left by the riverbanks. The European slave traders who stole and enslaved and raped and murdered African people, carried them, chained, across continents. Puerto Rico, seized, exploited, first by Spanish colonizers, then by Americans who conferred citizenship to Puerto Ricans only so they could be drafted into military service during World War I, but didn't allow us the same voting rights as other US citizens. The Puerto Rican women sterilized by the

American government without their consent. Pueblos that turned to ghost towns, all the schools closing because there were no more children. Büreкün, Borikén, Borínquen, Puerto Rico. Our history, our culture, our blackness, our names, our people. Stolen. Erased. Had Lolita heard the stories? Had she read them in her father's books before she became a freedom fighter? Did she carry them with her? Lolita climbing the stairs to the Ladies' Gallery, cocking her Luger pistol, Büreкün, Borikén, Borínquen, Puerto Rico, viva Puerto Rico libre, all those people on the streets of Ponce singing along as the band played "La Borinqueña," the priest's sermon still fresh in their minds from that morning's Catholic mass, the word of God, the palm fronds in their hands, their faces as that first shot rang out, Tommy Guns blasting, the earth opening up like a wound.

"Yo estoy sola," she said, but what she really meant was *I am a woman.*

Miami, 2018

MY FRIEND KEITH and I arrive in Miami together. We're here for a benefit reading for PageSlayers, a nonprofit organization that provides public school kids with free creative writing summer camps taught by writers of color, a mission close to my heart. Keith and I volunteer to read at the fundraiser, and Dana, the founder—and my former student—picks us up at the airport.

Keith and I spend the day checking out my old haunts in Miami Beach and Wynwood. We walk on Ocean Drive for a while, I show him Ida M. Fisher Elementary, some of the buildings where

I lived as a kid. We stop at a cart where a woman is selling jewelry, keychains, bracelets. Keith picks up a bracelet that says *Best Friends*.

"Aw," he says, "we should get some of these." He holds it up and asks the woman, "How much?"

I pick a blue one, my favorite color, put it on, and after we pay her, we're walking down the street in our friendship bracelets, like two kids.

The night before the reading, Keith and I pick up China, head to Duffy's in North Miami Beach for drinks and burgers. Dana meets us there, and then my friend Evy, and we sit outside, at a table by the pool, the DJ playing an old school hip-hop mix, Salt-N-Pepa and L.L. Cool J. and Biggie. We take shots of Patrón, pick sweet potato fries off Keith's plate, take selfies with our eyes crossed, tongues sticking out. Keith and I take pictures holding up our wrists, showing off our friendship bracelets. Keith says, in a sing-song voice, "Best Friends."

When Keith is talking to Dana, China leans over to me, asks, "Are you guys dating?"

"We're friends," I say. "I love him, but not like that."

China gives me a look.

"Stop that shit," I say.

"You look like you're together," she says, "the way you look at each other."

"It's the same way I look at you," I say. "The same way I look at all the people I love, like family."

She smiles, hugs me. "I love you, too, bitch."

I catch Keith smiling at us.

Evy tells the story of how when we were in Nautilus, in seventh grade, China wanted to fight her. "Jaqui and I were so close, we were partners in crime. But China *hated* me! I don't even know why."

I take a sip of beer, throw my head back, laughing, loud. "Because she was in love with me and she was mad jealous!"

Everybody laughs.

China hides her face in her hands. When she pulls her hands away, she says, "Because I was a kid. I was immature. And also, because I loved my friends and I was overprotective."

I turn to Keith. "She's *still* like that."

The waiter brings another round, and I raise my shot glass. Dana smiles at me from across the table, raises hers, too. China downs hers, fast.

"Bitch, I was gonna toast!" I say.

"I'm driving," Evy says, and leaves her shot on the table.

Keith isn't drinking—he never drinks. So I take his shot and China takes Evy's.

"Salud, dinero, y amor," I say, "que belleza sobra." And we drink.

Evy leans across the table. "So how did you guys meet?" she asks, meaning Keith and me.

"We met a few years ago, at a writers' conference," he says.

We keep talking, telling stories, joking, drinking, and it's strange, but also cool, that my best friend and my writing friend and my childhood friends, all of them from completely different worlds, are sitting at the same table laughing at the same jokes.

Before the night is over, the music will get louder, and we'll all get up, leave our drinks behind, and I will take Keith's hand

and we'll all scatter across the makeshift dance floor by the pool and dance without thinking, the whole restaurant watching, the people at the next table laughing, then all of them getting up, too. Then the lights will go down and the dance floor will be full and I will be surrounded by people I love. I will think of my friends: Boogie and me, not even fifteen yet, the two of us in black dresses and heels, singing at a club on Ocean Drive. Shorty and me, walking up and down Bayside, flirting with all the boys, dancing salsa on the party boats. Evy and me, passing each other notes in Civics class, swimming with Beba in the Forte Towers pool. China and Flaca and me, the three of us posing for pictures outside Miami Beach High, me catching China by surprise, putting my hands on her shoulders, jumping onto her back, and China, screaming, laughing. And Keith, signing his chapbook for me, *Generation Oz*, how he writes, *I love you!*, and how I tell him I love him, too, the day after the 2016 election, and later, when the news gets especially grim, black person after black person after black person murdered by police, and months after that, when he asks for a simple favor. *You know I love you*, I say. *I would slay dragons for you.*

All these years later, I'll be back on that dance floor. I will be swaying and the music will fill me and I will be a girl again. My friends will be there, and we'll dance all night, one song after another, and we will be laughing and laughing in each others' arms. I will be thirteen again, or fourteen, or twenty-six, or thirty, breath and rhythm, everyone awkward and ridiculous and perfect. We will be young, we will be alive, and I will be deeply grateful for these friends. I will know that I was lucky to find them, the kind of friends who bring you halfway across the world, who fly with you to Puerto Rico, who hold you at your grandmother's funeral, who invite you into their home, invite you into their families, take care of you, check on you, fight for you, who make you want to be better, who give you their time and attention, share their secrets, their dreams, their communities, who show up, who see you, who hear you calling from hundreds of miles away, and slowly, slowly, love you back to life.

Ordinary Girls

S ometimes in dreams, I return to those places where we spent our childhoods, where we started our lives, where we dreamed of being women. Sometimes I can see us: girls walking down Lincoln Road in their Halloween costumes, ballerinas and punk rockers and brides of Frankenstein; girls twisting and twirling each other on the dance floor at the Miami Beach Community Center on Ocean Drive; girls chasing each other on the PE field at Fisher; girls fighting at the bus stop across from Nautilus Middle School. And sometimes it's just me: a girl holding her father's hand in the Ciales town square, a girl reading her father's books, a girl running her fingers over moriviví.

We're not girls anymore. We are women now. China is a medical assistant in a cosmetic surgery clinic, and a single mother, raising three kids on her own. Boogie is a nurse, her kids already grown. Shorty is the general manager of a resort in the Florida Keys. Flaca is an executive assistant at real estate firm.

But some of us didn't make it: Beba. Chanty. I think of them almost every day. I carry them with me, their smiles, their loud as fuck laughter rising above the bleachers in the school gym, the way they dove into the pool and made a splash that was larger than our entire group. The way Chanty's nostrils flared when she smiled. Beba always turning something into a cartoon.

This is who I write about and who I write for. For the girls they were, for the girl I was, for girls everywhere who are just like we used to be. For the black and brown girls. For the girls on the merry-go-round making the world spin. For the wild girls and the party girls, the loudmouths and troublemakers. For the girls who are angry and lost. For the girls who never saw themselves in books. For the girls who love other girls, sometimes in secret. For the girls who believe in monsters. For the girls on the edge who are ready to fly. For the ordinary girls. For all the girls who broke my heart. And their mothers. And their daughters. And if I could reach back through time and space to that girl I was, to all my girls, I would tell you to take care, to love each other, fight less, dance dance dance until you're breathless. And goddamn, girl. Live.

NOTES

1. Page 13: Nelson A. Denis, *War Against All Puerto Ricans: Revolution and Terror in America's Colony* (New York: Nation Books, 2015).

2. Page 186, 188: "Lightning in our limbs." From John Murillo's "Renegades of Funk" in *Up Jump the Boogie.*

3. Page 187: "We knew nothing but what eyes could see." From John Murillo's "Renegades of Funk" in *Up Jump the Boogie* (New York: Cypher Books, 2010).

4. Page 188: "All of us." From T Kira Madden's "The Feels of Love" in *Guernica* (December 12, 2016).

ACKNOWLEDGMENTS

First, foremost, always: Abuela. A black Puerto Rican woman raised me, loved me, carried me all those years. Carries me still. Te quiero y te adoro.

For your generous support during the years it took to write this book, thank you to the MacDowell Colony, the Virginia Center for the Creative Arts, the Ragdale Foundation, the Wisconsin Institute for Creative Writing, Kenyon College and the *Kenyon Review*, the University of Central Florida Creative Writing Program, the University of South Florida MFA Program in Creative Writing, the Ohio Arts Council, the Bread Loaf Writers' Conference, the Sewanee Writers' Conference, the Tin House Writers' Workshop, the Center for Women Writers at Salem College, the National Endowment for the Arts, the Hambidge Center for the Creative Arts and Sciences, the John D. and Catherine T. MacArthur Foundation, the Mrs. Giles Whiting Foundation, the Elizabeth George Foundation, and the Florida Individual Artist Fellowship.

Thank you to the faculty at University of Wisconsin–Madison's Program in Creative Writing: Amy Quan Barry, Ron Wallace, Ron Kuka, Amaud Jamaul Johnson, Sean Bishop, Jesse Lee Kercheval, and Judith Claire Mitchell. What a dream it's been to come back and finish this book in Madison. And thank you to the staff, fellows, and my students. You all are amazing.

I am so grateful to my agent, the brilliant and wonderful Michelle Brower, who sits down with me every chance she gets and listens to my dreams and then works her ass off to make them come true. I am so lucky to have you. Thank you to my generous editor, Kathy Pories, for her guidance, for listening, and for believing in this book. And huge thanks to all the folks at Algonquin Books who rallied behind this book, especially Lauren Moseley, who heard it and believed in it before it was even a book. And to Michael McKenzie and Carla Bruce-Eddings. Thank you!

Thank you to the editors and magazines who supported my work, especially Jonathan Franzen and Robert Atwan at *The Best American Essays,* Celia Johnson and Maria Gagliano at *Slice Magazine,* Krista Bremer, Molly House, Derek Askey (you were right about Nicki Minaj), and all the folks at *The Sun Magazine,* Sari Botton at *Longreads,* Lance Cleland, Michelle Wildgen, Thomas Ross and all the folks at *Tin House,* The Pushcart Prize Anthology, Dinty Moore, Jessica Reed at the *Guardian,* Chekwube O. Danladi at *Ninth Letter,* Dinah Lenney, Cara Blue Adams, the *Kenyon Review,* Marcia Aldrich, Karl Taro Greenfeld, Ryan Rivas and Shane Hinton at Burrow Press, *The Fader,* Deesha Philyaw and *The Rumpus, T: The NYT Style Magazine,* Dr. Ivelisse Rodriguez, Kathie Klarreich, Jennifer Maritza McCauley, *Rolling Stone, TriQuarterly,* G.C. Waldrep and *West Branch,* John D'Agata and The Essay Prize at the University of Iowa.

For your friendship and unconditional support during the darkest times, Margaree Little and Rebecca Seiferle (and Oso!). Thank you, Geeta Kothari, Dr. Clara Román Odio, Dr. Ivonne Garcia, Dr. Sarah Heidt, for all your support. Thank you to the

University of Miami, the Miami Book Fair International, the Center for Writing and Literature at Miami Dade College, the Betsy Hotel, Books & Books, Siân Griffiths and Weber State University, YoungArts Foundation, Dana DeGreff, Andrew Boryga and PageSlayers, Write a House, the Notre Dame Arts & Culture Center, Kyle Dacuyan and PEN America, Rosebud Ben-Oni, Nicole Cullen and Mehdi Tavana Okasi, Jill Talbot and the University of North Texas, the Blue Field Writers House in Detroit, Jamie Lyn Smith, Ru Freeman, Nita Noveno, and Sunday Salon, Lilliam Rivera, Kima Jones and the entire Jack Jones Literary Arts team. Thank you, Miami. To the writing teachers and workshop leaders who saw something, even when I didn't: Douglas Williamson, Cecilia Rodríguez Milanés, Jocelyn Bartkevicius, Terry Ann Thaxton, Dan Wakefield, John Henry Fleming, Rita Ciresi, Ira Sukrungruang, Jo Ann Beard.

There were so many friends (too many of you to name) who've kept me going all these years, during the writing of this book, in ways large and small: Walton Muyumba, for your friendship, for your words, for believing in me. Karen Russell, my Miami hermana, for your warmth and generosity. Sheree Renée Thomas, the world is a better place because of you. Adriana Páramo, for your generosity. Sharon Pinson, Shima Carter, M.J. Fievre, Adeline Oka, Amina Gautier, Anjanette Delgado, Melissa Chadburn, Jonterri Gadson, Joseph Earl Thomas, Yesenia Flores Díaz, Laurie Thomas, Melissa Falcon Field, Angela Palm, Shamala Gallagher, Kimberly Elkins, Tiana Clark, Chaney Kwak, Phillip B. Williams, Rion Amilcar Scott, Chelsea Voulgares, Christina Askounis, Randall Tyrone, Michelle Peñaloza, Kavita Das, Tabitha Blankenbiller,

Jeremy Hawkins, Julie Bloemeke, Julia Ridley Smith, Julie Alpert, Destiny Birdsong, Christina Stoddard, Kateema Lee, Courtney Sender, Doreen Oliver, Elisha Wagman. Thank you, Eric Sasson (Hilarious Ambassador of Gay). The MacDowell Queer Coven, Guinevere Turner, Naomi Jackson, Amy Lam, Melissa Sipin, and Kristin Dombek, who made me dance, laugh, and feel all the human feelings. Patricia Engel and Jennine Capó Crucet, for your Miami stories. We are lucky to have you. Aurielle Lucier, Kimberly Reyes, Erica Anyadike, Rebecca Fisseha, Nicole Sealey, John Murillo, you all made Nairobi and Loita Hills better, so much better. Maaza Mengiste, Marco Navarro, Jenny Zhang, and Gabriel Louis, for the crazy days and nights in Tbilisi and Istanbul. A heartfelt thank you to Luis Alberto Urrea and Cindy Urrea, who helped me see what this book could be, what I could be. And to my Bread Loaf homies, who gave (and continue to give) so much: Jen Choi, Aurvi Sharma, Elena Passarello, Laura Wagner, Casandra Lopez, Katie Moulton, Nick Robinson, and Char Gardner. Thank you. To Vanessa Mártir, for your friendship and encouragement and your light. I can't wait to see your book in the world. Kenyatta Rogers, for all the hours we've spent talking shit and dancing and laughing. Keith S. Wilson, my homie, YA writing partner, best friend. You stole my alien socks. But I forgive you.

Thank you, T Kira Madden, John Murillo, Sandra Cisneros, Nelson Denis, Audre Lorde, Julia Alvarez, and Karen Russell for your words.

Lázaro Figueroa. Que en paz descanses.

Gracias a mi pueblo, y gracias a toda mi gente del caserío. Pa'lante, que Puerto Rico se levanta.

To my girls, to my family, to Cheito, and all of you I haven't named, or whose names I've changed, for privacy: I'm alive because you loved me. Thank you for trusting me with your lives and your stories. For the good days and bad days, for all the days that were full of joy. Thank you for forgiving me again and again. Sister, I miss you, always. Papi, thank you for the stories. Cheito, you always believed in me, always supported me. Thank you.

Lars: You gave me skies, torpedo fish, so much music. You are every river, every ocean, stingray, seahorse. Swan and minotaur. Electric. Ultramarine. Every single shade of blue.

WHAT IS HIP-HOP IF NOT POETRY:
I/I\I/I\I//I\I/I\I//I\I/I\I//I\I/I\I//I\I/I\I//I\I/I\I//I\I/I\I//I\I/I\
An Interview with Jaquira Díaz

Rebecca Godfrey: In *Ordinary Girls*, your depiction of coming-of-age in Miami is so vivid and rich. The book is full of specific details—dancing to "Pop that Pussy," drinking orange sodas at Miami Subs, wearing oversize T-shirts over bikinis, listening to Bone Thugs-N-Harmony. How did you excavate that? Was it from memory? Or did you draw on journals and other sources from the time?

Jaquira Díaz: I'm still friends with all the girls in the book, the ones who survived, and we often talked about these things. I was part of a group of girls that took lots of pictures. My friend Flaca took photography in high school, and worked in a photo lab, so she always had a camera, and later a camcorder. So much of our adolescence was recorded because of her. But we were all kind of obsessed with documenting our lives. We all had diaries, slam books, scrapbooks. We had a huge shared diary we passed to each other where we wrote entries, and we'd keep it for a few days, then pass it on. I also wrote so many letters to my friends. I was always writing, taking notes. I already believed myself a writer, and was always sketching out ideas. I thought I would write about my life, even though I didn't even know what memoir was.

RG: Why did it feel important to you to portray the music and style of your friends? Why was it important for you to include details of youth culture, of style and music that are so often absent from "literary" work?

JD: *Ordinary Girls* is in some ways about navigating a certain kind of black and brown girlhood. So many of the details that were present during our girlhood are erased or disparaged in our literary culture. The details of my life are the details of a working-class life, of growing up in poverty in Miami Beach and in the Puerto Rican housing projects. The music I reference, the music that was the soundtrack to my life, was music of the streets. Hood culture is not considered high art, but what is hip-hop if not poetry? 2Pac was a poet. So was Nas. The old salsa I grew up on was made up of storytelling and myth and poetry. Héctor Lavoe and Willie Colón and Lucecita Benítez were storytellers and poets as well as singers. Music taught me to write sentences. I learned more about writing from The *Miseducation of Lauryn Hill* than I ever learned from Hemingway.

RG: The writing about style and clothing is not purely descriptive. The details reveal so much about how femininity is exaggerated, celebrated, rejected. You capture how girls use style as armor, as code, whether it's the innocent "red hearts on the bodice" of your little sister's bathing suit, or the swagger of your friend Boogie in her "skintight Brazilian jeans," or you and your friend Shorty about to cause mayhem in "Daisy Dukes and chancletas."

JD: When I think of the details of style, of clothing, I think about how much of those years were performance. The way we dressed was as much about expression as it was about resistance. We were not the girls people wanted us to be, as I write in the book. We wanted to control at least what we wore, since we didn't feel we had control of much else. But we were definitely performing. Or at least I was. I wore boys' clothes—baggy jeans, basketball jerseys—because I was hiding. I'd started getting all this unwanted attention from men, and I wanted none of it. I dressed like a boy because I wanted to hide my body, but also, I wanted to seem much tougher than I was. I wanted to feel safe in my own body, which was often impossible.

RG: Suicidal young women occupy this very romantic place in white literary culture, from *The Bell Jar* to *The Virgin Suicides*, which you reference directly. In your community, there's nothing romantic about death. "We were trying to live, but the world was doing its best to kill us." How does your own experience inform or challenge that "sad girl" archetype that's so prevalent in our culture?

JD: In parts of the book when I talk openly about suicide, I try to speak to something larger, to say something about mental illness and its effect on me, on us. I was a girl suffering from depression. I was later diagnosed with major depressive disorder, anxiety, and insomnia, all of which I've struggled with my entire life. I also write about my mother's mental illness. She was diagnosed with paranoid schizophrenia when I was a girl. Years after my mother's diagnosis, it became clear to me that my mother went undiagnosed and untreated for years. But even after she started getting treatment, I realized she never really got adequate mental health care because we were poor. This is a problem and a reality for many communities, for so many people across the US who don't have health insurance or access to health care, or who simply can't afford adequate mental health care because even with insurance, they can't make ends meet.

I wasn't sad—I was ill. I was in so much pain I wanted to die. And there was such a stigma around depression that I couldn't really talk about anything I was feeling. I was so alienated that I thought dying would be easier. My story wasn't, and isn't, unique. So many of us go through this, suffering in silence. And then, when I was finally ready to talk openly, I could only see a therapist a handful of times in a year, because that's all that my father's insurance would cover.

I wish this were what we were all talking about in our current literary culture—our experiences with mental illness and the ways it affects our communities—rather than romanticizing "sad girl" narratives. I think we're moving in that direction. In the past year alone we've had the work of Esmé Weijun Wang's *The Collected Schizophrenias* and Bassey Ikpi's *I'm Telling the Truth, but I'm Lying*, both necessary and beautifully written.

RG: There's been a lot of interest in playing with linearity in memoir recently. Your book shifts between place and time. Part of this feels formally innovative, but it also feels necessary to capture the dislocating nature of your life. You were, as a young girl and then as a young woman, constantly moving between homes, countries, races—nothing felt particularly permanent. Your book artfully examines how colonialism and poverty and other factors create this destabilizing current. Did you purposely avoid a more traditional chronological structure?

JD: I gave up the idea of writing a memoir that was strictly chronological because that felt forced, like I was fabricating a sense of chronology. It felt like lying. So instead, I let things emerge organically. I wanted the book to feel similar to the way we experience memory, which is often in flashes, linked by association or sensory details or images. But I also wanted there to be an arc in each chapter, a theme, a relationship explored. And I wanted each chapter to speak to a larger story, not just my personal story, but to say something meaningful about the larger world, about girlhood, about race, about colonialism, about sexual violence and who is silenced. There were times when I needed to slow something down, because I wanted the readers to spend more time in a certain place, to think about a certain character and what that character meant to the overall theme. Such as in "La Otra," when I focus on my mother, and her fight with our neighbor, and the neighbor's daughter, Jesenia. I took this moment, carried it with me my whole life, so much so that I keep returning to it. So I slowed the narrative down, then flashed forward.

But there were also moments when I needed to speed things up, when I wanted the reader to get a sense of the chaos, of the disorder, of a life like mine, when everything seemed to move faster, when everything seemed to be headed toward disaster. I needed the reader to feel a sense of discomfort. Trying to tidy that up, to make it cleaner somehow, also felt like I was fabricating a sense of stability.

RG: Your book veers away from the traditional coming-of-age memoir, the ones in which the pivotal experiences in a young girl's life are usually related to love and sex. For you, violence, not love, was transformative. "Learn to fight dirty, to bite the soft spots on the neck and inner thigh, to pull off earrings and hair weaves." I haven't read such a nonchalant, candid portrayal of a young girl's rage, power, and physical anger. This is so rarely discussed or portrayed when it comes to young women. Can you talk about the process of writing these scenes? Did you ever feel you were in new territory, that there would be unease or discomfort from readers?

JD: Writing the scenes themselves didn't feel new to me, because I spent so many years being that person, living that life. I did sometimes stop and marvel at the fact that I'm alive, still here, still breathing, and that I was ever that person, that I was in such a state of rage.

But I did feel shame when I thought about readers who didn't live in neighborhoods like mine, who didn't grow up in poverty, who didn't live this kind of life. In order to keep writing this book, I had to stop thinking about readers outside my community, about how they might judge me or perceive people like me. What got me through was to keep looking back toward home, to remember that the people I was writing about were the same people I was writing for, and that those people, my people, they saw me, they knew me. It was important to show them that our stories, our neighborhoods, and the ways we live and love are just as important as those that get much more attention. I wanted to show that my voice, and this book, is made up of the places that made me, the people who brought me up.

RG: At one of your readings, a woman asked you something to the effect of, "How did you get out of the Miami world you depict, how did you get *better*?" The implication being that becoming part of an academic or literary community was superior. And you replied, "I'm not better." Your book also avoids a redemptive ending. Instead, you remain loyal to and fiercely aware of the struggles of your friends, of a demonized murderer, of Puerto Rico's history. Was there any pressure—internal or external—to provide readers with the more traditional ending of an individual's triumph?

JD: The truth is I'm not better, and I'm not sure I ever will be. Even though I've had access to education, to a graduate writing program, to a literary community, to the publishing world, even though I've been a professor and writer, I will always feel like I'm that same poor girl. Growing up poor means that we learn—we're taught—that the ways we live and love and work and speak and think are wrong, that we're not good enough. We're expected to perform for those in power, and often that means performing a certain kind of redemption story. We're expected to perform survival and resilience and overcoming obstacles. There has been pressure to provide that kind of traditional ending, but my life has never been like that.

People keep asking, "What was the one moment or event that turned your life around?" But the truth is there wasn't a single event or a single moment or a single person that turned my life around, and there was no Aristotelian reversal because this is not a novel. Real life doesn't work like that. I'm still living my real life, and I'm still struggling. Puerto Rico is still in crisis. Black Puerto Ricans have always been in crisis. Every day is a struggle. But also, every day is a blessing.

Rebecca Godfrey is the author of
Under the Bridge: The True Story of the Murder of Reena Virk.

QUESTIONS FOR DISCUSSION

1. Often, the parts of our lives that are exceptionally traumatic tend to impress themselves most on our memories. On page 15, Jaquira Díaz says she is both "determined to remember" and "prohibido olvidar (forbidden to forget)." Do you find yourself more capable of remembering the exceedingly bad times in your life? What about the exceedingly good? Why is Jaquira forbidden to forget?

2. Most of the memoir is centralized in the spaces where Díaz is with her family and the friends that become like family to her. When she joins the navy, Díaz, and the story itself, is uprooted from this sense of place. In what ways, and why, was this time a turning point for her? What new difficulties did her time in the navy present?

3. Think about the image of the mouse that Jaquira and Anthony encounter in Abuela's house. Why does Jaquira say she is "part monster, part mouse"? What does she mean by this? Does she think her act is forgivable? Do you?

4. At the beginning of *Ordinary Girls*, Díaz grapples with the question of whether home is a place. In the section titled "Regresando," Díaz continues to come back to Miami Beach. What are the different occasions that cause her to return? Do you think she sees

Miami Beach as a place she can call home, or not, and why? How are her feelings about Puerto Rico different from those about Miami? Is home a place, and what else do you think home could be, if not a place?

5. Abuela and Grandma Mercy are set in contrast to each other throughout Díaz's account of her childhood and young adult life. In what ways do each of her grandmothers inform Díaz's perception of herself, her heritage, and her worth?

6. Consider the two settings of Puerto Rico and Miami Beach. How does the author characterize the two differently? How do these differences reflect the changes in the family's dynamic over time?

7. Violence seeps into much of Jaquira's experiences. As a result, the parts of her life associated with love and community are also intermingled with fear and pain. What are some examples of these instances?

8. What are some of the "monster stories" told in *Ordinary Girls*, both in Díaz's own life and in the media that she is consuming? What is the scariest part about La Llorona, according to Díaz? What is her biggest fear regarding her relationship to her mother?

9. Cheito reminds Jaquira of Puerto Rico and Boricua culture. Despite the comfort this brings her, she is also acutely aware of the ways that his family is far different from hers. Does her experience

with Cheito give her motivation to change her future or cause her to resent her own family?

10. Music is a crucial part of the lives of Jaquira and her friends. Pick one of the songs she names in the memoir and listen to it. What was happening to Jaquira at the time in her life that she listened to this song? What parts of it do you think resonated with her? Why is music so important?

11. Díaz compares herself to Holden Caulfield. Compare the lives and characteristics of the two. Why do you think she identifies with him?

12. The chapter titled "Secrets" recounts Díaz's experiences from a young age involving violence against women. Discuss the parts of this chapter that shocked you or impressed upon you most. Then discuss the line "It will be a long time before you buy another pair of strappy sandals. But you will." Why is this statement so powerful?

13. Consider the quote, "I know something about the in-between, of being seen but not really seen" (p. 291). Compare Jaquira to the character she creates of Puerto Rico. Discuss why, at the end of the memoir, she delves into the topic of injustice in Puerto Rico, including Oscar López Rivera and Hurricane María.

14. What is an ordinary girl? Whom is Díaz addressing and what message does she want to send to them?

© MARIA ESQUINCA

JAQUIRA DÍAZ was born in Puerto Rico. Her work has been published in the *New York Times Style Magazine*, the *Guardian*, Longreads, *Condé Nast Traveler*, and included in *The Best American Essays 2016*. She is the recipient of a Whiting Award, two Pushcart Prizes, an Elizabeth George Foundation grant, and fellowships from the MacDowell Colony, the *Kenyon Review*, and the Wisconsin Institute for Creative Writing. She splits her time between Montréal and Miami Beach with her partner, the writer Lars Horn.